Timber Supply, Land Allocation, and Economic Efficiency

Timber Supply, Land Allocation, and Economic Efficiency

William F. Hyde

Published for Resources for the Future, Inc.
By The Johns Hopkins University Press
Baltimore and London

Published for Resources for the Future
By The Johns Hopkins University Press, Baltimore, Maryland 21218

Library of Congress Catalog Card Number 80-8021
ISBN 0-8018-2489-3

Library of Congress Cataloging in Publication Data

Hyde, William F
    Timber supply, land allocation, and economic efficiency.

    Includes index.
      1. Timber—Economic aspects—United States.
2. Forest reserves—Economic aspects—United States.
3. Forest management—United States.　4. United States
—Forest policy.　5. Forest management—Northwest,
Pacific.　I. Resources for the Future.　II. Title.
SD427.T5H92   635.9′2   80-8021
ISBN 0-8018-2489-3

Contents

List of Tables

List of Figures

Foreword

The biological, managerial, and economic potentials of future production of all forest outputs in the United States are highly important and deserving of serious study. The United States has the capacity to produce substantially more of all forest outputs than it currently does, but realizing that potential will be neither easy nor simple. Past experience is an informative but insufficient guide to the future, for alternatives exist for management of forests in directions and degrees not hitherto experienced.

General considerations arising out of this situation led Resources for the Future to recruit William F. Hyde to its staff in the fall of 1973. In the intervening years, he alone or in collaboration with others, has produced several articles and chapters in books edited by others. This book is the capstone and the culmination of his research at Resources for the Future. In this book he substantially extends and makes more realistic the standard theories of forest economics, and in the process has modified that body of theory to a major degree. He has applied more sophisticated analytical tools to the practical future management problems of the Pacific Northwest and of one specific forest area within that region. His results are a striking demonstration of the utility of modernized theory applied to future forest management.

This book is a major contribution to RFF's expanded program of research in forest economics and policy. This program is supported by Resources for the Future, the Weyerhaeuser Company

Foundation, and the U.S. Forest Service. Other books and studies in this general program have been made by Sedjo, Krutilla, Radcliffe, Bowes, Wilman, and others, as well as those by myself. This work by Hyde fills an important intellectual niche in the broad spectrum of RFF forestry studies.

I find great professional and personal satisfaction in the publication of this book because I have been closely identified with it and its author since its inception. I commend this book to all serious students of natural resource problems, for I think it has much to offer outside of, as well as within, forestry and outside of, as well as within, the United States. My judgment is that this book will long stand as a major landmark in the development of thinking about natural resource matters.

June 1980   Marion Clawson
                                       Resources for the Future

Preface

This text is one of many on the topic of timber supply, a perpetually central issue in forest economics and policy. But it is also something else: It is an attempt to examine the economic efficiency of investments in timber production. Special attention is directed to the increasingly important issue of investments in forestland, particularly public forestland, where allocation of land between timber production and other forest uses is an issue of national policy importance.

The first step in making any analysis is to identify the perspective from which it originates. Our perspective is that of the congressman who asks, "Will there be a timber shortage? Can I introduce a bill which will improve upon the situation? What form should this bill take?" In order to respond to these questions, we have to project timber supply in the absence of congressional action, that is, under current statutory public policies and assuming producer response to the market. We will obtain different projections than we might with a statistical analysis of historic trends, if only because historic trends include trends in public policy. We expect an answer which considers the timber industry's full investment response to price expectations—and the public land management agencies' full investment response to price expectations within the limits of current public law. If these responses would be satisfactory, but do not appear to be forthcoming in reality, then our congressman must ask "Why not?" The public policy issue is, "What prevents efficient investment levels in forestry?"

We develop the conceptual framework for such a projection and apply it in an illustrative case study. Once the projection is complete, our congressman can more meaningfully judge the merits of legislative action.

Land is one of the basic factors in timber production. This work is a first-generation effort to incorporate the conceptual with the applied problems of economically efficient allocation of forest-land among market and nonmarket uses. Our main contribution is the methodology, but even with poor data, we can provide a perspective on some issues which trouble timber managers and environmentalists alike. This perspective is particularly relevant for public land managers because much of the timber-environmentalist conflict occurs on public land.

Our applications raise some important issues which cannot be analyzed within the scope of this book. Analysis of competing nonmarket land uses is one issue; the applied economics of multiple use is another; an important third issue is public responsibility for community stability and overdecentralization of resource use. (Overdecentralization is a term used by Mason Gaffney to describe isolated small communities, sometimes lacking the necessary social services, which exist on the subsidized extraction of public resources.) There is considerable theoretical as well as applied work remaining to be done on these issues. Finally, there is the question of what our forests will look like in the future as a more croplike timber production technology replaces the current technology emphasizing protection and harvesting.

The research for this book was encouraged by Marion Clawson and supported by Resources for the Future. In fact, many of the ideas developed herein were previously discussed in one form or another with Dr. Clawson. He and I first published a preface to this work in Walter J. Mead and William McKillip, eds., *British Columbia Timber Policy* (Vancouver, University of British Columbia, 1976). John Krutilla of RFF and William Bentley of Crown Zellerbach encouraged me, lent their own insights, and kept me on the topic when I ventured astray. Much of the credit the book receives belongs to these gentlemen. Thanks are also due to Cassandra Madison, Colleen McCoy, and Vera Ullrich, most reliable and patient people and persevering typists; to Doris Sofinowski, who saved me from many programming errors and, therefore, from much embarrassment; and to Ruth Haas, who made it all readable, no easy task.

In addition to the above, Charles Wilbur, G. Robinson Gregory, John Cross, W. H. Locke Anderson, Gunter Schramm, and Frederic M. Scherer have my thanks for showing me the rationale of an economic approach. Thanks are also due to those who have led previous discussions of the issues covered here, notably Henry Vaux of the University of California, and George Staebler of the Weyerhaeuser Company. Ralph W. Marquis also deserves citation for his article on bromides and folklore in forest economics (*Proceedings,* 1947 National Convention, Society of American Foresters, pp. 76–81).

Grant Ainscough of Macmillan-Bloedel; Gilbert Baker of Weyerhaeuser; David Cox of the Industrial Forestry Association; Donald Gedney, Charles Bolsinger, Robert Burns, and Lewis Manhart of the Forest Service; John Walker of Simpson Timber Company; Charles Chambers and Timothy Gregg of the Washington State Department of Natural Resources; Stephan Anderson, formerly with Sierra Club Research but now with College of the Atlantic; Nicholas Dennis of the University of California at Berkeley; and particularly Irving Hoch and Winston Harrington of RFF and Donald DeMars of the Forest Service made specific, and significant contributions to individual chapters. Emery Castle, RFF; Henry Peskin, RFF; Clark Row, USFS; Mason Gaffney, University of California at Riverside; Robert Burt, Gail Blattenburger, and George Moore, former classmates; Darius Adams and Joe B. Stevens, Oregon State University; and members of John Krutilla's seminar in applied analysis all did yeoman service as reviewers. Much of the merit of this book is due to the thoughtful attention of these reviewers.

June 1980   W.F.H.

Symbols and Abbreviations

Frequently Used Mathematical Symbols

A	number of acres
A_A	allowable cut derived variable land production function
A_E	efficiency derived variable land production function
A_f	idle (fallow acres)
A_g	acres of old growth
A_m	regulated (managed) acres
A_r	residual acres
C	cost
CT	commercial thinning volume
D	demand
E	silvicultural effort
F	final harvest volume
G	old growth value; old growth volume in chapter 2
p	stumpage price
P	weighted stumpage price reflecting qualitative differences in product
Q	quantity, production, biological yield, harvest, volume
ρ	rate of relative stumpage price change
r	cost of capital
R	economic rent
S	supply; indicator or site quality in chapter 5
S_A	allowable cut derived supply function

S_E efficiency derived supply function
t_h age of stand at harvest
t_r regeneration lag in years
T $t_h + t_r =$ age of the timberstand *inclusive* of regeneration lag
T_c conversion period in years
T_k time required to grow a tree of some minimum diameter
T_m harvest timing constraint
V present value
x access cost
w wage rate
Y annual harvest volume calculated under the allowable cut
          rule
α proportionality constraint
θ operator instructing choice between CT and F

Forestry Abbreviations

ACE   allowable cut effect
CAI   current annual increment
cunit   100 cubic feet
dbh   diameter at breast height
FSM   Forest Service Manual
MAI   mean annual increment
Mbf   1,000 board feet
MMbf   1 million board feet
NF   National Forest
PLIM   piling unutilized material

1

Introduction

Concern that the United States is running out of timber has once again achieved some currency. Competing recreational demands on forestland and increasing environmental restrictions on timber production reinforce this concern. Together, these demands make modern forest management a controversial public policy issue. Examination of timber production, however, reveals substantial inefficiencies in both the public and private sectors. Our objective is to examine how a shift to more efficient timber management would affect this controversy.

We demonstrate that the expectation of timber shortage is a consequence of simplistic projection methods coupled with outmoded, inefficient timber management practices; and that increasing recreational and environmental demands are more apparent than real constraints on timber production. Moreover, if timber supply is less of a problem than anticipated, then conflicts between timber and nontimber uses of forestland are also less of a problem than anticipated. The important question for public policy is *not* whether timber production should be encouraged by subsidies and special tax treatments; *rather,* it is the efficiency with which timber management and land allocation are carried out among competing uses—particularly timber and dispersed recreation.

Background

Projected "timber famines" of the past have never materialized—despite their pronouncement by chiefs of state, official public agency reports, and distinguished scientists.[1] Nevertheless, the concern persists. Moreover, there are just enough data supporting such a view to grant it a measure of validity. Current concern focuses on the coastal Pacific Northwest (the Douglas-fir region), which is the source of one-quarter of the nation's annual timber harvest. Projections indicate that region's industrial timberlands will deplete their inventory by the year 2000.[2] Exports to Japan only reinforce this concern.

The public owns one-half of the forestland in this region and is, therefore, in a position to meliorate the projected industry shortage. Reservation of public forestlands as a Wilderness area, however, decreases timber production—and current proposals recommend up to 268,800 additional acres in this region, 29 percent of the national forest total, for the Wilderness System.[3] Moreover, multiple use requirements, restrictions on clearcutting (the predominant harvest method for Douglas-fir), and high logging road standards all increase harvest costs on the remaining public lands where harvests are not prohibited.

Together these factors have made forest management, particularly forest management on public lands, one of the more controversial areas in all resource and environmental management. Because of this, the President's Advisory Panel on Timber and the Environment was formed, the Monongahela and similar federal district court cases on timber harvest practices received national attention, and Senator Hubert Humphrey initiated legislation known as the Renewable Resources Planning Act (RPA) in 1974, which was amended by the National Forest Management Act (NFMA)

[1] For example, the Viceroy of Mexico City in 1546, the American Association for the Advancement of Science in 1873, President Theodore Roosevelt, and periodic U.S. Forest Service reports in this century.

[2] For example, U.S. Forest Service, *The Outlook for Timber in the United States* (October 1973); Donald R. Gedney, Daniel D. Oswald, and Roger D. Fight, "Two Projections of Timber Supply in the Pacific Coast States," U.S. Forest Service (1975); Robert E. Wolf, "The Douglas-Fir Region Timber Supply Situation and Log Export Regulation as Proposed by H.R. 5544," The Library of Congress, Congressional Research Service, Environmental Policy Division, May 8, 1975; and John H. Beuter, K. Norman Johnson, and H. Lynn Scheurman, "Timber for Oregon's Tomorrow" (Corvallis, Oregon State University, School of Forestry, Research Bulletin no. 19, 1976).

[3] Oregon Wilderness Coalition, "The Oregon Alternative" (Portland, September 1978) B-9; Citizens for Washington Wilderness, "Citizens Wilderness Alternative" (Seattle, 1979).

in 1976. Each addresses timber harvest issues and each has environmental overtones. Our analysis bears directly on the long-term planning requirements of RPA and the explicit economic efficiency criteria in NFMA.[4]

Economic efficiency criteria justify expanding production until benefits derived from the last unit of output just equal its factor costs. At this point profit is maximized. Existing public and private timber management demonstrates independent cases of both under- and overproduction in these terms. Their harvest criteria tend to resemble volume maximization over time, and the timberland base, at least for public land, is only vaguely related to profitability. Perhaps these deviations from efficiency can be explained as historically appropriate management practices which have failed to adjust to changing market conditions and social values. Regardless of their explanation, they are inappropriate today.

Public agency deviations from market solutions often derive additional justification from nonpriced services and externalities, both of which are important aspects of public land management, and from the public law. We shall demonstrate, however, that observations of land allocation by public agencies do not support these arguments. Strict adherence to market solutions results in more efficient allocation of both timber and nonpriced resource services.[5] Furthermore, agency interpretations of the public law may be unnecessarily narrow. A reading of the law does not require these interpretations. Neither RPA nor NFMA, nor any other applicable law, contains any clause that substantially impedes efficiency.[6] These administrative interpretations and their resulting inefficiencies are discussed in chapter 2. Economically efficient use

[4] Section 6(k) of NFMA requires identification of "lands within the management area which are not suited for timber production, considering physical, economic, and other pertinent factors"; formulation and implementation of "a process for estimating long-term costs and benefits to support the program evaluation requirements of this Act"; and identification of "timber sales made below the estimated expenditures for such timber."

[5] For evidence in an illustrative case, see William F. Hyde, "Compounding Clearcuts: The Social Failures of Public Timber Management in the Rockies," in John Baden and Richard Stroup, *The Environmental Costs of Government Action* (proceedings of a Liberty Fund conference at Big Sky, Montana, September 1978).

[6] John V. Krutilla and John A. Haigh, "Toward a Coherent Public Lands Management Philosophy," *Journal of Business Administration* vol. 10, no. 2 (Spring 1979).

of the public lands requires a sharp shift in agency interpretations of the legislation. These interpretations are obvious candidates for serious public scrutiny.

Analytical Approach

After examining the conceptual basis for much of existing timber management practice in chapter 2, we turn to the rules for efficient timber management. Subsequently, we apply the efficiency rules in an empirical test for the Douglas-fir region. The projections for efficient price and quantity, as well as their land use implications, can be contrasted with current levels. The differences provide a measure of the gains from efficiency.

The focus of current controversy is on long-term forest management. Projections of timber shortage are for the years 2000–2020; RPA requires fifty-year planning, and statutory Wilderness designation is probably permanent. Conveniently this period, thirty to fifty years, frames what is generally thought to be one complete economic timber growing cycle, or rotation. Thus, it is appropriate for us to examine efficiency in the economic long run when everything is variable, that is, all factors of production, including currently standing timber, can change. This is the same as assuming that all forestland stands idle, fallow, available for allocation to any use including timber production according to that technology which returns the greatest timber value.

It is difficult to estimate the impact of this timber production technology, however. Historical observations provide no guideline because (1) existing timberstands reflect years of timber growing, or silvicultural, practices which are inefficient in the modern market and (2) forestry is entering a period of rapid technical change. In the long run, market pressures may cause private timber producers to shift from traditional harvest criteria that are no longer profitable, toward modern market efficiency. In fact, a broad-stroked picture of industrial timberlands in the past ten years shows just such a shift. The direction of public timberland management is less certain, but NFMA encourages movement toward efficiency.

Timber production is changing from the harvest of "volunteer" stands to a more sophisticated cultivation technology. In any field, the early years of development promise to be years of rapid learning. This is particularly true where much of the learning, and the technology, can be transferred intact from a related field, as from agriculture to forestry.

In the past, timber growth was relatively unmanaged, and the technology focused on harvesting and processing instead of cultivation. In the economic long run, all this may change. All existing timberstands will be replaced and all currently known timber-growing technologies, ranging from planting to harvesting, can be implemented in the new stands. Furthermore, new, currently unapplied, or even unknown, short-run technologies can be added during the new rotation. An example of the latter might be new fertilizers derived from presently unknown chemical compounds and introduced to partially grown timberstands, thereby producing larger harvest volumes than presently anticipated. This all suggests that production estimates might be based on observations of best current technologies. For our purposes they must further be carefully chosen to reflect efficiency. We can obtain information about such production frontier functions by surveying recent technical literature and by inquiring of forest technicians the least costly way to produce each of several harvest levels.

Specifically, our approach begins with construction of the behavioral production model. We use the familiar static profit maximization model based on competitive theory of the firm. Competition (or public ownership that acts as a price taker) characterizes the timber-producing market in the Douglas-fir region. The standard model requires modification, however, for important local factors. We examine the characteristics of this model in chapter 3.

The second step is to estimate the model's parameters from the technical data, which vary with land quality and location, and with ownership objectives. This leads us to one of our goals, which is the determination of efficient long-run input and harvest levels. These levels are appropriate for a given expected harvest price. By summing efficient harvest levels across all land and ownership classes, we obtain a point on the least-cost or efficient long-run supply schedule. By examining efficient harvest levels associated with alternative price expectations and summing across land and ownership classes, we can trace out the full regional supply schedule.

Any projection of a thirty- to fifty-year future must be based on some highly probabilistic assumptions. We should never forget that our projected supply schedule assumes full adjustment to market efficiency in both the public and private timber-producing sectors. In the public sector this requires a considerable shift in existing administrative policy.

Application

Given some exogenous knowledge of the demand price and the capability of existing timber inventories to meet demands in the period less than one rotation from now (known as the "conversion" period), we can project the long-run price–harvest–volume relation. In chapter 4 we develop a measure of the inventory sufficient for the conversion period. (Determination of the optimal harvest rate during the conversion period is an important forestry problem, but is not our problem here.)

In long-run supply analysis, the demand price is explicit. That is, unlike short-run supply analysis where production is only a function of variable factor costs, long-run production decisions are a function of expected output prices as well as factor costs. We review this theory in chapter 4. In our empirical analysis we use demand prices consistent with historical trends. We also test other demand price trends for their impacts on harvest volumes.

Knowledge of both supply and demand enables us to comment on the likelihood of a timber shortage at any given price. If demand exceeds projected supply at the chosen price, then a shortage would be apparent—except that the price will rise until projected demand and supply are in equilibrium. If projected supply exceeds demand, however, then either the observed equilibrium price will be lower or we have overestimated actual supply. The latter may occur where either the public or private sector has failed to respond fully to efficiency criteria.

Investments in the factors of production, as well as harvest volumes, are related to expected prices. Perhaps the most important investment for public policy analysis is the investment in forestland. As higher timber prices attract ever poorer land into timber production, we can relate production to the land from which it originates. The timber price–land use relation is a feature of our analysis.

Knowledge of land use enables us to comment on environmental gains from efficiency. The steep slopes, shallow soils, and rocky outcrops that characterize land of poorer quality also make it more environmentally risky for timber production. Removing marginal land from timber production as part of any shift from traditional management criteria to efficiency, therefore, creates environmental gains.

A convenient encapsulation of these relationships is shown in figure 1-1. In the first quadrant, expected prices are read on the vertical axis and annual harvest volumes on the horizontal axis. As the price level increases, the volume supplied increases according to the function $S(p)$. If forestland is arrayed from better to poorer quality along the vertical axis in the second quadrant, then rising expected timber price levels attract both more intensive management practices and poorer land into timber production. This is reflected in the variable land production function $A(p)$. Given a known demand price p_1, we expect a long-run annual harvest of Q_1 originating from the first A_1 acres.

We can demonstrate a measure of the timber production opportunity value on any acre. If we select an acre, say a_x, then q_x is its average annualized harvest volume and X, the area between the cost (supply) function and the expected price level, is the net annual timber value for that acre. There is no consumer surplus associated with this value because acre a_x is only a small portion of the good timberland, its impact on aggregate timber supply is marginal, and there is no price effect. The timber opportunity value is similar to Ricardian rent. It differs only in that Ricardo assumed a constant level of management across all land. The opportunity value is the value which net competing nontimber values must exceed if they are to replace timber production on this acre.

The residual forest acres, which are poorer for timber production than the first A_1, can be reserved—and at zero cost in the way of net timber opportunities forgone. Indeed, there is a benefit gained by avoiding timber production costs that exceed returns on these acres. The reserved acres provide flexibility to adjust to unforeseen future events. Meanwhile, they can be, without further justification, fully devoted to reversible nontimber uses. We later allude to

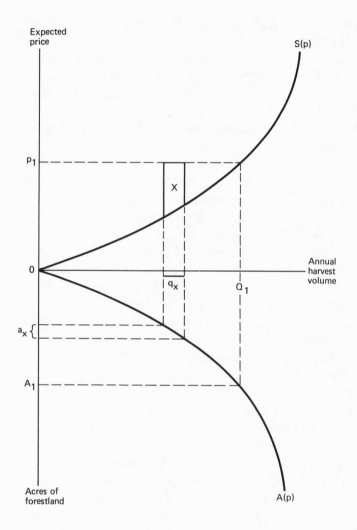

Figure 1-1. Efficient determination of timber supply and forestland allocation.

the community, employment, recreational, and environmental impacts of restricting timber production from these acres, as well as the relation of this restriction to public law.

So far we have discussed market efficiency without considering multiple uses. Multiple use implies a different *socially* efficient allocation of forestland on those acres where timber production and a joint use together create positive net benefits, but timber alone has a negative net value. This condition requires serious study beyond our effort. A useful starting point can be found in the literature on applied welfare economics in multiple-purpose river development.[7]

Meanwhile, we can reasonably assert that among all forest uses only a few compete with timber production to an extent that is important for our analysis. Besides timber, the usual classes of forest uses are recreation, forage, fish and wildlife, water, and wilderness. Only (1) dispersed recreation, including some hunting, fishing, and hiking and (2) other wilderness uses, perhaps including biological reserves, compete with timber production. These uses cannot exist jointly with timber production on the same forestland base. They probably have very low direct production costs; therefore our estimate of the timberland that composes the unprofitable residual approximates a lower bound for land available for competing uses. Furthermore, the opportunity value of timber on profitable forestland approximates the value that must be exceeded if additional land is to be devoted to competing uses.

Our empirical estimations of the timber opportunity value are based on an assumption of economic efficiency. Where efficiency is not the rule in timber management, as it often is not today, then the observed opportunity values for timber are lower than the potential values; fewer acres can be justified for timber management and competing uses are even easier to justify so long as inefficiencies in timber management persist.

In anticipation of an objection, we note that there is no conceptual reason that land allocation decisions could not be based on the value of competing, nontimber opportunities, and the land allocated to timber production only when the value of the latter is demonstrably greater than competing values. In application, however, data on these values are less available; therefore they are more difficult to calculate than timber values.[8] In fact, a merit of using the

[7] See John V. Krutilla and Otto Eckstein, *Multiple Purpose River Development: Studies in Applied Economic Analysis* (Baltimore, Johns Hopkins University Press for Resources for the Future, 1958); and Arthur Maass, M. Maynard Hufschmidt, Robert Dorfman, Harold A. Thomas, Jr., Stephen A. Marglin, and Gordon M. Fair, *Design of Water-Resource Systems* (Cambridge, Mass., Harvard University Press, 1962).

[8] One might begin with V. Kerry Smith, "The Estimation and Use of Models of the Demand for Outdoor Recreation," in *Assessing Demand for Outdoor Recreation,* Appendix B, p. 89, Committee on Assessment of Demand for Outdoor Recreation Resources, National Academy of Sciences, Washington, D.C., 1975;

timber opportunity cost is that knowledge of absolute competitive values is never necessary for decision making. We must only assess their magnitude as greater or less than known timber values.

A Comment on Engineering Functions

Functions such as production and supply are known in the economics literature as "engineering" functions because their parameters are really a function of technical or engineering estimates. Chenery introduced them to the economics literature[9] and Vaux introduced them to forest economics.[10] This book generalizes Vaux's approach by distinguishing among ownerships of forestlands and allowing variable rotation lengths, a variety of silvicultural inputs and input levels, and changing relative prices.

Engineering functions can capture the shift to efficiency criteria and the implementation of technical change. Statistical, or econometric, functions are an alternative, but there are insufficient cross-sectional data for statistical estimation of efficient, technically current, timber production. Statistical functions based on historical data can only arbitrarily adjust for our predicted, historically discontinuous, shift in technology. Furthermore, while they may be attached to historical or other timberstand growth models, these latter models run without price feedbacks. That is, statistical supply functions fail to anticipate investment responses to price expectations.

and John V. Krutilla and Jack L. Knetsch, "Outdoor Recreation Economics," *Annals of the American Academy of Political and Social Sciences,* vol. 389 (May 1970) pp. 63–70. Citations in these can lead one to other useful sources.

[9] Hollis B. Chenery, "Engineering Production Functions," *Quarterly Journal of Economics* vol. 63, pp. 507–531. For further reference, see James M. Griffin, "The Process Analysis Alternative to Statistical Cost Functions," *American Economic Review* vol. 62, no. 1 (March 1972) pp. 45–56; and James R. Marsden, David E. Pingry, and Andrew B. Whinston, "Engineering Foundations of Production Functions," *Journal of Applied Economics* vol. 4, no. 4 (December 1972) pp. 279–290.

[10] Henry J. Vaux, "Economics of Young-Growth Sugar Pine Resources" (Berkeley, University of California, Division of Agricultural Sciences, Bulletin no. 78, 1954). Vaux applied engineering functions for just our sort of long-term problem in "How Much Land Do We Need for Timber Growing?" *Journal of Forestry* vol. 71, no. 7 (July 1973) pp. 399–403.

Engineering functions, however, have problems of their own. They require explicit assumptions about owner and manager behavior. Our assumptions are that there is static profit maximization in competitive markets with fixed but different expected marginal internal rates of return for each ownership. As previously noted, competitive profit maximization is a reasonable assumption for the Douglas-fir region. Analyses using engineering functions can easily overlook a factor of production and the functions themselves ignore risk and uncertainty. The first problem can be guarded against through regular review by technical experts, the second by sensitivity analysis—which effectively indicates the degree of confidence that can be placed in the conclusions. In addition, rates of return greater than true expected marginal rates of return can protect against the risk of overenthusiastic long-term benefit projections.[11] In our empirical analysis of the Douglas-fir region, we further hedge our long-run production estimates by (1) conservatively estimating production levels associated with efficient current technologies, (2) precluding the introduction of any new short-term technologies, and (3) disregarding any expansion of timber management into currently agricultural land as timber prices rise relative to agricultural prices.

We devote the second part of the book to application of the resulting functions. With them, in chapter 5 we examine the efficient timber price and harvest levels and the general land allocation question for the Douglas-fir region. In chapter 6 we discuss how these results might vary within the region and as traditional timber management criteria substitute for efficiency. We also devote more attention to land allocation. In chapter 7 we draw the policy implications of this analysis.

[11] Documentation of this risk in public projects is the theme of Robert H. Haveman, *The Economic Performance of Public Investment: An Ex Post Evaluation of Water Resources Investment* (Baltimore: The Johns Hopkins University Press for Resources for the Future, 1972).

2
Allowable Cut

This chapter describes current timber management practice; its biological, financial, and land use implications; and, particularly, its departures from economic efficiency. These departures occur because harvest rules that were efficient in the past are no longer appropriate in the modern market and in the presence of modern timber production and harvest technologies. Departures from efficiency in intensity and land use, and in resulting timber prices and harvest volumes are substantial. They account for economists' arguments in favor of expanding short-run public agency harvests and also for economists' belief in the capacity of North American producers—public and private—to respond to rapidly expanding world demand for wood fiber. Marion Clawson has estimated that, for the National Forest System alone, one impact of these departures is a forgone annual timber harvest opportunity worth six hundred million dollars.[1] Moreover, the apparently inefficient use of land by some public agencies is at the root of conflicts over use of forestland for either recreation or growing timber.

The multitude of timberland ownerships, each with its own objectives, makes it difficult to describe current management. We can, however, divide ownership into three general classes—public, industrial, and nonindustrial private—and concentrate on the basic model, which provides a point of departure for the timber management plans of the first two. The third ownership class is the most

[1] The National Forests," *Science* vol. 191, no. 4227 (February 20, 1976) pp. 762–767.

diverse, ranging from second homes to farm woodlots to large commercial ownerships unaffiliated with forest products firms. As such, it is the most difficult to characterize. Nevertheless, Clawson has found that nonindustrial private timberstand structures are similar to those of industrial timberstands.[2] By implication, their management must be similar.[3]

The basic model common to federal and state timberland management agencies, as well as to many industrial firms, is known as the allowable cut model. "Allowable cut" is a generic term for a class of models which apply where there are substantial inventories of mature timber and which focus on harvest volumes rather than net revenues. In this chapter we initially develop the basic conceptual allowable cut model used for harvest level determination and discuss its association with cash flow justifications for timber investments. Subsequently, we review a simplified version of the U.S. Forest Service variation on this allowable cut model, and then discuss the separate Forest Service timber price appraisal system. A final section summarizes and compares allowable cut results with those obtained using economic efficiency.

The Forest Service provides a useful focus for our analysis because it is the single largest timber producer—public or private—in the country, producing one-quarter of our aggregate annual harvest volume and managing one-half our standing timber inventory. It also manages the bulk of the lands over which there is a timber–recreational use controversy. As the most important public timber manager, the Forest Service is the agency most able to effect a significant change in timber management practice.

[2] *The Economics of U.S. Nonindustrial Private Forests,* Resources for the Future, Research Paper R-14, Washington, D.C., 1979.

[3] Alternatively, nonindustrial private owners have multiple objectives and a variety of entrepreneurial skills and abilities to finance forest investments. Therefore, their timberstands, taken as a unit, appear quite different from what we would expect if each owner maximized returns on timber investments alone. The apparent similarity of nonindustrial private timberstand structures to industrial timberstand structures only reflects the fact that both industrial and nonindustrial private ownership objectives differ from simple profit maximization, and that both vary in a significant way from stand structures and ownership objectives for the third, or public, ownership class. For further discussion of nonindustrial, private landowner objectives, see an often-overlooked series of articles by H. Chapmen, H. Conklin, L. James, R. Keniston, J. Landstrom, W. Lord, A. Mignery, D. Quinney, C. Stoltenberg, H. Webster, A. Worrell, and J. Yoho in the *Journal of Forestry* and *Land Economics* (various issues, 1951–66).

land component, then, at the end of the conversion period, the second term of Eq. (2-1a) disappears; acres previously stocked with old growth become a part of the regulated timberland base; and a steady state develops [Eq. (2-1b)] in which annual harvests equal annual growth perpetually—and at maximum annual growth level.

$$Y_i^1 = \max_{T} (A_m + A_g) Q(T)/T \qquad \text{for all } i > T_c \qquad (2\text{-}1b)$$

Management focus is generally on Eq. (2-1a) for the practical reason that timber rotations and conversion periods are so long. An illustrative example may be helpful. Assume we manage 160 acres of which 60 acres are regulated stands of Douglas-fir. Representative stands of Douglas-fir may grow according to the schedule:

Age (years)

40	50	60	70	80	90	100

Volume (ft^3)

5,250	7,050	9,000	10,220	11,350	12,390	13,270

MAI (vol./age)

131	141	150	146	142	138	133

Since culmination of MAI occurs at age sixty, there are 1-acre stands for each age class from zero to 59. Aggregate annual growth is 9,000 ft^3 (60 acres, each averaging 150 ft^3 per year). We harvest 1 acre of sixty-year-old trees each year—which is also 9,000 ft^3 —and immediately replant. The remaining 100 acres are unregulated stands of old growth Douglas-fir averaging, say, 15,000 ft^3 per acre. Given a conversion period of 100 years, we harvest and replant 1 acre of 15,000 ft^3 of old growth each year. Total annual harvests are 24,000 ft^3.

Equation (2-1a) may be applied in either of two basic forms known as *area* control and *volume* control. Volume control focuses on the annual harvest level, irrespective of its area of origin. Area control focuses on the land from which annual harvests originate. The usefulness of this distinction becomes clearer if we recognize that the "stock" of old growth is really not stagnant as we assumed, but continues to both grow and decay over time. This dynamic nature of old growth is ignored in Eq. (2-1a). Accordingly, we might focus on the eventual regulated forest, and harvest equal *areas* of old growth annually throughout the conversion period while annual old growth harvest volumes, and, therefore, total annual harvest volumes, fluctuate. Or we might focus on annual harvest *volume* uniformity throughout the conversion period and vary the number of acres of old growth harvested—only to find the eventual timber management area nonuniformly regulated.

Uneven-aged Management

Foresters recognize Eqs. (2-1a and b) as the Hanzlik formula.[7] It was intended for even-aged Douglas-fir stands, but can be adapted for uneven-aged and selectively managed forest types. The short- and long-term management objectives remain a steady flow of timber and a fully regulated forest producing at its biological maximum, respectively.

In the uneven-aged and selectively managed forest there may be several species and several age classes of each species mixed in each timberstand. The younger age classes are always ready to replace their older siblings as the latter are harvested. Therefore, one stand may be indistinguishable from the next and the forest must be managed as a single unit, rather than as T^* identical, equal acreage segments. That is, *all* acres move into the regulated component A_m when the initial management decision is made. *None,* however, produces at its sustainable biological maximum until conversion is complete. Meanwhile, the older trees imply that actual inventory G_a exceeds desired inventory G_d, the inventory which will eventually obtain on an acre of regulated forest. The difference $(G_a - G_d)$ is drawn down over the conversion period much as the old growth inventory is drawn down in the Hanzlik formula:

$$Y_i^2 = \max A_m [Q(T)/T] + A_m [(G_a - G_d)/T_c]$$
$$\text{for all } i = 1, 2, \ldots, T_c \qquad (2\text{-}2a)$$

$$\text{where } G_d = (1/T) \sum_{i=1}^{T^*} Q(i) \cong Q(T^*)/2$$

[7] E. J. Hanzlik, "Determination of the Annual Cut on a Sustained Basis for Virgin American Forests," *Journal of Forestry* vol. 20, no. 5 (May 1922) pp. 611–625.

which is also the volume of timber standing on an acre of regulated forest. Once again, the second term on the right-hand side of Eq. (2-2a) disappears at the end of the conversion period and, if $T_c = nT^*$ where n is a positive integer, then a steady state develops.

$$Y_i^2 = \max A_m Q(T)/T \qquad \text{for all } i > T_c \qquad (2\text{-}2b)$$

Equations (2-2a and b) are known to foresters as Heyer's formula or the Austrian formula and actually preceded Hanzlik historically.

Financial Returns

There are no financial parameters in the conceptual models for either even- or uneven-aged forests; therefore, there are no grounds for judging timber investments. Nevertheless, such judgments are often made on the basis of the implicit annual cash flows: from receipts, regardless of their source, to investments, regardless of their allocation.

For example, consider the rate of return on investments in previously idle land. Following the even-aged case, Eq. (2-1a), the impact on annual harvests of planting A_f (the quantity) previously idle (fallow) acres, and thereby adding them to the regulated component, is given by

$$Y_i^3 = \max_T \{ (A_m + A_f) Q(T)/T$$
$$+ [A_g - A_f Q(T)/G]G/T_c \}$$
$$\text{for all } i = 1, 2, \ldots, T_c \qquad (2\text{-}3)$$

Annual growth of the newly planted seedlings $[\max A_f Q(T)/T]$ justifies increasing annual harvests, but the increase cannot be drawn from the immature trees of the regulated component. Alternatively, we harvest an equal volume from the inventory of old growth. We harvest this volume each year throughout the rotation period, or until the newly planted seedlings reach maturity. Therefore, we schedule a portion of the old growth acreage to satisfy the new regulated harvest level. Remaining old growth acreage continues to be harvested evenly throughout the conversion period.

Recalling our previous numerical example for 160 acres of timberland, assume we own an additional 10 acres of former cropland on which we now plant Douglas-fir seedlings. Seedling growth justifies increasing annual harvests by 1,500 ft^3 (10 acres × 150 ft^3 per acre per year) and these harvests must come from our stock of old growth. There are 15,000 ft^3 of standing timber on each old growth acre; therefore we schedule 0.1 acre each year, or 6 acres for the sixty-year rotation, to satisfy the new regulated harvest level. Ninety-four of the original 100 old growth acres remain; therefore unregulated old growth harvest must be decreased by 6 percent, or 900 ft^3 annually, throughout the conversion period. The immediate and continuing net gain due to planting ten previously idle acres is 600 ft^3 (1,500 − 900).

The rate of return is that rate which equates the discounted sum of the value of the annual harvest differential with the cost of the planting investment that made it possible:

$$\sum_{i=1}^{T_c} p_i \, (Y_i^3 - Y_i^1) \, (1+r)^{-i} = C \qquad (2\text{-}4)$$

where $p_i =$ timber (stumpage) price in year i
$C =$ investment cost
$r =$ rate of return

Continuing our numerical example while introducing prices of $150 per 100 ft^3 and planting costs of $100 per acre, we calculate a 90 percent annual return on our investment.

Calculations similar to Eqs. (2-3) and (2-4) can be made for returns to other silvicultural (i.e., timber management) investments in regulated stands. Growth becomes a function of silvicultural activities such as thinning and fertilizing, as well as of time, and harvest expansion is a result of additional growth per acre instead of growth on new acres as in Eq. (2-3). Fertilization, for example, increases average annual growth on the A_m regulated acres and, therefore, justifies expanded annual harvests just as planting initially idle acres justified expanded annual harvests in Eq. (2-3).[8] The

[8] When growth is expressed only as a function of time, the expected returns to silvicultural inputs such as fertilization are necessarily zero regardless of observations to the contrary. In this case, timber investments are restricted to planting— the case of old growth and idle acres. Enoch Bell, Roger Fight, and Robert Randall show that this is an important irrationality in public agency accounting in "ACE: The Two-Edged Sword," *Journal of Forestry* vol. 73, no. 10 (October 1975) pp. 642–644.

rate of return is that rate which equates the discounted value of annual harvest differentials with the cost of fertilization. Annual returns as great as 390 percent have been calculated in this manner.[9]

The immediate increase in annual harvest volume due to silvicultural investments is known to foresters as the "allowable cut effect" or ACE. It should be clear that both the allowable cut effect and the rate of return calculated from it are limited by the existing old growth inventory. Exhausting this inventory also exhausts the opportunity for immediate harvest expansion and immediate financial return. It should also be clear that, where "excess" old growth inventory exists (there were 94 acres of excess old growth in our idle acre example), profitable old growth harvest opportunities can be held hostage for want of an idle acre or other silvicultural opportunity.

The allowable cut effect is an artifact of combining two *independent* decisions. Even where both old growth and idle acres or other silvicultural opportunities exist, if silvicultural investments cannot be independently justified on their own grounds, then tying them to old growth harvests on other acres is the same as taxing good investments to support bad. In our continuing example, harvesting old growth with an infinite *independent* rate of return combines with planting sixty-year rotation Douglas-fir, which has an expected 2.2 percent *independent* annual rate of return, to create a 90 percent *allowable cut* rate of return. With real interest rates in excess of 2.2 percent, we can justify planting only by taxing old growth harvests. Herein lies the crux of economic objections to the allowable cut model. To maximize profits, operationally independent decisions, such as harvesting one acre and planting another, must stand on their own.[10]

[9] USDA Forest Service, Pacific Northwest Forest Research and Experiment Station (PNWFRES), "Douglas-Fir Supply Study" (1969).

[10] The sensibility of the allowable cut model, as well as the sensibility of using it to judge the merit of timber investments, is the subject of much critical discussion by forest economists. See Dennis L. Schweitzer, Robert W. Sassaman, and Con H. Schallau, "Allowable Cut Effects," *Journal of Forestry* vol. 70, no. 7 (July 1972) pp. 415–418; Dennis E. Teeguarden, "The Allowable Cut Effect: A Comment," *Journal of Forestry* vol. 71, no. 6 (June 1973) pp. 357–369; David W. Klemperer, "The Parable of the Allowable Pump Effect," *Journal of Forestry* vol. 73, no. 10 (October 1975) pp. 640–641; and Jack Hirshleifer, " 'Sustained Yield' Versus Capital Theory," in Barney Dowdle, ed., *Economics of Sustained Yield Forestry* (Seattle, University of Washington, forthcoming).

Many profit-oriented, large, timberland ownerships, nevertheless, apply their own variations of the allowable cut model. The managers of each have their own justifications and their own perceptions of reality. For example, the Weyerhaeuser Company's requirements for an annual source of operating funds and stockholders' dividends make the annual cash flow feature of the model attractive. Concern for its mills' future requirements for logs makes a tie between harvests and investments attractive. And, finally, the generally high productivity of Weyerhaeuser lands saves the company from falling into one of the most obvious and frequent traps of the allowable cut model—planting poor lands which generate virtually no independent returns. The Washington State Department of Natural Resources is another example. It must provide a continuous flow of funds to the state school system, therefore the annual cash flow feature of the allowable cut model is attractive to it as well. The department takes more recognition of cyclical price variations than many ownerships and modifies its annual harvest volumes accordingly. Several federal land management agencies (Bureau of Land Management, Bureau of Indian Affairs, Forest Service) also apply the allowable cut model, usually in a very constrained form. In the following section we examine the Forest Service application in more detail.

U.S. Forest Service Application

The U.S. Forest Service is the country's single largest timberland manager, public or private. The Forest Service is additionally critical in the context of our discussion because, as a decentralized public agency, it is in a good position to respond to changing public policy. In particular, it is in a good position to alter administrative decisions to reflect expanding demands for timber and outdoor recreation. Not only does the Forest Service manage a large number of acres with the largest single inventory of old growth, but many of these acres are of low potential timber productivity and located at higher elevations; that is, they are the marginal timberlands that should be carefully scrutinized for allocation among alternative uses.

Forest Service timber management decisions are composed of three distinct pieces: (1) land allocational decisions, (2) harvest and investment decisions, and (3) timber pricing decisions. Forest Service Manual (FSM) 2410 (May 1972) provides a guide for these decisions.[11] We examine each of them in turn.

Land Allocation

The fundamental land unit for timber production is the so-called "commercial" forestland base. Commercial forestland is the residual left after unusable land is subtracted from the total area in the National Forest System. It is further divided into components according to acceptable timber management activities.

PRODUCTIVE TIMBERLAND.   Acres of nonforestland and unproductive forestland, as well as the surface area of rivers and lakes, are subtracted from the total area managed by the Forest Service. The remaining, *productive,* forestland is divided among productive reserved, productive deferred, and *commercial* components. Reference to figure 2-1 may be useful. The productive reserved component includes that part of Wilderness, scenic, and geologic areas which, except for statutory or administrative reservations, qualifies for the commercial component. (As of 1976, productive reserved is 44 percent of all reserved land, but only 7 percent of all productive land.[12] The remaining 56 percent of reserved land is nonforestland, unproductive forest, or water.) The productive deferred component includes that part of all land under study for addition to the reserved component which would otherwise qualify for the commercial component (38 percent of all deferred, but only 5 percent of all productive land).[13]

[11] See also Daniel Navon, "Timber RAM," USDA Forest Service Research Paper PSW 70 (1971) and Robert Q. Sullivan, Enoch F. Bell, and Jack Usher, "Information Relating to RPAT Timber Policy Issue #1 (Harvesting Schedules)," USDA Forest Service Timber Harvesting Issues Study Team, 1975, p. 4.

[12] There are 14.8 million acres of national forests in the Wilderness System. Only 48 percent (7.2 million) are productive timberland.

[13] Some believe that *Sierra Club v. Butz* and a principle of similar treatment for similar land units require that nonselected (for Wilderness classification) roadless areas also be included in the deferred component until their status is resolved. The Forest Service puts these in the new category "unclassified" but leaves them in the commercial forestland base for harvest determination. See Charles McKetta, Charles Hatch, Lee Medema, and Kjell Christophersen, "The RARE II Process in Idaho" (Moscow, University of Idaho Forest Range and Wildlife Experiment Station, July 1978).

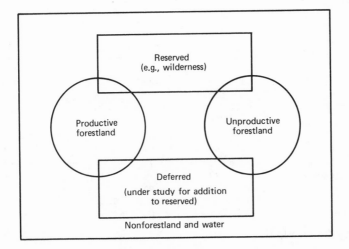

Figure 2-1. The national forests. The Venn diagram segments the total area managed by the Forest Service into its major components: productive and unproductive forestland and nonforestland. Additional distinction is made between reserved and deferred components, which cut across the first three categories, and commercial forestland, which is the remaining productive land.

All harvesting occurs on the commercial component. The term "commercial," however, is a misnomer. It includes no economic measure of cost or value, therefore its definition has only mild market relevance. Commercial forestland consists of acres that are capable of producing in excess of 20 ft^3 of industrial wood fiber per annum. The definition is restricted to a unique unit of measure and void of any allowance for changes in mill utilization or market condition.[14]

Commercial forestland is itself divided among four components: unregulated, standard, special, and marginal. The *unregu-*

[14] It is calculated at culmination of MAI for natural stands; trees must be at least 5 inches in diameter at breast height (dbh); tops are excluded above where they are less than 4 inches in diameter, measured inside the bark. Smaller trees are excluded from the inventory, although some mills currently saw trees as small as 4 inches dbh. The MAI calculation is not adjusted for either advance regeneration or periods when the land may lie idle between harvesting and subsequent regeneration. Furthermore, it only considers species currently growing on the acre—in spite of the fact that other native species (species occurring within the natural successional sequence) may grow at different rates.

Table 2-1. Acres of Productive Forestland (1975), U.S. Forest Service (thousands)

Component	Total West	Alaska	East	Total
Reserved	6,394	2	762	7,158
(Total) a	(14,749)	(397)	(1,069)	(16,215)
Deferred	4,632	97	277	5,006
(Total) a	(10,534)	(2,567)	(148)	(13,249)
Commercial (total)	64,837	4,799	9,389	79,025
Standard	40,011	3,056	7,342	50,409
Special	5,103	917	1,451	7,471
Marginal	16,493	732	481	17,706
Unregulated	3,230	94	115	3,439
Total productive	75,863	4,898	10,428	91,189

Source: USDA Forest Service, *The Outlook for Timber in the United States* (October 1973) appendix I.

a Including unproductive.

lated component is that small portion of the national forests which is devoted to experimental forests, recreational and administrative sites, and to isolated sites which would otherwise be in the regulated (standard, special, and marginal) components. The *standard* component includes those lands on which timber "should be managed intensively." The *special* component includes those lands on which timber "should" be managed with consideration for environmental or multiple use constraints. The *marginal* component includes those lands economically submarginal due to various harvesting constraints (those specified in the Forest Service Manual are insufficient demand or funding, silvicultural practice, and environmental and multiple-use considerations) or access barriers (high road costs) which may disappear within the ten-year Forest Service planning period.[15] In practice, the ten years for removal of harvest and access barriers are ignored. The marginal component becomes all remaining acres approximately meeting the 20 ft^3 criterion.

MULTIPLE USE IMPLICATIONS. The 1976 distribution of acreage within these components is shown in table 2-1. Keeping in mind the FSM 2410 definitions given above, this distribution is revealing in its implications for land allocation between timber and competing nontimber or multiple uses of the forest.

[15] FSM 2412.15 and 2415.4.

First, assume that "productive" timberland is, indeed, productive in the sense that timber production is a profitable use of the land. (We examine this charitable assumption more carefully in the empirical analyses in chapters 5 and 6.) Then, recognizing that complementary forest uses pose no allocational problem, we can focus on competitive uses: We can disregard multiple uses which are in harmony with timber production because provision for them does not require modification of timber management criteria. We can also disregard multiple use opportunities on the rangeland and unproductive timberland managed by the Forest Service.

The market is inoperative for many of the multiple uses of forestland (e.g., recreation in its various forms, watershed, and environmental services). This provides justification for the Forest Service to depart from market efficiency criteria in its timber management. That is, relying on the free timber market to do the allocating would lead to one distribution of productive timberland. Where nonmarket multiple use values compete with timber production, provision for them at levels reflecting their social values implies a different distribution—with less land allocated to timber production. Thus we expect table 2-1 to reveal some allocation of productive timberland to competing multiple uses. The allocation we observe should be indicative of the Forest Service assessment of social valuation for these forest uses.

There are 91,189,000 acres of productive timberland under Forest Service management. Of these, the allocation of 5,006,000 acres is deferred for future decision. Of the remaining 86,183,000 acres, only 8 percent (7,158,000) is reserved for nontimber multiple uses, in contrast with the 58 percent (50,409,000) designated for "intensive" timber management where multiple use benefits are implicitly complementary and coincidental. On the remaining 33 percent (28,616,000), timber production is constrained, often by market conditions, but sometimes by competing multiple use values.

These allocations are equally as impressive on a regional as on a national basis. Apparently, nontimber uses have small impact on land allocation in our national forests. Consideration of nontimber multiple use values causes only a small shift in land allocation from that which would occur if these values were disregarded altogether. Three hypotheses are possible: (1) Conflict between timber and nontimber uses is not the difficult issue we sometimes think it is. Timber may be better suited to more productive sites while competitive uses are generally better suited to poorer, unprofitable timber-growing sites. (2) Intensity of timber production is constrained in a manner that reflects nonmarket-valued uses—although there are no statements to this effect in the definitions of the standard timber-land component in FSM 2410. (3) The Forest Service is mostly a dominant use agency wherever timber is a profitable alternative. Whichever hypothesis one prefers—and there is probably some truth in each—it is saved from being a universal truth by the fact that the special component requires multiple-use constraints. In this component, *some* timberland is used to *some* degree for competing, nontimber uses.

Constrained Optimization

Let us now turn to the Forest Service version of the allowable cut model for harvest and investment determination. The Forest Service Manual delegates implementation of this model to the nine Regional Foresters, who may redelegate to the 154 Forest Supervisors. The latter apply the model independently (therefore, without perfect consistency) to each of the national forests as if it were a separate and complete timbershed supporting local market demand by itself. Therefore, the fundamental land unit for harvest computation is the commercial component of each national forest.

Once the commercial timberland base is determined, each national forest maximizes annual harvests subject to constraints on product quality, harvest flow or "sustained yield," multiple use, and environmental protection. Multiple use and environmental protection enter as professional judgments rather than as formal constraints. In fact, environmental protection is not even stated in FSM 2410; nevertheless, the threat of litigation under the National Environmental Protection Act and Section 208 of the Federal Water Pollution Control Act makes it a very real implicit constraint.

In conclusion, a simplified version of the Forest Service model resembles Eq. (2-1a) for even-aged stands under area control, but with two constraints: product quality and sustained yield.

$$Y_i^4 = \max_T A_m\,[Q(T)/T] + Y_i\,(A_g/T_c)$$

$$+ \lambda_1 (T - T_k) + \lambda_2 (Y_i^4 - \alpha Y_{i-1}^4)$$
$$\text{for all } i = 1, 2, \ldots, T_c \qquad (2\text{-}5)$$

where $Y_i(A_g/T_c) =$ volume of old growth harvested from the A_g acres in year i

$T_k =$ time required to grow a tree of some minimum size

$\alpha =$ proportionality constant

λ_1 and λ_2 are lagrangian multipliers; in economic terms, they are the shadow prices (costs) of unitary shifts in the product quality and sustained yield constraints, respectively

The required conversion period is an arbitrary one-and-one-half times CMAI or approximately 120–150 years for the most important commercial species.[16] If harvesting at CMAI is equivalent to the economic harvest age using a zero interest rate, then harvesting at one and one half times culmination of MAI is equivalent to economic harvesting with a *negative* interest. This irrationality is reinforced in some applications for which the conversion period remains unchanged as each year passes. In such cases the regulated forest and harvesting at culmination of MAI are only approached asymptotically.

Value per unit of volume increases with tree diameter, which increases with tree age. Thus, age and diameter are proxies for quality, and the constraint $(T - T_k)$ ensures that harvested trees are of some minimum quality. Without a price variable in this part of the model, there is no empirical rule for assessing the quality standard. Various standards might be used [e.g., board feet, which requires trees of $11\frac{1}{2}$ inches in diameter at breast height (dbh); cubic feet, which requires 5 inches dbh; biomass, which counts everything], each leading to a different empirical growth function with its own T_k, its own age at CMAI, and its own harvest volume. The Forest Service uses the board foot measure, although many mills saw lumber from trees considerably smaller than $11\frac{1}{2}$ inches dbh.[17]

---

[16] FSM 2410.3 (1), Emergency Directive No. 16 (May 1973).

[17] For example, Roger D. Fight and Dennis L. Schweitzer, "What If We Calculate the Allowable Cut in Cubic Feet?" *Journal of Forestry* vol. 72, no. 2 (February 1974) pp. 87–89. Sullivan, Bell, and Usher suggest that a purely measurement change to include trees from 5 inches dbh would result in a 10–30 percent increase in current Forest Service harvests. Sullivan, Bell, and Usher, "Information Relating to RPAT Timber Policy Issue #1."

These two requirements ($T_c = 3T/2, T \geq T_k$) are intended to protect against the uncertainties of imperfect growth and inventory estimates and decreasing inventory quality, respectively. Long conversion periods and large minimum size imply reduced annual harvests from the stock of old growth or, what is the same, greater inventory available to meet uncertain future demands. Norstrom demonstrated the reasonableness of this response by proving that the optimal rotation is longer under uncertainty.[18] He drew no empirical conclusions, however, about the optimal magnitude of adjustment for uncertainty. Timberstand growth decreases in the years subsequent to CMAI. Therefore, the Forest Service pays an opportunity cost, in the form of growth forgone in the second and subsequent rotations, to protect against uncertainty. The opportunity cost is substantial for conversion periods as long as 120 years and diameters as large as 11½ inches.

The second constraint, known as sustained yield or "even-flow," guards against an eventual "falldown" in annual harvest volumes after the final harvest of old growth by ensuring that no single annual harvest level is less than some proportion α of the previous year's level. Today, the Forest Service applies an extreme version of this constraint, called nondeclining, or strict, even flow. It specifies that $Y_i \geq Y_{i-1}$, or $\alpha = 1$.[19]

There are two major impacts of the even-flow constraint: First, it reinforces the rationing of old growth harvests over time. By postponing harvests it delays receipts, thereby decreasing the present net worth of the old growth inventory. Keane has shown that under even flow, some volume may even be lost forever. For example, the Timber Management Plan for the Lassen National Forest calls

[18] Carl J. Norstrom, "A Stochastic Model for the Growth Period Decision in Forestry," *Swedish Journal of Economics* vol. 77, no. 3 (1975) pp. 329–337.

[19] Even flow is a requirement of the Multiple Use–Sustained Yield Act of 1960 and the National Forest Management Act of 1976 (NFMA), although neither act requires strict even flow. NFMA permits annual harvest level fluctuations as long as they balance out by the end of each ten-year forest planning period. It also permits decennial departures from even flow in order to meet overall multiple use objectives of the forest plan. (See Section 11 of the act.)

The Forest Service normally calculates harvest levels upwards of *400 years* into the future—dependent on an unchanging acreage base, although it knows this base is decreasing and, therefore, that its even-flow calculation is imperfect. It should also expect technical change in timber growing over the 400-year period. The absence of land base and technical change variables decreases the reliability of the even flow annual harvest calculation.

for annual harvests of 150 million board feet (MMbf) perpetually. Keane estimated that harvests could be increased to 268 MMbf annually for the first decade and continued at 150 MMbf annually thereafter simply by relaxing the even-flow constraint. Thus, under the Forest Service plan, 1,180 MMbf are lost forever.[20] Second, by restricting harvest volume adjustments in response to changing market conditions, this constraint only encourages price fluctuation, and forces volume adjustments on private timberland owners, loggers, and timber processors. Only public agencies, such as the Forest Service, can ignore prices and at the same time isolate themselves from questions of market entry or exit. Even those private landowners who apply some form of the allowable cut model must be price responsive. Their continued existence depends on a degree of price competitiveness.

The Forest Service and those who supported inclusion of an even-flow clause in NFMA justify it on grounds of local community stability, but leave the questions "at what cost?" and "to whom?" unanswered. Furthermore, given technical change, substitution among factors and products, depreciation of fixed capital and equipment, and labor mobility, it would be unique if strict even flow were the best guarantee of community stability—to say nothing of social welfare.

In addition to these constraints, the national forests in Oregon and Washington have been operating under a rule of cutting old growth first. They calculate annual harvest levels from Eq. (2-5) but take the actual harvests, whenever possible, from the old growth inventory. While it is true that this rule saves some decaying wood, it amounts to an antieconomic worst-first rule because remaining old growth timber tends to be on the poorest sites and in the least accessible areas—otherwise it would have been harvested earlier, before this rule was implemented.

Finally, a word about labeling is in order. Annual harvests calculated in the manner of Eq. (2-5) are often called the "allowable cut." Actually, allowable cut was the term for periodic Forest Service harvests under a previous timber management model. Harvests calculated in the manner of Eq. (2-5) are properly labeled the "potential" harvest if they refer to the ten-year forest plan, or the

[20] John Keane, "Mimeo #6025" (San Francisco, Western Timber Association, November 11, 1974).

"programmed" harvest if they refer to the harvest planned for the next single year.[21]

Timber Pricing

Our analysis would not be complete without examining the procedure for pricing Forest Service timber. Timber is sold on the stump—hence, the term "stumpage"—at a price assessed independently of the allowable cut model for harvest volume determination. Other timberland owners besides the Forest Service use allowable cut models, and each has its own stumpage pricing scheme. The Forest Service uses an appraisal approach based on the sound economic concepts of derived demand and reservation prices.[22]

We might examine these concepts for a moment. To understand the market exchange price for any good, we need to know about its demand and its supply. The *demand* price for any resource is set in the market for final goods and is related to quantity demanded. The theory of derived demand explains primary resource demand price as the final good demand price minus the costs of intermediate production. Thus, stumpage demand price is the market price of lumber or paper minus the production costs (sometimes known as product conversion costs) for mill and logging operations.

Supply prices are different for the long and the short run. In the *long run,* when all factors of production are variable, the supply

---

[21] There are five different items sometimes known by "allowable cut": (1) the harvest optimizing model, (2) the potential harvest, (3) the programmed harvest, (4) the *ex ante* planned harvest, and (5) the *ex post* harvest. The potential harvest originates from the three regulated (standard, special, and marginal) components of the commercial forestland base. It is calculated for a ten-year period. The programmed annual harvest is the next single year's planned harvest from the standard, special, and unregulated components. The marginal component is excluded, while unregulated harvests are not calculated according to Eq. (2-5). The *ex ante* planned annual harvest varies from the programmed harvest by several lesser adjustments: thinning, salvage, and protection cuts; product cuts; and harvests required by presidential edict. *Ex post* annual harvests are less than *ex ante* by the volume offered but unsold, but more than *ex ante* by the volume previously sold but uncut till this year. (Contracts normally allow three years to complete the harvest. As a result, the actual harvest level shows greater variation than the potential, programmed, or *ex ante* harvest levels.)

[22] FSM 2420 (May 1972).

price of a unit of output is its incremental production cost. For timber, the factors of production are land, silvicultural inputs such as seedlings and fertilizer and the labor and entrepreneurial effort associated with them, and growing time. The production costs are the land rent, silvicultural costs, and the cost of holding invested capital. The *short-run* supply price, on the other hand, is only the cost of putting an already completed product, a unit of standing timber inventory, on the market. For timber, this short-run supply price is the timber sale administration cost minus the value of the forgone opportunity to wait another year and collect any appreciation in timber volume and value.

In the long run, the expected demand price must equal or exceed the supply price or the firm will lose money and go out of business. In the case of the Forest Service, we hardly expect it to go out of business, but we do expect land to be removed from timber production where long-run production costs exceed expected demand prices. In the short run, a firm still hopes demand prices cover production costs, but, if they do not, it cuts its losses by selling at any price above the short-run supply price. In a volatile market or a market where the short-run supply price may be but a fraction of long-run supply price—both characteristic of the stumpage market—producers may establish a reservation price above the short-run price but below which they will not sell.

So much for the theory. The Forest Service, as previously indicated, uses the derived demand and reservation pricing concepts to establish its stumpage prices. It appraises demand price by subtracting from the market lumber price (1) production costs and (2) a margin for the processor's risk and profit according to the formula[23]

$$D = D = L - N - M \tag{2-6}$$

where D = stumpage demand price

L = demand price for lumber taken (realized) by the mill

N = production costs for mill and logging operations

M = margin for risk and profit

If access to the timber requires road construction, then road costs are also subtracted.

[23] It is not clear where the Forest Service received the quasi-regulatory authority to set returns for profit and risk.

The result is the derived demand appraisal. It is the advertised sale price only if it is sufficiently high to cover reforestation costs and an arbitrary, that is, noncost-related, base rate ($3 per Mbf for high-priced species, $2 for medium, and $1 for low-priced species). Together, the reforestation costs plus the base rate are a reservation price. Bids are accepted and stumpage is sold at a price equal to or greater than the advertised sale price. Consider the following example:

Appraisal price	$150 per Mbf
Road costs	$148 per Mbf
Derived demand appraisal	$2 per Mbf
Reforestation costs	$25 per Mbf
Base price	$3 per Mbf
Reservation price	$28 per Mbf

The advertised price is $28 per Mbf, the greater of either the derived demand appraisal or the reservation price.

Where road construction is necessary and the advertised price exceeds the derived demand appraisal, that is, where the reservation price exceeds appraised price minus road costs, as in our example, the Forest Service is acknowledging that its appraisal may be less than that of some bidders. It is, furthermore, offering the stumpage in return for a road. The rationale for such an exchange is difficult to understand on these grounds alone. The road should be justified on its own grounds. If future timber receipts from subsequent rotations or if nontimber multiple use benefits justify building roads, they should explicitly enter the equation.

Such cases where the advertised price exceeds the derived demand appraisal—regardless of road construction—are known as deficit sales. The term "deficit" clearly *does not mean* that Forest Service receipts are less than would be obtained at the reservation price. In fact, deficit sales are often bid considerably above the advertised price and, conversely, nondeficit sales are occasionally not bid upon at all. Each case implies that the appraisal itself neglected or misestimated some important element of current market conditions. (The Forest Service receives a lot of meaningless objections from loggers who freely bid on deficit sales but subsequently argue they are paying too much. If the loggers themselves did not appraise the timber at a higher value than the Forest Service, they should not have bid.)

The appraisal process is administratively costly and even unnecessary except in those markets where the Forest Service is facing colluding buyers or a monopsonist, that is, a single bidder with attendant control over the final price. Where there is competition, the final price would be set in the market regardless of the appraisal. Widely varying bid and advertised prices are sufficient indication that the appraisal system is faulty. Likely reasons are (1) failure of the system to consider anticipated product price increases, (2) misestimates of adequate returns for profit and risk, and (3) scale economies or misestimates due to the lack of a relationship between prices or costs and quantity in Eq. (2-6).

Long-run production costs, which should help the Forest Service determine whether or not to continue managing any particular parcel of land for timber production, are never assessed. When Barlow summed the most identifiable timber production costs (sale costs themselves and road costs excluding the cost of Forest Service-built roads—the most apparent exclusions were payments to counties in lieu of taxes; fire, insect, and disease control; administration; and carrying costs on invested capital) for the years 1970 through 1973, he found they exceeded timber sale revenues each year in at least three of nine Forest Service regions.[24] This implies that the land from which the average sale was made in those three regions either (a) should have been withheld from sale while its timber appreciated, (b) should have been managed less expensively, or (c) should be removed from timber production altogether. If production costs in these three regions are indicative of

[24] The Forest Service is in the process of reallocating funding in some of these regions. A frequently heard defense of misallocation to timber is that budgets for other Forest Service activities are often inadequate and that timber budgets provide personnel and equipment that can be employed on nontimber activities during slack time. A Forest Service budgeting and accounting system allowing full comparison of costs and revenues for the various forest outputs would allow assessment of nontimber budgets on their own merits as well as more defensible timber budgets. For a first cut at budget comparisons, see Marion Clawson, "The National Forests"; Thomas J. Barlow, "Forest Service Pricing Mechanism for National Forest Timber Sales," as submitted by Congressman George Brown of California in *The Congressional Record*, May 10, 1976, H4169-4172; and William F. Hyde, "Compounding Clearcuts," in John Baden and Richard Stroup, eds., *The Environmental Costs of Government Action* (Proceedings of a Liberty Fund conference at Big Sky, Montana, September 1978).

costs in the remaining regions, then some sales in the latter should also be reevaluated.[25]

Summary and Comparison of Allowable Cut with Economic Efficiency Results

We have examined the basic allowable cut model for harvest level determination and its Forest Service application. There are three independent parts to it: (1) land management decisions, (2) harvest and investment decisions, and (3) the pricing decision.

The land area to be managed is often not an important decision for private timberland owners. They tend to possess good land and they use it in the production of timber unconstrained by other forest uses. Public agencies, on the other hand, generally possess some poorer land less well suited for timber production. They also have responsibilities to provide land for competing, nonmarket, forest uses. The Forest Service determines its land base for timber on an arbitrary criterion (i.e., land able to naturally produce 20 ft^3 of wood fiber per acre per year) that reflects biological productivity and bears only a coincidental relationship to either socially or financially efficient use of the land.

Annual harvests from this land base are determined by an application of the allowable cut model itself. The basic objective of the model is to maximize annual harvests over time, while converting previously unmanaged land in the timberland base into managed, or regulated, timberland. In the Forest Service application,

[25] For another view of Forest Service timber appraisal, see Sidney Weintraub, "Price-Making in Forest Service Timber Sales," *American Economic Review* vol. 49, no. 4 (September 1959) pp. 628–637. There is an extensive literature on appraisal, a review of which might begin with (1) William R. Bentley, "An Economic Model of Public Timber Sales," *Journal of Forestry* vol. 67, no. 6 (June 1969), pp. 405–409 and the succeeding discussions by Robert A. Jones and Walter S. Mead on pp. 410–414; and (2) literature on timber sale policy: W. R. Bentley, "Forest Service Timber Sales," *Land Economics* vol. 44, no. 2 (May 1968) pp. 205–218; and Dennis E. Teeguarden, "Allocating Public Timber by Transferable Purchasing Quotas," *Natural Resources Journal* vol. 9, no. 4 (October 1969) pp. 576–589. See also Walter J. Mead, *Competition and Oligopsony in the Douglas Fir Lumber Industry* (Berkeley, University of California Press, 1966); and Ronald N. Johnson, "Competitive Bidding for Federally Owned Timber," (University of Washington, Ph.D. dissertation, 1977).

the conversion of previously unmanaged land occurs at a very slow rate for the ostensible purpose of leaving an untapped inventory of mature timber as protection against poor data and uncertain future demands. The Forest Service further constrains the allowable cut objective to guarantee a minimum timber quality and an even harvest flow year after year.

Within these constraints the model acts to tie together operationally independent harvest and investment decisions. New growth, in response to investment, is realized immediately in the form of harvests from the previously unmanaged land. In fact, investments in new growth are a prerequisite to such harvests. Receipts from the incremental harvests are compared with investment expenditures to calculate an internal rate of return, which is really a measure of annual organizational cash flow and not the usual measurement of investment efficiency.

The basic allowable cut model is largely unresponsive to market prices although some applications of it are modified to allow some price response. In the Forest Service application, determination of harvest volume and setting the offer price are wholly independent activities. The offer price is set by subtracting logging and processing costs from lumber prices. If this appraised price exceeds an arbitrary minimum reservation price, timber is advertised for sale to the highest bidder. Since there is no comparison of prices with production costs, neither appraisal nor eventual sale price provide any guide to long-run timber investments.

It is apparent that the allowable cut model incorporates a number of departures from economic efficiency. In the remainder of this chapter we suggest the direction of shifts in prices, harvest levels, and land use that would occur if economic efficiency criteria replaced allowable cut. Initially, we examine the period of old growth conversion and later, the truly long run where all investments are variable, the entire timberland base is regulated, and annual harvests are steady and sustainable.

The Short Run

Under allowable cut criteria, the old growth inventory is harvested over a period equal to or exceeding the rotation age (assuming an economic land base). The intent is to obtain an even stream of annual harvests while eventually transforming the land containing old growth stands into the uniform annular segments of a fully regulated forest. In contrast, under economic criteria, old growth is treated like a stock resource. The inventory of old growth is optimally "mined" at a rate such that the marginal net return (MNR) from the last unit of volume harvested (mined) equals its user cost. User cost is the discounted value of expected appreciation resulting from volume growth and relative price increases. *Ceteris paribus,* discounting causes the optimal flow of old growth harvests to be rapid initially and to decline from year to year.

For large producers with an impact on market prices, MNR declines with increases in quantity sold. That is, for producers who perceive a downward sloping demand curve, additional volume harvested is absorbed by the market only at ever lower prices. Eventually this year's market price is so low that it pays to postpone additional harvests until the following year. Thus, the rational large producer does not harvest his old growth all at once. He does, however, harvest at a rate faster than the constant annual rate suggested by allowable cut criteria. The present net value of his old growth harvest stream is greater using economic efficiency criteria, but his timberland is divided into more uniform annular segments if he uses allowable cut criteria.

Large private producers may own some old growth, but they do not tend to own land which is unprofitable for harvesting. Most marginal timberland is managed by public agencies. For public agencies, some land in the allowable cut base may actually be beyond the perimeter of efficient management regardless of standing timber volumes. In this case, delayed harvest of old growth—which occurs under allowable cut criteria—can serve efficiency ends. That is, it delays harvest from land which should not be in the timber management base in the first place. This justification fails, however, where a "worst first" rule prevails and there is a rush to harvest the inefficient timberland.

Small producers perceive market stumpage prices as unchanging with respect to the volume they offer. Their MNR is constant. It is easy to calculate the difference in the present net value of their old growth harvested under allowable cut and efficiency criteria. Assume an unchanging stock of old growth, constant relative stumpage prices, a capital opportunity cost of 5 percent, and a 100-year conversion period,

$$V^1 = \sum_{i=1}^{100} (pG/100) \ (1.05)^{-i} \cong 1/5 \ pG \qquad (2\text{-}7)$$

where V^1 = present net value
p = stumpage price
G = volume of old growth

The present net value of old growth harvested under allowable cut criteria is approximately one-fifth its value under efficiency criteria. For longer conversion periods or greater opportunity costs of capital, the value of old growth harvested by small producers under allowable cut criteria is even less than one-fifth of its value if harvested under efficiency criteria.

The Long Run

In the long run, old growth is not an issue; the forest is fully regulated and annual harvests are steady and sustainable. The issues of importance are the level of sustainable annual harvest flow and its cost. We begin our long-run comparison of harvest criteria by stating the efficiency solutions and, then, by demonstrating how allowable cut solutions vary from efficiency solutions.

Efficiency solutions are least-cost solutions by definition, therefore they result in the greatest sustainable annual harvest volume associated with any given set of stumpage prices and input costs. The efficient model can generally be described by

$$V^2 = \max_{T,E} \ [\, pQ(T,E)e^{-rT} - wE - R \int_T e^{-rT} \, dt \,] \qquad (2\text{-}8)$$

where production is now a function of both time and E, a measure of silvicultural effort (or all factors of production other than time and land), r is the opportunity cost of capital, w the cost of a unit of silvicultural effort, and $R \int e^{-rT}$ is the rental fee for a fixed unit of timberland. From this model and the expectation of regular additions of marginal acres for higher and higher stumpage prices, we can diagram the aggregate supply schedule as S_E in figure 2-2.

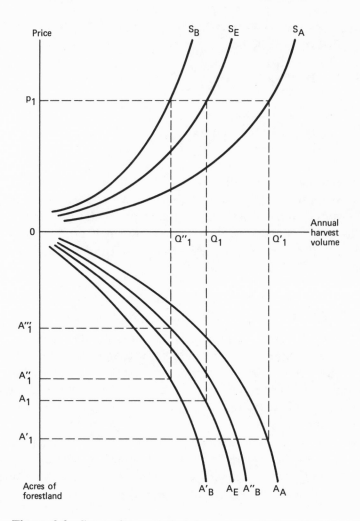

Figure 2-2. Comparison of timber supply and forestland use under allowable cut and efficiency criteria.

Furthermore, we can compare supply directly with its requirements for timberland, A_E, also in figure 2-2.[26]

With this background on efficiency, we can return to the allowable cut model and contrast its results in terms of figure 2-2. After old growth conversion, the allowable cut model becomes a cash flow model for the entire regulated forest. It supports silvicultural management on one part of the forest with receipts from harvests on a

[26] We develop this model with greater attention to detail in chapters 3 and 4.

different part. Harvests are restricted, however, to timberstands that have achieved CMAI or, what is the same, the harvest timing parameter T_m is chosen such that it maximizes $Q(T,E)/T$. The mathematical formulation for the model is:

$$V^3 = \max_{T,E} [\, pQ(T,E) - wE - R + \lambda_3 (T - T_m)\,] \qquad (2\text{-}9)$$

such that $T_m = \max_{T} Q(T)/T$, where λ_3 is a lagrangian multiplier, the shadow price of increasing the minimum harvest age one more year. We can see a direct relationship between Eq. (2-9) and Eq. (2-4), the ACE formulation, if we consider $Q(T,E)$ to be the harvest volume difference $(Y^3 - Y^1)$ for a single year and if silvicultural costs and the annual land rent in Eq. (2-9) combine in the single cost term in Eq. (2-4).

Since capital carrying costs are not charged in Eq. (2-9), and receipts are reinvested internally, for a given stumpage price more cash remains to be spent on all timber investments (that is, capital or an extended rotation, silvicultural effort, and land). The annual harvest volume associated with any price exceeds that associated with the same price in the efficiency formulation, Eq. (2-8). The allowable cut supply curve S_A is to the right of the efficiency supply curve S_E in figure 2-2.

An alert investor will discover that this allowable cut result arises from the combination of two independent investment decisions. He can obtain receipts from one segment of his forest without reinvesting on another. Instead, he can spend his cash wherever it promises greatest returns, either within or outside of forestry. He will remove his ready cash from timber investments until he finds the independent investment which can be justified on its own grounds, or until

$$V^4 = \max_{T,E} [\, pQe^{-rT} - wE - R \int_{T} e^{-rT}\, dt + \lambda_3 (T - T_m)\,] \qquad (2\text{-}10)$$

Assuming the constraint on harvest timing is binding, this formulation leads to a supply curve like S_B in figure 2-2. It would shift from S_A directly to the efficiency supply curve S_E except for the constraint. Equation (2-10) rids us of extramarginal land previously justified as timberland because of a subsidy from the better acres.

It also rids us of excessive, inefficient, levels of silvicultural effort. Due to the binding constraint, however, Eq. (2-10) still implies an overinvestment in capital carrying costs (extended rotation) in comparison with investments in land and silvicultural effort. (The returns to an extra dollar invested in extending the production period to meet the constraint are less than the returns if that dollar had been spent on additional land or silvicultural inputs.)

Let us interject here that labor is an important component of silvicultural effort. Since the harvest timing constraint gives preference to capital over labor, it acts against the interests of timber-producing communities with significant unemployment—and the community stability concern of Forest Service timber management.

We can also compare the land use requirements of the allowable cut and the constrained efficiency models with the land use requirements of the efficiency model. We begin with reference to A_E in figure 2-2, the efficiency-derived variable land production function. The allowable cut model, Eq. (2-9), justifies additional investment per acre with resulting additional annual harvest volume per acre. This is consistent with the common belief that the allowable cut approach produces older trees at harvest time. The variable land production function A_A derived from the allowable cut model is to the right, or above, the efficiency-derived function A_E. Furthermore, for a given market price p_1, the allowable cut approach uses more land A_1' than the A_1 acres required by the efficiency approach. Some part of the extra investment justified by the allowable cut approach is this investment in land.

We can derive the position of the constrained efficiency variable land production function and compare it with the efficiency-derived function A_E. The relative position of the latter is less certain. For a given acre, a less than efficient combination of *carrying costs and silvicultural effort* is used; therefore, a less than efficient annual harvest level results, and A_B' is to the left, or below, A_E. There is also a tradeoff between carrying costs and acreage, however, and it results in a less than efficient *number of acres* being required for any given harvest level. This suggests that the constrained efficiency production function A_B'' is to the right, or above A_E. The dominating effect, therefore the true position of the constrained efficiency production function, is unknown without additional information. We do know, however, that for a given market price, some acres which would otherwise be used for timber production are unprofitable producers in the constrained case. These are the A_1A_1'' or the A_1A_1''' acres, depending on whether A_B' or A_B'' respectively, is the correct constrained efficiency production function.

Conclusion

The magnitude of price-quantity difference between allowable cut and efficiency approaches is not fully known, but four recent empirical analyses have considered it. Jones examined costs and timber harvests in the Beaverhead National Forest.[27] He found that supply curves for timber and wilderness are greatly influenced by management constraints. A recent Forest Service study supports this point, although it bases its analysis on the allowable cut model. The empirical results of this study support the conclusion that multiple use managerial constraints are so severe as to dissipate all opportunity for timber managerial discretion and optimization.[28]

Kutay and Walker examined specific Forest Service applications of the allowable cut approach. Kutay examined the removal of roadless land from the timberland base in western Oregon.[29] Removal of this land causes a decrease in allowable harvests. It also decreases road-building costs. Kutay found that reappropriation of road-building funds from roadless areas to other timber management activities in previously roaded areas increased annual harvest levels. In summary, as we depart from allowable cut criteria in the direction of efficiency criteria, *for the same costs more timber can be grown and harvested and more roadless land* (Kutay's interest) *remains for nontimber uses.*

[27] J. Greg Jones, "Economic Costs of Allocating Land to Wilderness" (Iowa State University, Ph.D. dissertation, 1977).

[28] Roger D. Fight, K. Norman Johnson, Kent P. Connaughton, and Robert W. Sassaman, "Roadless Area-Intensive Management Tradeoffs on Western National Forests" (USDA Forest Service, 1978).

[29] Kurt Kutay, "Oregon Economic Impact Assessment of Proposed Wilderness Legislation," in Oregon Omnibus Wilderness Act, publ. no. 95-42, Part 2, 1977, pp. 29–63, Hearings before the Subcommittee on Parks and Recreation of the Committee on Energy and Natural Resources, United States Senate, 95 Cong., 1 sess., April 21, 1977 (Washington, GPO).

In an examination of the Stanislaus National Forest, Walker demonstrated that constraints on tree diameter and harvest flow, as well as a worst-first rule favoring old growth harvests, can be so binding as to reduce harvest levels calculated by the allowable cut approach below harvest levels calculated by efficiency rules.[30] This reduction holds both before and after all old growth is harvested. *In summary, more timber is available at lower costs* (Walker's interest) *using efficiency criteria. Moreover, Walker found no reason to justify harvest of less accessible old growth stands. Again, more land remains for nontimber uses.*

In this chapter we have reviewed the most common alternative to economic efficiency criteria for guiding timber management decisions. In this concluding section we have contrasted the alternative or allowable cut results with those obtained under economic efficiency. Our contrast has been conceptual. Empirical analyses by Kutay and Walker support our conclusions. They suggest that both timber volume and nontimber acreage gains, as well as financial savings, are forthcoming when managers switch from allowable cut to efficiency criteria for timber management. These empirical analyses each focused on gains to efficiency in the economic short run when some factors are fixed, and none dealt with both a fully unconstrained efficiency model and its land use implications. These are our focus in subsequent chapters.

[30] John D. Walker, "Timber Management Planning," Western Timber Association, August 1974.

3

The Economics of
Timber Production

We have examined the general model for timber production familiar to public agencies and many private firms and we have suggested the direction of its departures from economic efficiency. In this chapter and the next we develop the contrasting efficiency model. Here we define efficient timber production for the competitive firm with a fixed land base.

On some unit of available land, seedlings appear—naturally or with man's assistance. Over time they grow in volume and appreciate in value until the decision is made to harvest them and convert them into a useful product. During the transition from seedlings to maturity, trees themselves are both inventory and capital as the needles or leaves combine light, water, and soil nutrients to produce new wood fiber accumulating on the bole of the trees. The time rate of this accumulation is a function of land quality, the genetic characteristics of individual trees, and the natural and artificial flows of energy inputs; that is, the light, water, and soil nutrients.

Forests possess a number of interesting biological characteristics (see appendix A), but from an economic perspective, they are only a particular form of growing capital. We first explain their general growth or production function and then introduce the economic variables, prices and costs. The inputs of choice are (1) *the length of the production period* (rotation age), adjusted for a chosen lag in reforestation and (2) the *level of silvicultural effort*.

Silvicultural effort includes both labor and capital aspects of the various timber management activities, as well as entrepreneurial skills. Our presentation of the production model is static and deterministic and this remains a shortcoming in a dynamic and stochastic world.

The decision as to when to harvest has fascinated economists for much of the 200-year modern history of their discipline.[1] When to harvest, how much to harvest, and how quickly to expend the inherited stock of mature timber are all problems in traditional *capital theory*. Where to harvest, a problem in *location theory*, is less well developed in the economics literature.[2] This problem includes not only which acres to allocate to timber production, but also locational variations in the optimal rotation age and the optimal level of silvicultural effort. Determination of the optimal rotation age and the optimal level of silvicultural effort follows directly from our presentation of the production model. From here it is a simple step to determine the optimal harvest level both per rotation and per year. We postpone discussion of the inherited stock of mature timber until chapter 4. In that chapter we direct attention to the underlying location theory and its application in forestry before discussing the relationships explaining locational variance

[1] Martin Faustmann is credited with the first correct capital theory model, "On the Determination of the Value Which Forest Land and Immature Stands Possess for Forestry" (1849), in M. Gane, ed., *Institute Paper 42* (1968), Commonwealth Forestry Institute, Oxford University. The best-known critiques of Faustmann and succeeding timber management models are M. Mason Gaffney, "Concepts of Financial Maturity of Timber and Other Assets" (Raleigh, North Carolina State College Agricultural Economics Information Series, no. 62, 1957); William R. Bentley and Dennis Teeguarden, "Financial Maturity: A Theoretical Review," *Forest Science* vol. 11, no. 1 (March 1965) pp. 76–87; and Paul A. Samuelson, "Economics of Forestry in an Evolving Society," *Journal of Public Inquiry* vol. 14, no. 4 (December 1976) pp. 466–492. See also Peter H. Pearse, "The Optimum Forest Rotation," *Forestry Chronicle* (June 1967) pp. 178–195; Orris C. Herfindahl and Allen V. Kneese, *The Economic Theory of Natural Resources* (Columbus, Ohio, Charles E. Merrill, 1974) pp. 81–85; and Colin W. Clark, *Mathematical Bioeconomics* (New York, Wiley, 1976) pp. 256–269. Each of these is well done. Disregard statements by economists suggesting that natural forests are composed of evenly distributed trees from all age and size classes.

[2] The basic reference is Johann H. von Thünen, *Der Isolierte Staat in Beziehung auf Landwirtschaft und Nationalökonomie* (The Isolated State in Relation to Land Use and National Economy) (Berlin, Schmaucher Zarchlin, 1875). See also G. Robinson Gregory, *Forest Resource Economics* (New York, McGraw-Hill, 1972) pp. 255–256, 352–353.

in the optimality conditions. In summary, we find the optimality conditions each have the standard intuitive logic, that is, at optimal investment levels the discounted time stream of expected marginal returns equals the discounted stream of marginal investment costs.

Readers who are interested in pursuing the topic further may refer to appendix B, "Special Cases of the Production Model." It compares (1) the biological management model and (2) the standard economic model with (3) our revision of the economic model. The former two are special cases of the latter, each with economic justification in its own historical context. The appendix goes on to suggest a trend toward perennial management, that is, timber management of more than just a custodial nature for the years between reforestation and final harvest. The ultimate in perennial management is for weeding, fertilizing, thinning, pruning, or the like, to occur in virtually all of these intermediate years. Rotation age has been the classic measure of comparison for biological and economic models. As we introduce technical change and perennial management, rotation ages for biological and economic models tend to converge.

The Conceptual Model

The forest manager's or landowner's objective is to maximize the present value of timber production from variable inputs of silvicultural effort and time, where time is really the use of something for a period (1 acre for one year). Present value is the expected total timber revenue minus the costs of silvicultural effort and periodic land rental fees, all discounted.

In this chapter we look at production from the perspective of a competitive firm with a *fixed* land base. Our focus on a single acre is in keeping with the tradition of the literature, but it requires the implicit assumption of constant returns to scale for the fixed factor. We discuss this assumption in greater detail in chapter 4 before varying the land base.

We make the further temporary assumption that our acre is representative: all other acres in the productive region possess the same biological potential. They vary from our acre only in their access to markets (i.e., mills) and in their relative logging difficulty, both of which are reflected in stumpage prices. Once we determine the optimality conditions, the assumption of uniform biological potential can be dropped, and we can determine new optimality conditions for an acre of each different productivity class. (Alternatively, we could show production as a function of land quality, as well as of time and effort, and find the optimality conditions for land quality directly.)

The Productive Process

Our representative acre first becomes available for reforestation in year zero. It may have been growing another crop of trees which was just harvested, or the land may have been previously used for an altogether different purpose, but it becomes idle, awaiting reforestation only in this year. Seeds first germinate, or sprouts first emerge from the roots or stump of their parent stock, to begin their characteristic growth path t_r years later. The period, t_r years, is the regeneration lag. It is positive if the land lies idle for a while, zero in the case of immediate restocking, or it can even be negative if there is advance natural regeneration or if transplanted seedlings are older than the idle period is long.

The regeneration lag is important, because the owner must pay for idle land, either in real land rent fees or in terms of lost opportunity to grow more timber. In actual application, the regeneration lag may become critical. On dry sites in the Rocky Mountains, for example, natural regeneration may take decades, and even artificial regeneration may not succeed the first time. Disregard for the regeneration lag on such sites was a fundamental issue in the Bitterroot controversy in the 1960s.[3] Some Pacific Coast firms, on the other hand, are considering planting three-year-old seedlings within a year of the previous harvest for an effective regeneration lag of minus two. Forest managers are aware of the importance of the regeneration lag,[4] but even if they were not, they would develop

[3] See *A University View of the Forest Service,* Committee Print 115, Senate Committee on Interior and Insular Affairs, 91 Cong. 2 sess. (1970), better known as the "Bolle Report."

[4] For example, Kenneth P. Davis, Philip A. Briegleb, John Fedkiw, and Lewis R. Grosenbaugh, "Determination of Allowable Annual Timber Cut on Forty-Two Western National Forests," Report of the Board of Review, Forest Service, U.S. Department of Agriculture, M-1299, September 3, 1962, p. 23. Here we begin to expand upon (and complicate) the simple capital theory models cited in footnote 1, above.

an awareness as they approached the final harvest of existing mature timber and expected to face a fully regulated forest—including no idle land but only land with trees of age classes ranging from one year to maturity. Instead, they would observe much idle land and no mature trees. Their plans would call for harvesting mature trees of age t_h. Instead, they would observe trees of maximum age $t_h - t_r$.

Starting in the year zero, the land produces some volume of timber greater than or equal to zero over the next T years. Biological yield, however, is normally given in terms of tree age at harvest t_h. Therefore, ignoring silvicultural effort for the moment, volume per acre in T years is the biological yield Q placed in the context of the regeneration lag, or $Q(t_h + t_r)$. Starting in year zero, in $(t_h + t_r)$ years we can harvest a volume of timber equal to $Q(t_h + t_r)$ per acre and begin another rotation, eventually repeating output $Q(t_h + t_r)$ in $2(t_h + t_r)$ years and again in $3(t_h + t_r)$ years and so on for an indefinite number of rotations. The regeneration lag may decrease for later rotations as management intensifies. We concentrate on the first rotation and assume that further regeneration lags are similar to the first because discounting over the long growing periods characteristic of timber considerably diminishes the economic impact of changes in subsequent regeneration lags. (Technical change may also occur, altering the level of production in the second and subsequent rotations. See the discussion of seed improvement in appendix B.)

The two time periods represented by t_r and t_h may create confusion if continued throughout our discussion. To prevent this, we introduce a single summary symbol T for the production period such that $T = t_h + t_r$ hereafter. We can now identify the production function for a given acre.

$$Q = Q(T,E) \qquad (3\text{-}1)$$

Volume of wood fiber Q is a function of time T and the level of initial period silvicultural effort E. In the absence of management, land lies idle until it regenerates naturally, and only time affects the production level. On the other hand, when positive amounts of effort are applied, it can affect the biological production level at a given time indirectly, by decreasing regeneration lag, as well as directly, by changing the growing stock, for example, by improving seed quality or by adding soil nutrients. Therefore, the level of effort affects both the level and the rate of production.

Production as a function of time is described by the following relations:

$$Q_T = 0, T \leq t_r, T \geq t_1$$
$$Q_T > 0, t_r < T < t_1$$
$$Q_{TT} \geq 0, T \leq t_2 \qquad\qquad (3\text{-}2)$$
$$Q_{TT} < 0, T > t_2$$

where subscripts denote first and second partial derivatives with respect to the subscript and t_1 is the time at which the maximum volume is attained. The second derivative becomes negative at some time t_2 (an inflection point) after t_r (see figure 3-1). This is the logistic growth function characteristic of density-determined biological populations. Both single trees and even-aged stands demonstrate the logistic growth pattern—although competition among individual trees for sunlight, water, and soil nutrients causes

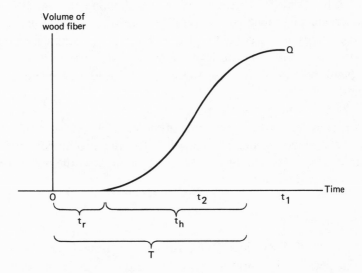

Figure 3-1. Production. Notes: Q is the logistic production function, variable only in time. As shown, it has a positive regeneration lag t_r. The timberstand itself grows for t_h years before harvest, and would attain a maximum volume in year t_1. Silvicultural effort (not shown) would reduce regeneration lag, shifting the production function to the left.

fully stocked stands to stretch their horizontal axis such that they attain maximum volume at a later time.[5] This means expressions (3-2) are correct whether one is clearcutting entire stands or selectively harvesting single trees.

Once again, silvicultural effort E includes labor and capital aspects of timber management activities such as planting, thinning, and fertilizing, as well as entrepreneurial skills. It is measured in terms of some standardized unit (such as one man and one machine for one hour). We can, for ease of exposition, restrict silvicultural treatments to one initial application and assume that only natural or "wild" seed is used. This restriction on silvicultural treatments is in keeping with the more familiar literature.[6]

Where silvicultural effort is justifiable, that is, where its expected returns exceed its costs, it is reasonably applied as soon as the land is available, in year zero. There can be no rationale for forgoing positive net economic return while simultaneously paying a land rental fee. Biological difficulties, furthermore, encourage earlier initial silvicultural effort: regeneration costs increase logarithmically as competing grasses, brush, and pioneer species establish themselves on idle land. Therefore,

$$E(0) \geq 0$$
$$E(T) = 0 \qquad \text{for all } T > 0, \text{ and}$$
$$Q_E > 0, Q_{EE} < 0, \quad \text{for some } E > 0 \qquad (3-3)$$

Under these conditions, Eq. (3-1) resembles biological yield functions for volunteer timberstands (wild trees). We eventually relax the restriction on silvicultural treatment and the natural seed assumption for our empirical analyses in chapters 5 and 6.

Economic Variables

We now consider the expected prices and costs associated with production which bring economic meaning to our model.

[5] See appendix A for a review of forest successional patterns.

[6] Moreover, the dynamic calculus of variations model with periodic silvicultural treatments converges with our static, point input–point output model where rotation ages are great and silvicultural investments subsequent to the initial one are small. As rotation ages become large, the influence of returns from subsequent rotations becomes very small. As post-planting costs decrease to zero, the variational functional also decreases to zero until the harvest. Both assumptions tend to negate the need for maximizing an integral.

Timber is sold as "stumpage," the product as it stands on the stump. Assuming perfect competition in the product market, stumpage prices p taken by a particular seller are invariant with quantity sold. They may vary spatially, however, due to locational differences in logging costs and accessibility to the productive site which, together, we call extraction costs, $x \geq 0$. Forests tend to be in mountainous regions and mills tend to locate at the perimeters of these regions or in the valleys between them. Therefore, as loggers go further from the mill to obtain stumpage, they log deeper into the mountains, into more difficult terrain. As they log further from the mill, road maintenance, hauling, and logging costs increase per unit of product. Since prices are quoted on the stump, they must be adjusted for these differences.

$$p - x \geq 0 \tag{3-4}$$

where $p = x$ implies that unit prices equal unit extraction costs and, therefore, defines the perimeter of efficient extraction.

Total revenues are stumpage prices—adjusted for uniform extraction costs—times volume sold. If the discount rate is a constant $r > 0$, then present value of the total revenue stream for each acre, at the moment idle land becomes available for timber production, is

$$(p - x)\, Q(T,E)e^{-rT}$$

The discount rate is the result of the landowner's portfolio balancing and asset demand.[7] It is his opportunity cost of capital.

Costs include initial silvicultural costs, if regeneration is not natural, and the cost of land. Recall that we assume no silvicultural effort after the planting date. Total silvicultural cost is the unit factor cost w times the volume of effort,

$$wE \geq 0 \tag{3-5}$$

where $w, E \geq 0$

Each acre of land must be either purchased or rented or, for those who already own their land, an opportunity cost must be paid

[7] See J. E. Stiglitz, "Growth with Exhaustible Natural Resources: Efficient and Optimal Growth Paths," *Review of Economic Studies, Symposium on Exhaustible Resources* (1974) pp. 123–137.

for its use. This opportunity cost is the dollar amount the owner forgoes by not renting or selling the land to someone else. He expects that, by putting the land to use growing timber, it will produce revenue sufficient to compensate him for all opportunities forgone. Land costs or, in economic terminology, land rent R is, therefore, the periodic return to ownership. The discounted value of this periodic return is equal to the rental value of land for T years.

$$\int_0^T Re^{-rt}\,dt = R \int_0^T e^{-rt}\,dt \geq 0 \tag{3-6}$$

The Complete Economic Model

We are now prepared to make the full statement for maximizing economic returns over the duration of a timber production period. In accordance with our earlier statements, we maximize the expression for discounted revenues net of silvicultural costs and land rent:

$$V^5 = \max_{T,E} \left[(p-x)\,Q(T,E)e^{-rT} - wE - R \int_0^T e^{-rt}\,dt \right] \tag{3-7}$$

If both the product and factor markets are perfectly competitive, and silvicultural costs include returns to entrepreneurial skills, as well as to the labor and capital inputs of timber management activities, then rent accounts for the entire residual between optimally determined revenues and costs. The only rents are locational and rent is zero at the extensive margin of economically productive timberland.

But, in general, the optimal land rental value is unknown, and without it we cannot determine optimal production levels. This suggests that we should look at land for its highest valued use. If timber production is the highest valued use, both now and in the future, then, as an alternative to Eq. (3-7), we can look at the case of successive rotations on the same land—or perpetual timber production.

Following this approach, the problem can initially be stated as

$$V^6 = \max_{T,E}(p-x)\,Q(T,E)e^{-rT}$$
$$- wE\,(1 + e^{-rT}\ldots + e^{-nrT}..)$$
$$= \max_{T,E}[(p-x)\,Q(T,E)e^{-rT}$$
$$- wE]\,(1-e^{-rT})^{-1} \tag{3-8}$$

since $(1-e^{-rT})^{-1}$ is equal to the infinite series. Successive optimal rotation lengths are identical because relative stumpage prices and all other parameters are constant. This form is familiar to foresters as the Faustmann equation. rV^6 is the "soil expectation value."[8] .

Samuelson proved that Eq. (3-7), the single rotation model *with land rental payments*, and Eq. (3-8), the perpetual timber production model, possess identical optimality conditions.[9] Since rent accounts for the entire residual between optimally determined revenues and costs in Eq. (3-7), then $V^5 = 0$ at its maximum and

$$V^6\,(1-e)^{-rT} = R\int e^{-rT}\,dt.$$ Samuelson proved this equivalence

for one optimally chosen rotation and for an infinite time period. It is important to recognize the difference between the single period production model with provision for land rent V^5 and the single period production model *without* provision for land rent. The latter is in error and *cannot* be shown as equivalent to V^6, Eq. (3-8).

Optimality Conditions

We can now examine the optimality conditions. Differentiating Eq. (3-8) with respect to E and T and setting the derivatives equal to zero, we find the necessary conditions for a maximum.

$$V_E = [(p-x)\,Q_E e^{-rT} - w]\,(1-e^{-rT})^{-1} = 0 \tag{3-9}$$

$$V_T = \big\{(p-x)\,Q_T(1-e^{-rT}) - r[(p-x)\,Q - wE]\big\}$$
$$e^{-rT}\,(1-e^{-rT})^{-2} = 0 \tag{3-10}$$

[8] See footnote 1.
[9] Samuelson, "Economics of Forestry."

where the subscript denotes the partial derivative with respect to the subscript.

The sufficient conditions for a maximum are:

$$V_{EE} = (p - x)Q_{EE}e^{-rT} (1 - e^{-rT})^{-1} \leq 0 \qquad (3\text{-}11)$$

$$
\begin{aligned}
V_{TT} = \Big\{ & (p - x)Q_{TT} (1 - e^{-rT})^2 \\
& - 2r (p - x) Q_T(1 - e^{-rT}) \\
& + r^2 [(p - x) Q - wE] \Big\} e^{-rT} (1 - e^{-rT})^{-2} \leq 0
\end{aligned}
$$

$$(3\text{-}12)$$

and that $V_{EE}V_{TT} > (V_{ET})^2$, where

$$
\begin{aligned}
V_{TE} = V_{ET} = \Big\{ & (p - x) Q_{TE}(1 - e^{-rT}) \\
& - r[(p - x) Q_E - w] \Big\} e^{-rT} (1 - e^{-rT})^{-2}
\end{aligned}
$$

$$(3\text{-}13)$$

Solving Eqs. (3-9) and (3-10) yields E^* and T^*, the optimal level of silvicultural effort and the optimal rotation age, respectively. With this information and knowledge that $Q = Q(T,E)$, we can solve for the optimal harvest level Q^* and the variations in E^*, T^*, and Q^* caused by locational or extraction cost differences.

Silvicultural Effort

For the moment, let us hold rotation age constant at T^* while we examine silvicultural effort. Conditions (3-9) and (3-11) and figure 3-2 demonstrate the impact of changing the level of effort. From Eq. (3-9) we determine that effort should be increased until the marginal product of the E^*th unit of effort equals its factor cost.

$$V_E(T^*) = 0 \qquad \text{implies } (p - x) Q_E e^{-rT^*} = w \qquad (3\text{-}14)$$

The sufficient condition for an optimum, Inequality (3-11), reduces to $Q_{EE} < 0$ if $p > x$. The marginal product of effort is positive but decreasing if per unit expected revenues exceed per unit extraction costs. It is clear that permanent price increases or decreases in the factor cost/stumpage price ratio $w/(p - x)$ justify higher levels of silvicultural effort.

Figure 3-2a shows the total revenue product and total factor cost association with these conditions. Figure 3-2b shows marginal

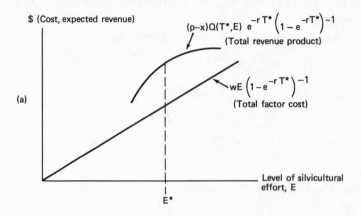

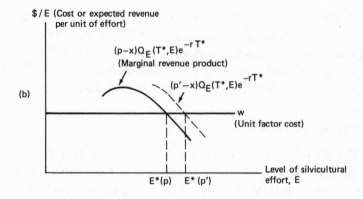

Figure 3-2. Silvicultural effort.

revenue product and marginal factor cost, the necessary and sufficient conditions in terms of conditions (3-14). Maximum economic returns occur at the level of effort E^* for which total revenues are in greatest excess of factor costs or, in accordance with
condition (3-14), where decreasing marginal revenue product
equals the unit factor cost. It is apparent from figure 3-2b that
stumpage price increases and access cost decreases shift the marginal revenue product curve to the right such that its new intersection with unit factor costs indicates a higher optimal level of effort.

Rotation Age

Now, holding silvicultural effort constant at E^*, let us look at rotation age. Conditions (3-10) and (3-12) and figure 3-3 demonstrate the impact of changing the rotation age. Rewriting Eq. (3-10), we determine that harvests should be postponed until the declining marginal revenue product equals the increasing opportunity cost of delaying harvests.

$$V_T(E^*) = 0 \quad \text{implies } (p - x)Q_T \, (1 - e^{-rT})$$
$$= r\,[(p - x)Q - wE^*] \tag{3-15}$$

Stated another way, the optimal rotation age occurs when the value of an additional year's growth is just offset by the implicit loss incurred by postponing net harvest revenues for one year. For coastal Douglas-fir, this is in the range of thirty to fifty years, depending on land quality, stocking density, regeneration costs, stumpage prices, and the opportunity cost of capital.

We can examine the harvest age more closely by segregating condition (3-15) into three components.

Component		*Description*
(a)	$(p - x)Q_T$ $(1 - e^{-rT})$	(a) Expected value of volume growth in the marginal investment period.
(b)	$r(p - x)Q$	(b) Revenues forgone by delaying harvest one year.
(c)	$r\,wE^*$	(c) Gain from delaying planting costs one year.

The value of marginal volume growth is the biological capital appreciation expression. It is restricted to a single rotation in a perpetual sequence and to those acres within the perimeter of efficient extraction. Because biological, hence value, growth of timber eventually decreases, at some moment in time it becomes profitable to harvest a slow-growing, mature timberstand and to replace it with vigorous young growth. From this moment forward, the timberland owner who fails to harvest suffers a loss from what

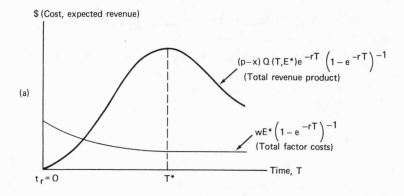

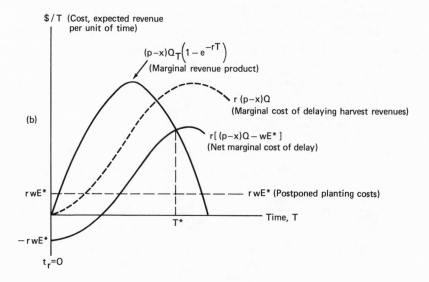

Figure 3-3. Harvest timing.

he could have made—an opportunity loss described by postponed revenues, $r\,(p - x)Q$. This loss is partially offset by the gain obtained by postponing planting costs for the subsequent rotation. (The planting cost term disappears if the landowner relies on natural regeneration.) Together, the postponed revenues and planting costs are the net marginal cost of delay.

From condition (3-15) it is clear that the rotation age is dependent on relative stumpage prices. We shall demonstrate this more fully in the next chapter. For the moment it is sufficient to argue that permanent increases in the expected price or permanent decreases in the factor cost/stumpage price ratio justify shorter rotations.

Figure 3-3 diagrams the harvest timing decision for $E = E^*$ and $t_r = 0$. Figure 3-3a shows the total revenue product and total factor cost associated with these conditions. Figure 3-3b shows the marginal functions, the necessary and sufficient conditions in terms of condition (3-15). The marginal cost in forgone revenues from delaying harvest and the marginal gain from postponing planting costs are shown as dashed lines. They combine as the net marginal cost of delay. Maximum economic returns occur for the rotation age at which total revenue product is in greatest excess of total factor costs or when marginal revenue product equals the net marginal cost of delay.

Summary

In order to learn about timber supply, we must first assess efficient timber production. In order to learn about land allocation to timber, we must first determine what land can efficiently produce timber. The purpose of this chapter is to gain insight into both of these judgments.

We need only to array all costs and expected revenues, each identified with their times of occurrence, and then compare them in present value terms. Costs include the cost of land. Timberland managers cannot ignore this cost because, even if they own their land, they have the alternatives of (1) managing for a more valuable product or (2) selling the land. After payment of all labor, capital, and managerial expenses, remaining revenue is the return to land ownership—"rent" in economic terminology. Efficient landowners maximize rent; timber is produced from the combination of inputs and timing that maximizes economic rent. *Abstracting from nonmarket-valued services of the forest,* forestland is efficiently allocated to timber on those acres where the rent from timber production is positive.

Timber production varies as forestland is cultivated more or less intensively—or even allowed to lie idle until it reforests naturally. Intensity relates to the level of silvicultural effort applied. Higher expected prices attract more intensive silvicultural investments. More intensive silviculture results in greater harvest volumes. Beyond some level, however, increased silvicultural costs exceed the expected value of increased harvests. At the optimal level, the cost of the last unit of silvicultural effort equals the value of additional product, or, in economic terms, marginal factor costs equal marginal revenue product.

Timber production also varies with time, increasing independently of the level of silvicultural intensity. Optimally, harvests should be delayed until the moment when additional gain from further delay is exactly offset by the net additional cost of delay. Beyond this moment, the value of volume increases in the current crop is more than offset by greater opportunity returns forgone (defined in terms of delayed receipts adjusted for delayed new crop silvicultural costs).

For an acre of given biological quality and access characteristics, and for a given stumpage price, there is only one optimal level of silvicultural intensity and one optimal rotation. Thus, there is only one optimal harvest volume, and only that volume maximizes rent. Since ours is a long-run model, this harvest level is sustainable in perpetuity if relative prices and technology remain unchanged.

With this knowledge, we can examine changing stumpage prices as well as acres of varying biological productivity and accessibility, and proceed to determine timber supply and land allocation. Efficiency is our guiding criterion throughout; that is, we assume the landowner always intends to maximize rent.

4
Timber Supply

In the preceding chapter we developed a deterministic model for competitive timber production on a given acre, a model that emphasizes location and intensity of productive activity. The model was simplified by the assumption that all silvicultural activity occurs in the first period. In this chapter, we apply the model to develop a single-acre supply schedule. By applying the supply analysis to each class of land and by aggregating (1) across acres in each class, under the assumption of constant returns to scale, as well as (2) across the classes themselves, we can determine the sustainable aggregate annual timber production at various stumpage prices—a long-run timber supply schedule. A straightforward extension of this analysis provides insight into locational rents accruing from timber production.

With some knowledge of expected demand, we can discuss efficient forestland allocation between timber and competing non-timber forest resource uses. This is the focus of the second portion of the chapter. Allocation is a direct result of our knowledge of (1) the demand price for stumpage, (2) the per acre timber production model, and (3) approximate recreation values. In the succeeding chapters we make an empirical application of this supply model and compare timber production and land allocation results with those prevailing under current practice, which often resembles the allowable cut approach of chapter 2.

There remains the question of the time path of harvests between now and the time when sustainable harvest levels can become effective. For a current standing inventory below some level, it may never be possible to arrive at the projected sustainable harvest levels without some form of rationing. Prices will rise in excess of our anticipations and new growth will be harvested before it reaches our anticipated optimal age. The final portion of this chapter discusses "conversion" period inventories and develops a measure of sufficient standing inventory that is useful for our empirical analysis.

Supply

Each change in cost or public policy is reflected in the price to the producer and, therefore, in his management and harvest decisions. Supply is the locus of least-cost or efficient harvest levels associated with given prices. We discuss derivation of the single-acre supply schedule before turning our attention to the impact of a variable land base and determination of aggregate regional supply.

We can derive the single-acre supply schedule using Hotelling's Lemma as it relates to profit functions.[1] That is, the partial derivative of the profit function with respect to the expected output price is the output supply function. If $V^* = V^* (p, r, x, w)$ is the neoclassical profit function derived by (1) solving the necessary conditions for a profit maximum and (2) substituting into the definition for profit, then, given perfect competition in the product and factor markets, the supply offered is dV^*/dp or Q^*. Return to the Eq. (3-8) formulation of our objective function. Simultaneously solving Eqs. (3-1), (3-9), and (3-10), the production function and first-order conditions, respectively, we find the optimal harvest level or supply.

$$Q^* = Q_T (1 - e^{rT*})/r + wE^*/(p - x) \qquad (4-1)$$

Q^* is offered every T^* years; therefore our landowner offers the sustainable annual harvest equivalent of Q^*/T^* from each acre. This implies a fully regulated forest—$1/T^*$ acres of each age class

---

[1] The earliest statement known to the author is H. Hotelling, "Edgeworth's Taxation Paradox and the Nature of Demand and Supply Functions," *Journal of Political Economy,* vol. 40 (1932) pp. 577–616. A more recent statement is found in Ronald W. Shephard, *Theory of Cost and Production Functions* (Princeton, N.J., Princeton University Press, 1953).

from ages one year to T^*—by the economic long run when the sustainable harvest can become effective.

Equation (4-1) tells us the harvest level associated with a given price. To find how annual harvests vary with price, we find the derivative of sustainable annual harvests with respect to price of $d(Q^*/T^*)/dp$. The result is a complex mathematical form with an uncertain sign because Q^*, Q_T^*, T^*, and E^* are all functions of p. Alternatively, we propose to examine the supply function for two special cases with empirical meaning: (1) natural forests with no intentional silvicultural inputs and (2) those with a fixed, positive, level of silvicultural inputs. The general case with fully variable silvicultural inputs is most amenable to a simple intuitive argument.

NATURAL FORESTS.   Historically, North American forests consisted of wild trees naturally grown and this is still an accurate description of many public forests in the West. In this case there are no intentional silvicultural investments; rotation age is the only decision variable for accessible land.

Supply for an acre of natural forest is given by Eq. (4-1) where silvicultural effort E is equal to zero, or

$$Q^* = Q_T(1 - e^{-rT^*})/r \qquad (4\text{-}2)$$

and $d(Q^*/T^*)/dp = 0$ $\qquad\qquad\qquad (4\text{-}2a)$

This is a fundamental, and well-known, theorem of forest economics. Timber supply from the natural forest is completely price inelastic. It responds only to changes in r, the opportunity cost of capital. Maximum sustainable annual harvests occur when the interest rate is zero.[2]

FIXED SILVICULTURAL INVESTMENTS.   In this frequently observed case, there may be a fixed, positive level of initial period silvicultural investments, such as site preparation and planting, but none, such as thinning or fertilizing, in subsequent periods within the timber rotation. Initial period investments may be fixed by law—as in required reforestation—or by managerial rule of thumb. Their observed level has not necessarily been an economic decision.

---

[2] This conclusion is conditional upon a fixed level of all productive inputs other than time, and constant relative prices. See appendix B for further discussion.

The expression for supply is:

$$Q^* = Q_T(1 - e^{-rT^*})/r + wE_0/(p - x) \qquad (4\text{-}3)$$

where E_0 is a positive constant. The change in annual harvest associated with a change in price is a function of output prices as well as factor costs. It can be most easily examined diagrammatically.

First, rewrite Eq. (4-3) such that

$$Q_T/[Q^* - wE_0/(p - x)] = r (1 - e^{-rT^*})^{-1} \qquad (4\text{-}3a)$$

With rotation age on the horizontal axis of figure 4-1, the right-hand side of Eq. (4-3a) can be represented by the family of curves $r' > r'' > r'''$ corresponding to decreasing values for r. Superimposed on this family of curves is the curve with vertical axis y corresponding to the rate of growth, the left-hand side of Eq. (4-3b). Intersecting curves show the optimal rotation associated with each interest rate r. As expected after our discussion of natural forests, higher interest rates imply reduced optimal harvest ages and smaller optimal harvest volumes.

The left-hand side of Eq. (4-3a) is an increasing function of the factor cost–adjusted price ratio $w/(p - x)$. That is, a price increase (or wage decrease), perceived as permanent, causes y in figure 4-1, the rate of growth curve, to shift leftward. Or, in other words, a price increase (or wage decrease) causes a decrease in optimal harvest age, therefore a decrease in optimal harvest volume and a decrease in sustainable annual harvest volume. Or, yet another expression of this unexpected result is that a price increase (or wage decrease) raises annual land rental costs (rV) more than it raises the present value of gross revenues $[(p - x) Qe^{-rT}]$, thereby implying shorter economic rotations and, hence, a decrease in sustainable annual harvest volume. This result is due to the fixed nature of investments[3] and their declining relative costs as stumpage

---

[3] We have constant returns to scale (CRS) within an acre, or class of equally accessible acres, because output bears a constant relation to the number of acres. CRS may be a reasonable assumption as we observe vertically integrated firms where gross sizes are apparently uncorrelated with the volume of their land holdings. Nevertheless, this all suggests future research on land as a variable factor of production. Clark Row has examined scale economies in the use of other factors in "Probabilities of Financial Returns from Southern Pine Timber Growing" (Ph.D. dissertation, Tulane University, 1975). I owe these points on CRS to Irving Hoch.

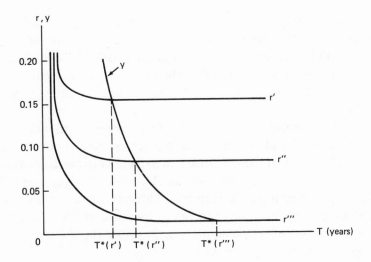

Figure 4-1. Harvest timing.

prices increase. It can be confirmed by consulting any conceptual or empirical biological yield data, as we will do in chapter 5.

If one long-run impact of a price increase is to shorten the optimal rotation, then, in the short run, there will be a period of adjustment during which some standing timber will be older than the new optimal harvest age but younger than the old optimal harvest age. This timber, which is overmature as a result of the price increase, contributes a short-run harvest expansion. Thus, where silvicultural investments are fixed, the short-run effect of a one time only, but permanent, price increase is to expand annual production by harvesting the now overmature stands. The long-run effect, however, is to decrease annual harvests as the higher price causes a reduction in optimal harvest age. The short-run supply schedule has the usual positive slope, but the long-run schedule has an unusual negative slope.[4]

[4] The foregoing exposition originated with Colin W. Clark, *Mathematical Bioeconomics* (New York, Wiley, 1976) pp. 259–263. The earliest demonstration of the backward bending supply curve associated with a fixed resource base known to the author is Parzival Copes, "The Backward Bending Supply Curve for Fisheries" *Scottish Journal of Political Economy* vol. 17, no. 1 (February 1970) pp. 69–77.

A More General Analysis

Our analysis has been partial, restricted to a fixed level of silvicultural investment and to a single acre or class of identical acres. Once the analysis is generalized to allow silvicultural effort and land use to vary with price, then we expect the supply schedule to follow economic theory and demonstrate a positive relation to price.

First consider silvicultural effort varying with price. From expression (3-14), we know that a price increase induces expanded silvicultural effort, which reflects in expanded harvests for rotations of any length t_0 Therefore, sustainable annual harvests $Q(t_0, E)/t_0$ are larger after the price increase. This effect counters the rotation reducing effect of a price increase described in Eq. (4-3a). It is unclear which effect predominates, therefore the slope of the *single acre* supply curve remains in question.

Now consider the effect of a price increase on land use. Recall the form of our profit maximization expression including explicit land rental payments, Eq. (3-7):

$$V^5 = \max_{T,E} \; (p - x) \; Q(T,E)e^{-rT} - wE - R \int_0^T e^{-rt} \, dt$$

For the competitive firm, rent is a residual accounting for the entire difference between optimally determined revenues and costs, therefore Eq. (3-7) is equal to zero at its maximum and we can restate it as

$$R \int_0^{T^*} e^{-rt} \, dt = (p - x) \, Q^* \, e^{-rT^*} - wE^* \qquad (4\text{-}4)$$

It should be clear that, for a given rotation age and level of silvicultural effort, price increases cause an increase in rent. Some land which was previously extramarginal for timber production now returns a positive rent and transfers from its previous use into timber production. Sustainable annual harvests increase by the share of harvests originating from the newly productive land.

Figure 4-2 shows another, perhaps clearer, picture of this. It describes how extraction costs and land rent vary as we move to less and less accessible acres of uniform biological productivity. Net

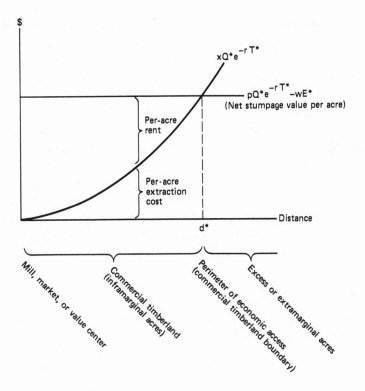

Figure 4-2. Rent and location.

value of physical product is constant as Q^*, T^*, and E^* are constant. The first acre is adjacent to the mill, extraction costs per acre are at a minimum, and rent per acre—the difference between net value of physical product and extraction costs—is at its maximum. Total collectable rent increases as we add less accessible, more distant, acres, but rent for each given acre decreases. Rent decreases to zero on the acre $Q^* e^{-rT^*}$ extraction dollars from the mill. This is intuitively clearer if we consider access only a function of distance d. Then rent is zero on the acre d^* miles from the mill, and d^* identifies the perimeter of rational timberland management. It is also apparent that a price increase to $p' > p$ shifts the net value of physical product upward, thereby creating additional rent on inframarginal timberland and allowing the expenditure of additional extraction dollars or, what is the same, shifting the perimeter outward. Thus, the price increase adds land to the timber management unit and, therefore, acts to increase aggregate harvests.

Introduction of a variable land base leads us to an important extension of our analysis, an extension to aggregate regional supply. If (1) all landowners are competitive or, where public agencies are involved, all landowners act as price takers and (2) landowners observe constant returns to scale for each land class, then the aggregate supply schedule is obtained by summing output horizontally across all ownerships. In our case, this is the same as summing across all acres in a land class and then summing across all land classes.

Given the opportunity cost of capital, extraction cost, and the wage rate, and recalling that production varies with the land class (and therefore, the optimal rotation age and level of silvicultural effort and the optimal harvest level all vary with the land class) then annual supply for a single acre of land class i is

$$S_i^*(p) = Q_i^*(p)/T_i^*(p) \qquad (4\text{-}5)$$

Supply originating from all acres A of land class i is $AS_i^*(p)$, and aggregate annual supply from all i land classes is:

$$S(p)^* = \sum_i A_i S_i^*(p) \qquad (4\text{-}6)$$

For higher prices, land classes which were previously agricultural become more profitable in timber production. Similarly, land classes which at lower prices were extramarginal due to either low biological productivity or expensive access (or stricter management requirements, that is, policy restrictions causing silvicultural treatments to be more expensive) also become profitable. As harvests from both of these land classes are added, long-run annual harvests expand.

In conclusion, we predict that the long-run aggregate supply schedule tends to be positively sloped, and annual harvests increase with higher prices for two reasons which may offset the negative harvest timing effect of higher prices: (1) higher prices justify increasingly land-intensive silviculture, therefore increased annual harvest, on a fixed land base, and (2) higher prices bring additional, less economically productive acres into timber production.

Figure 4-3 demonstrates this conclusion for a region with only two land classes, A_I and A_{II}. The horizontal axis shows the annual

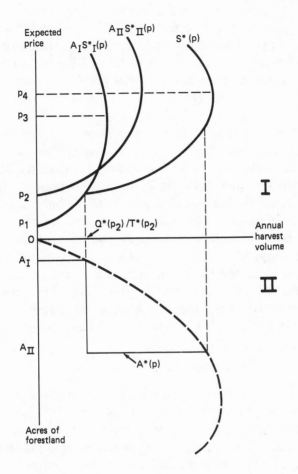

Figure 4-3. Aggregate supply schedule.

harvest level. The vertical axis in quadrant I shows prices (given a constant wage level); the vertical axis in quadrant II shows acres. The functions $A_I S_I^*(p)$ and $A_{II} S_{II}^*(p)$ describe supply schedules in land classes one and two, respectively. Their horizontal sum is $S^*(p)$. The function $A^*(p)$ describes the use of land for timber production associated with each efficient price–harvest level combination. For any land class there is no efficient harvest below some price. For example, at less than p_1, competitive timber production is uneconomic for the first class of acres $(\overline{OA_I})$. For higher prices, production on the first land class becomes economic, but the second $(\overline{A_I A_{II}})$ and succeeding classes remain idle. Aggregate supply

$S^*(p)$ is coincident with supply $A_1S_1^*(p)$ from land class A_1. For higher prices yet, land of poorer biological potential, more difficult access, or stricter management constraints becomes economic—as at p_2 for the second class of acres. For prices of a permanent level p_2, annual harvests are $Q^*(p_2)/T^*(p_2)$, and the best $\overline{OA_{II}}$ acres are used for timber production. The $\overline{OA_I}$ and $\overline{A_IA_{II}}$ acres are used with different degrees of intensity, however, and yield different efficient annual harvests per acre. The land production function is a step function in figure 4-3. It is continuous (like the dashed line in quadrant II) when land classification is continuous. It is not a production function in the usual sense with the only variable factor of production on the horizontal (vertical in our case) axis because the level of silvicultural management also changes throughout its range. If known silvicultural technologies are eventually exhausted, then, above some price p_3 for the first class of acres, annual harvests decline for the class as a whole. If all available land can also eventually be exhausted, then above some price, p_4 in our example, the aggregate of annual harvests from all land classes declines.[5]

Further Comment on Rising Prices

To this point we have examined the impacts of a permanent change in the price *level*. Empirical observations, however, confirm that stumpage prices are temporally increasing relative to all other prices. This introduces the question of input and output effects of a *rate* of price change, a sufficiently unusual question to justify special comment.

A positive annual rate of real stumpage price change has been the North American experience for the past 150 years and there is reason to expect its continuance.[6] The most likely explanations for this phenomenon are a previous low rate of technical change in timber production relative to that for substitute products and the slow depletion of the natural stock of mature timber.[7] As this stock

[5] Of course our declining supply ignores the likelihood of price-induced technical change.

[6] Harold J. Barnett and Chandler Morse, *Scarcity and Growth* (Baltimore, Johns Hopkins University Press for Resources for the Future, 1963) and Vernon W. Ruttan and James C. Callahan, "Resources Inputs and Output Growth," *Forest Science* vol. 8, no. 1 (March 1962) pp. 68–82 are the basic references.

[7] See Vernon L. Robinson, "An Estimate of Technical Progress in the Lumber and Wood Products Industry," *Forest Science* vol. 21, no. 2 (June 1975) pp. 149–154 for an empirical discussion of technical change in timber production.

is drawn down, we expect relative prices to rise, much as prices rise with the slow depletion of a mine that provides a large market share of some mineral.[8] Eventually this stock will be exhausted, all timber harvested will be the result of a price-induced renewable production process, and the rate of price increase due to this effect will disappear.

We can introduce this effect into the objective function as $\rho > 0$, the rate of price change. It quickly becomes apparent that the optimal rotation age is a function of ρ, that second and subsequent rotations are of different optimal ages, and that the objective function loses the simple form of Eq. (3-8).

Alternatively, we might recall the form including explicit rental payments, Eq. (3-7), and modify it to consider the rate of price change.

$$V' = \max \ (pe^{\rho T} - x) \ Q(T,E)e^{-rT} - wE - R \int_0^T e^{-rt}dt$$

Rent also changes as a function of ρ, but the changes are small in terms of periods as long as timber rotations, therefore we momentarily disregard it. The interesting impact of a positive rate of price change is on the optimally chosen rotation age. Holding silvicultural effort constant and taking the first derivative with respect to T and setting it equal to zero, we find that

$$V'_T(E^*) = 0 \qquad \text{implies } Q_T/Q = r - \rho \qquad (4\text{-}7)$$

Condition (4-7) tells us that the optimal rotation is a function of both the opportunity cost of capital and the rate of price increase. If the landowner perceives temporarily increasing prices, then he extends the rotation so as to gather more of the price increase. The greater the rate of price increase, the longer he extends the rotation.

Taking this result with our previous discussions of condition (3-15) and Eq. (4-3a), we conclude that the *price level and its rate of change work in opposition,* higher price levels and lower rates of change causing shorter optimal rotations than lower price levels and greater rates of change. Therefore, we cannot draw any *a priori* conclusions about the net impact of increasing prices on rotation age. We have all the more reason to expect a positively sloped supply curve.

[8] See Herfindahl and Kneese, *Economic Theory of Natural Resources* for a discussion of the optimal depletion of a mine.

Extraction: A Diversion

Before introducing the question of forestland allocation among competing uses, we momentarily turn our attention to further consideration of extraction costs and their impact on timber management. Land is allocated to timber wherever timber production is the highest valued use, yet extraction costs do not exceed the entire value of the land's product. We reviewed this in Eq. (4-4) and the adjacent discussion of figure 4-2. Casual observations of timber management suggest that for loggers and mills that are plentifully supplied from land within this economic range, extraction costs are not much of an issue. On the other hand, for mills not so plentifully supplied or operating in management areas (known as "working circles") with very large radii, extraction can be a critical variable. For example, the Weyerhaeuser Company, located at lower elevations in the middle of the rapid- and dense-growth Douglas-fir region of western Washington, does not include a transportation variable in its management calculus. George Staebler, Weyerhaeuser's Director of Forestry Research, has, nevertheless, related elevation, hence ease of extraction, to the value of land for growing timber.[9] Macmillan-Bloedel in coastal British Columbia is an example of a firm more affected by transportation costs. Long distances are a way of life where Macmillan-Bloedel operates, and M-B does include a transportation variable in its timber bidding calculus.

For firms with plentiful timber supply within the perimeter of economic access, this supply is an invitation to expand mill capacity. Until capacity expansion, however, access can be an important variable because for every nearby silvicultural management opportunity there exists the alternative of harvesting less accessible standing timber. Given the long production periods associated with timber, there is considerable uncertainty about eventual demand and supply. There is, therefore, abundant opportunity to trade off silvicultural management costs for extraction costs. Additional extraction costs for stumpage previously beyond the managed timberland but within the economic perimeter have the advantage of immediate payoff, whereas silvicultural investments pay off only

---

[9] George R. Staebler, "Concentrating Timber Production Efforts," *Proceedings, 1972 National Convention* (Society of American Foresters, Washington, D.C.) pp. 74–81.

after the timber responds to management and is subsequently harvested, perhaps many years later.

For example, if an insect epidemic infests a managed timber-stand, the landowner has the alternatives of (1) controlling the epidemic, thereby saving some volume of wood fiber within the infested area, or (2) expanding harvests to an equal forested area beyond the managed timberland. The intuitive economic solution includes some combination of both (1) and (2) such that incremental control costs equal incremental extraction costs.[10] If the epidemic occurs in a young, managed stand which will not be harvested for some time, then access will be unnecessary until that time, and extraction costs associated with the eventual harvest are discounted. Epidemic control costs, however, must be incurred upon discovery of the infestation. The suggestion is that expenditures can be postponed until the landowner is more certain of both the control technology and his markets. The same opportunity to postpone expenditures while gaining certainty exists wherever expansion of the harvest area is an alternative to silvicultural (for example, thinning, fertilizing, site preparation) or control (insect or disease epidemic or fire) operations for which cost outlays occur before the eventual harvest payoff. This is probably an important opportunity for public forest ownerships and the loggers and mills dependent upon them since the former are generally thought to include the bulk of the marginal as well as virtually all of the submarginal timberland.

Where timber is in less plentiful supply, further observation of Eq. (4-4) and figure 4-2 can show us the impacts of extraction on timber management. It should be clear that extraction costs and stumpage price work in opposition. Therefore, increases in extraction costs have the opposite effects of price increases on the optimal rotation and level of silvicultural effort, that is, rotation age increases and the level of silvicultural effort decreases.

---

[10] Note the variation from the standard least-cost-plus-loss solution—marginal control cost equals marginal damage. Here the solution is marginal control cost plus marginal extraction costs equals marginal damage. William F. Hyde and Mark F. Sharefkin, "A Simple Model for Pest Control" (Washington, D.C., EPA Pest Control Workshop, May 1975). In our example, the owner has the third alternative of taking early harvests from immature trees of the next working circle segments. This suggests the additional tradeoff between extraction costs and forgone value appreciation.

These observations are intuitively satisfying. Imagine that we know the optimal rotation age T^* for an acre on what we think is the perimeter of economic extraction. After trees of this acre are harvested, identical trees on the next, less accessible, acre continue growing. Eventually the value of stumpage grown on the less accessible acre may exceed the only incremental costs, those associated with extraction. At this time—a new, larger T^* for the less accessible acre—the less accessible acre is worth harvesting. This scenario cannot continue indefinitely, however, because access costs increase at a constant rate $(xQe^{rT} > 0$ dollars per acre) and timber eventually grows at a decreasing rate $(Q_{TT} < 0)$. Regarding silvicultural investments, Eq. (4-4) and figure 4-2 suggest that silvicultural effort decreases as the extraction difficulty increases. That is, equimarginal silvicultural applications yield diminishing net revenues as extraction costs increase—or for less accessible acres. Casual empiricism confirms these observations. We observe planting on some timberlands; on other lands which tend to be less accessible to the mill, we observe only naturally growing volunteer timberstands; and, finally, on some lands which tend to be even less accessible yet, we observe naturally growing stands which apparently may never be cut.

At the perimeter of economic extraction, silvicultural costs are zero and we can show that unit extraction costs equal the unit stumpage price. First solve Eq. (4-1) for x and take the limit as silvicultural costs go to zero.

$$\lim_{E^* \to 0} \left\{ p - rwE^*/[rQ^* - Q_T(1 - e^{-rT^*})] \right\} = p \qquad (4\text{-}8)$$

On such land, where silvicultural investments cannot be justified, but where naturally growing volunteer timberstands exist, periodic harvests are justified if stumpage revenues exceed extraction costs. This is the controversial case of many old growth stands on the national forests today. Our economics justify periodic "mining" of these stands. Since silvicultural costs are zero, the optimal rotation age is dependent only on the opportunity cost of capital. This is the "natural forests" case discussed earlier in the chapter.[11]

[11] Four recent papers consider the extraction cost–land rent issue: See William J. Milton, "National Forest Roadless and Undeveloped Areas," *Land Economics* vol. 51, no. 2 (May 1975) pp. 139–143, which includes comment on the relation of stumpage prices to marginal land; Mathew D. Berman, "Economic Impact of

Forestland Allocation

With knowledge of the long-run aggregate supply schedule, we can draw some general conclusions about forestland allocation. The aggregate supply schedule, because it sums across schedules for each acre and each land class, also reflects the summation of acres necessary to obtain any particular efficient price–annual harvest combination. We traced a simple case of this price–harvest–acreage relation in figure 4-3. In this section, we discuss implications of the price–harvest–acreage relation for efficient land allocation among timber production and competing land uses. Efficiency criteria require that land be allocated to its highest valued use, therefore we examine timber values relative to competing land use values.

The model can be diagrammed as in figure 4-3 if we assume continuous variations in prices, silvicultural inputs, harvest volumes, and land quality. The timber supply schedule $S^*(p)$ was described in detail earlier in this chapter. Price expectations determine the efficient level of technology (input combinations) and land base associated with any annual harvest level. Therefore, price determines the harvest–acreage relation, or the production function for land $A^*(p)$. (Once more, this is not a production function of the usual sort because other factors of production are changing along with land.) The most economically productive acres enter into production first or at lower prices, therefore land quality declines from the origin along the acreage axis, and the production function has a positive but decreasing slope.

For any given price, we know the number of acres that can efficiently be used for timber production—*if there are no competitive land uses.* Where there are competitive land uses, efficiency criteria require that land be allocated to its highest valued use. We

---

the Proposed Alaska National Interests Lands Conservation Act" (Anchorage, Trustees for Alaska, July 1978); and John Ledyard and Leon Moses, "Dynamics and Land Use: The Case of Forestry" in Barney Dowdle, ed., *The Economics of Sustained Yield Forestry* (Seattle, University of Washington, forthcoming). The first two are empirical, the latter develops the mathematically correct conceptual model. William R. Bentley also commented on this issue in "Security, Uncertainty and the Value of Public Forestry Investments" in Walter J. Mead and William McKillop, eds. *British Columbia Timber Policy* (Vancouver, University of British Columbia, 1976) pp. 132–141.

might classify the competitive uses broadly as recreation. Most forest-based recreational uses do not exchange in the market, therefore it is difficult to determine the value of recreational land, and it is difficult to determine efficient land allocation between timber and recreation.

One approach is to determine the timber opportunity cost, the net value of timber forgone, if the land is allocated to recreational uses. It is much easier to determine whether recreational values exceed or are exceeded by the timber opportunity cost than it is to determine them precisely and independently. Abstracting from multiple-use opportunities, only when recreational values exceed timber values is the land efficiency allocated to recreation.

The net value of timber forgone is the sum of consumers' and producers' surpluses originating from timber produced on the land in question. Consumers' surplus is approximately the area between the market price p_1 and the demand curve $D(p)$ and to the left of their intersection in figure 4-4. It is effectively zero if (1) there is nothing unique about timber grown on the land in question, that is, there are many good substitutes, such as timber grown on different land, and (2) the land area is so small that harvests from it have only a marginal impact on demand, that is, its withdrawal from timber management causes no change in stumpage price. Observation of the market suggests the first condition holds and the second condition is likely for currently prospective withdrawals for recreational forestland—at least for broad regional and national markets. There is no measurable consumers' surplus associated with forgone timber opportunities.

Producers' surplus is not a surplus at all. Rather it is a Ricardian rent, a payment for use of the land. It is approximately the area between the supply curve $S^*(p)$ and the market price p_1 and to the left of their intersection. If the highest valued non-recreational use of the land is for timber production, then rent R for a single acre for a single year is:

$$R = rV \tag{4-9}$$

where V is determined as in Eq. (3-8), the single acre firm's profit-maximizing function. The rental value for land *permanently* allocated to timber management, or the discounted perpetual stream

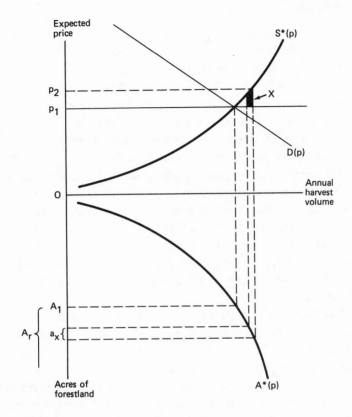

Figure 4-4. Timber supply and land allocation.

of annual timber rents, which is also the sale value of the land for
for a single acre for a single year is:

$$R \int e^{-rt} dt = V(1 - e^{-rT^*}) \qquad (4\text{-}10)$$

The relationship between Eqs. (4-9) and (4-10) can be further
demonstrated by showing that $R \int e^{-rt} dt = R(1 - e^{-rT})/r$.

With this background, there are two land allocational cases to
consider, one where timber opportunity cost, which is coincident
with the forgone timber rental value, is zero and one where it is
positive.[12] We will examine each and add a comment on multiple
use.

---

[12] We have not foreclosed the potential economic rationality of harvesting
existing stands on these acres if their *short-run* profitability justifies it.

Residual Timberland

We might label as residual all forestland where the net value of timber opportunity forgone is zero. These are the A_r acres of biologically productive timberland as determined by market price and the supply schedule. No rational manager would use any of the A_r acres, say acre a_x, for sustainable timber production because on this acre his costs would exceed his receipts by $p_2 - p_1$ per unit of output or by X dollars per annum. The A_r residual acres can be reserved from timber management, and at zero cost in the way of net timber return forgone. Indeed, there is a benefit gained by avoiding timber management costs that exceed revenues. Natural timberstands on the residual acres provide flexibility to adjust to unforeseen future events, including (but not restricted to) harvest expansion due to short-run stumpage price fluctuations and increases in long-run stumpage price expectations. Meanwhile, these acres can, without further justification, be fully devoted to *reversible* nontimber uses.

Nontimber benefits must still justify any expenditure made on the residual acres. That is, recreational benefits must exceed investments in picnic tables and improvement of wildlife habitat as well as carrying costs for garbage collection and trail maintenance, etc. Otherwise, efficiency criteria require that the residual acres remain in their natural condition and only the minimum custodial management, or stewardship, is justified.

There may be an additional rationale for restricting the A_r acres to recreational uses. The land most environmentally risky for timber production is typically marginal timberland, including both steep slopes and high elevations. The greatest environmental hazard of commercial timber production is the soil erosion problem caused by road building and the felling and skidding of logs. This hazard is reduced considerably if logging is restricted on steep slopes and shallow-soiled high elevations.

Positively Valued Timber Opportunity

What about those cases where the best timberland also possesses desirable, even unique, recreational characteristics? Should not some of the best land be allocated to recreational uses? For example, we know that campers and hikers like the tallest groves of trees, and we know the latter grow on the best land. Similarly, big game require low elevation winter range, and fish require shaded streams running through good timber sites. In each case we expect competition for use of the land, competition between timber and recreational values. For any particular acre, recreational values should be greater than the timber opportunity forgone in order to justify the acre's allocation to recreation. For permanent allocation to recreation, the timber opportunity is that acre's sale value.

For temporary allocation to recreation, the forgone opportunity is the annual timber rental value minus the net value of any timber growth during this temporary period. An interesting scenario would have recreationists desiring one last opportunity to visit some valley before timber management operations begin. To obtain this opportunity, they might actually pay a rent, perhaps in the form of admission fees, equal to the opportunity cost of delaying timber management.

For any payment greater than this opportunity cost, the private timberland owner is willing to sell because the payment is larger than the current value of the long-run profit he can make growing timber. Despite the nonexclusionary, therefore unpriced, nature of many recreational uses of forestland, there is some evidence of such reallocation occurring. Examples are purchases by the Nature Conservancy (which are held in trust until repurchased by public agencies), by hunting and fishing clubs, and by recreational home-owners. Some large timber-producing firms are finding the recreational home market—both permanent sales and more temporary leasing of land—a lucrative alternative use of their forestland.

For public land, any demonstration of recreationists' willingness to pay that is greater than the timber opportunity forgone shows the manager that public welfare is greater when the acre is allocated to recreation. Estimating willingness to pay is not an easy task, but the economics literature on the subject is well developed, and public agencies have some experience with it.[13]

13 Externalities and nonexclusion make it difficult for individuals to register their demands in the market. See footnote 8 in chapter 1 for an introduction to the nevertheless extensive literature on estimating such nonmarket values.

Multiple Use

Opportunities for multiple use imply an increase in projections arising from our analysis to this point. Multiple use has to do with more than one output arising from at least one common input, such as timber and recreation from a common land unit. Efficiency requires that the incremental output pay its own separable cost, including both its direct costs of production and the opportunity costs it may impose in the form of reduced production of the other outputs.

Consider that if some share of all silvicultural expenditure is really made for recreational purposes (for example, replanting an aesthetically displeasing old clearcut site that is within sight of a campground), then it is inappropriate to charge this share against timber receipts. In terms of figure 4-2 this suggests wE^* is smaller by the cost of planting the old clearcut, therefore $Q^*e^{-rT^*} -wE^*$ is larger. The perimeter of economic extraction shifts to the right, implying that there is more land profitable for timber management, therefore larger annual harvests. Recreation increases too, if the improved aesthetics result in expansion of campground use that is greater than the recreational loss on the former residual land, which is now within the timber production perimeter.

The pine beetle-infested forests (the common input) of Colorado's Front Range provide another example of multiple outputs from a single input. Timber grows naturally here, but too slowly to be a profitable venture. Inaccessibility is also a factor. The land is probably best allocated to recreation, range, and watershed. The beetle infestation damages recreational values and increases the likelihood of fire—implying further recreational damage. Where recreational values justify beetle control, infested trees are cut and destroyed. Trees would not be cut for their timber value, but, where they are cut for other reasons (for example, insect control), hauling costs are the only separable costs of timber production. Therefore, if timber receipts are greater than hauling costs, timber is an efficient multiple use as long as the epidemic lasts. If, however, hauling interferes with recreational use—perhaps logging trucks are a hazard to recreational users of the roads—then timber production costs include both hauling costs and the value of recreational opportunities lost.

It is easy to find other examples, including the opposite case where timber should pay for most of the basic inputs and recreational opportunity is essentially a by-product, but one which may interfere with some of the timber production process. We develop an illustrative example in chapter 6.

Limitations of the Supply and Land Allocation Model

The full conceptual model must be applied with care. The meaning of its conclusions is limited. We will discuss the causes of its limitations before proceeding to its implications for land allocation and other policy. Briefly, they are its static, deterministic, long-run nature, and an implicit underlying assumption about standing inventory. The latter is important to the feasibility of our harvest conclusions and we shall give it careful thought.

The model is static. Its basic data—acreage, production technologies, and input prices—are observed during a single moment in time. These observations change with time and as a result of exogenous factors. Since the model fails to anticipate such input data adjustment, its harvest results are constant and less dependable predictions the further from the present we project them.

Norstrom[14] and Holtman and Smith[15] independently demonstrated the impacts of stochastic factors. For a single production process with either uncertain output volumes or uncertain output prices, Norstrom demonstrated that longer rotations and larger harvests are optimal. For a variety of production processes with either uncertain output volumes or uncertain output prices, Holtman and Smith demonstrated a preference for durable processes as certainty increases. In timber production, investments in planting and in the seed itself are generally more durable—their impact continues throughout the full rotation—than investments, such as thinning and fertilizing, which may occur at various times within a rotation. In addition, silvicultural activities which are newer for the relevant species or region are likely to yield less certain results.

[14] Carl J. Norstrom, "A Stochastic Model for the Growth Period Decision in Forestry," *Swedish Journal of Economics* (1973) pp. 329–337.

[15] A. G. Holtman and V. Kerry Smith, "Uncertainty and the Durability of On-the-Job Training" (unpublished manuscript, 1977).

Regardless of the accuracy of the long-run acreage, technology, and price estimates, there will be *short-term* price and harvest fluctuations. Short-run flexibility is an important issue, perhaps more important than long-run supply. Stumpage prices show great cyclical variation, yet timber management often aims at producing a constant flow of timber. This text is not the place for a detailed discussion of the issue.[16] In our context, short-run price and harvest fluctuations can be discussed in terms of variations around the long-run expectations of the model, or in terms of sensitivity of long-run results to adjustments in acreage, technology, and price estimates.

In addition, short-run inventory problems can deny the feasibility of the long-run results; for example, if there were insufficient standing timber inventory to allow consumption in the years between now and the economic long run without causing significant relative price changes. In the United States there is an inventory of mature timber ("old growth"), some of which might be harvested whenever short-run market fluctuations interfere with orderly progress toward long-run results. This is the nature of the "conversion" problem laid out in succeeding pages. The existence of "excess" inventory, old growth or otherwise, implies that the long-run solution is feasible.

Conversion and Old Growth

Since standing timber is both working capital and product, short-run market adjustments (particularly short-run harvests) affect the time path to long-run results and, therefore, the feasibility of long-run price and harvest projections themselves. Our question is, *given some knowledge of demand, what level of standing inventory is sufficient to get us through the (conversion) period between now and the economic long run without significantly increasing relative stumpage prices?* The relevant inventory includes both old growth and vigorous younger stands. If the volume is only just sufficient

[16] Gould and O'Reagan demonstrated, in an illuminating simulation model, the gains from adjusting the harvest flow according to random changes in price expectations. Ernest M. Gould, Jr. and William G. O'Reagan, "Simulation: A Step Toward Better Forest Planning" (Petersham, Mass., Harvard Forest Papers no. 13, 1963).

and the age distribution is skewed toward younger stands, then, at some time, harvests of mature timber must come to a halt, a large volume of immature inventory will remain, immature timber may be harvested, substitution to products competitive with wood fiber may occur, and prices will adjust upward. Therefore, feasible long-run solutions require satisfactory age distribution as well as a sufficient volume of standing inventory.

It is not our intention to determine optimal conversion policy. That requires full knowledge of the time path of annual harvests— or the projection of demand and supply for each and every year in the conversion period. Rather, we only intend to determine the feasibility of attaining our long-run annual harvest level. Insufficient standing inventory renders our long-run calculation meaningless. A more than sufficient inventory, including satisfactory age class distribution, implies lower prices and greater harvest volumes than projected, or contraction of the efficient timberland base, or both, in the short run. Alternatively, the excess inventory may be stored as protection against uncertain future events and risky activities. Therefore, a more than sufficient current standing inventory may affect long-run optima, but it does not deny the feasibility of some time path to the long run.

Assume the conversion period does not exceed one timber rotation and assume demand at no time during conversion exceeds expected annual long-run demand. The first assumption is reasonable because the rotation length T^* defines the economic long run, the period in which all inputs are variable and the entire forest inventory age structure can be changed to a preferred age structure. The second assumption is reasonable unless wood fiber demand is decreasing—which it is not doing either in absolute or per capita terms—or our competitive share of demand is decreasing absolutely. (North America has an apparent worldwide comparative advantage in timber production, as does the region of our empirical case study.)

Then, if the optimally determined inventory expected in the fully regulated forest is sufficient to perpetuate long-run harvest levels, it is also sufficient to allow some time path to the long run. (If our competitive share were declining, then an inventory sufficient to perpetuate current harvest levels would be sufficient.) The problem reduces to describing the inventory of the fully regulated forest. Once again there are i land classes distinguished by their biological productivity and accessibility. Each class has its own optimal harvest age. In a fully regulated forest, the A_i acres in each land class are divided into T_i^* segments, one for a stand of each age from zero (or the negative of the regeneration lag t_r) to optimal harvest age. Therefore, long-run inventory I is:

$$I = \sum_i (A_i/T_i^*) \, [Q_i(-t_{r,i}) + Q_i(-t_{r,i} + 1)$$
$$+ Q_i(-t_{r,i} + 2) + \ldots + Q_i(T_i^* - 1)$$
$$+ Q_i(T_i^*) \qquad\qquad (4\text{-}11)$$

where $Q_i(T_i^* - 1)$ refers to volume in the stand of land class i of age $T_i^* - 1$. As $Q(T)$ approaches symmetry around $T^*/2$, our measure of sufficient inventory approaches

$$I = \sum_i (A_i/T_i^*) \, Q_i^* T_i^*/2 \cong A_i Q_i^*/2 \qquad (4\text{-}12)$$

where $Q^* = Q(T^*)$

The inventory shown by Eq. (4-12) is sufficient if it is distributed among time-ordered segments as in Eq. (4-16). Alternatively, any "short" segment from Eq. (4-11) can be substituted with equal *area* from the excess of segments with *older* stands. When stands from short segments reach maturity, it is obvious that only older, not younger, stands will also be mature and, therefore, able to substitute equally or better in the market. Since older stands grow more slowly, however, equal acres, not equal volumes, must be the substitution criterion. Any substitution, on this criterion, increases the minimum sufficient volume of Eq. (4-12).

Now let us inquire about the substitutability of old growth acreage for short segments. For our purposes, old growth is any stand of age greater than economic maturity T^*. (In other usage the term may mean any age from economic to physiological maturity —depending on the perspective of the user.) Much of the existing old growth is on unroaded land. The capital costs of new roads are high, and much unroaded land may not qualify as efficient timberland if it has to yield a return on these capital costs as well as on all other timber production expenditures. Old growth acreage can substitute for the short segments (1) if it is already in the efficient working circle and logging roads necessary to extract the old growth already exist, or (2) if the old growth is of sufficient value to pay competitive returns on necessary road-building investments.

In conclusion, some standing inventory volume $\sum_i A_i Q_i^*/2$ is sufficient to allow some time path to our anticipated long-run harvest level without significant short-run decreases in annual harvests or increases in stumpage prices. This volume is contingent on an equal distribution of acres in each age class in the working circle. In the absence of such a distribution, excess acres from older age classes can substitute where their harvest is efficient. Together, this volume and distribution, as well as the substitution criterion, determine sufficiency. Since conversion period demand is most likely less than annual long-run demand (demand in the year subsequent to conversion) and growth is positive (even on old growth acreage), a more precise evaluation would prove our three conditions *more than* sufficient to (1) prevent a short-run harvest decrease or price increase, and (2) make our long run feasible. As an aside, it is worth noting that this analysis sidesteps some difficult and controversial issues regarding both conversion period behavior and the desirability of achieving perfect regulation.[17]

Summary and Conclusions

To this point we have developed a method for analyzing questions of long-run timber investment and supply and then turned our attention to forestland allocation. We separated forestland uses into two competing categories, timber and recreation, and focused on the former. Efficient timber production is defined by the competitive economic model, with investment a direct response to price expectations. For a fixed positive level of silvicultural investment, sustainable annual *single-acre* harvests *decrease* with lower factor cost–adjusted price ratios. Regional supply is the aggregate of production across all classes of available forestland, and *aggregate* regional harvests may *increase* as lower factor cost–adjusted price

[17] Thomas R. Waggener summarizes these issues in "Some Economic Implications of Sustained Yield as a Forest Regulation Model" (Seattle, University of Washington, College of Forest Resources, Contribution no. 6, 1969).

ratios attract both more silvicultural effort and additional land to the productive management base, offsetting the negative single-acre price effect. A positive annual rate of price increase acts to further offset this effect. For each factor cost–adjusted price ratio there is one efficient investment level and one aggregate output level. Furthermore, since land use responds to price, there is one efficient acreage requirement associated with each price level. The output level speaks to our first problem, long-run timber supply—given sufficient current inventory to allow conversion to profitable long-run timber production levels.

After land allocation for timber is determined, remaining acres are of poorer quality for timber production. They can be reserved for reversible competitive uses at no cost in terms of forgone timber production. Efficiency criteria require that productive timberland also be allocated to competitive uses—reversible or otherwise—where the latter values exceed the value of the timber opportunity forgone. Our timber supply model helps us determine a first approximation of efficient allocation, even in the absence of good information about recreational land values. To this point we have abstracted from the likelihood of multiple products originating from the same land unit. The residual approximation of recreational land is conservative to the extent that multiple use is efficient but ignored.

There are, of course, other conflicts in forestland use besides those between timber and recreational uses. Once economically productive timberland is subtracted, our approach can be reapplied to conflicts between various recreational uses by apportioning extramarginal timber acres, or those acres plus multiple-use acres, among two competing recreational use categories. We can repeat this method, each time for a smaller group of residual acres, until efficient allocation of forestland among all uses is determined. The difficult, but not impossible, tasks are to develop supply schedules for many of the recreational use categories and to make some reasonable deductions about their demand. We avoided the latter task in this chapter by asserting a given demand price. We cannot be so cavalier in the case study applications in chapters 5 and 6.

5

The Douglas-fir Region:
A Case Study

In this chapter and the next we apply the analytical model of chapters 3 and 4 to a specific forestland area. We contrast the results with those which currently obtain from the aggregate of a variety of ownerships, each with its own behavioral model, but which in general resemble the allowable cut model of chapter 2. The analytical model of chapters 3 and 4 might be applied at two levels: (1) an aggregate or regional level and (2) the micro level of a single physical or land tenure unit. The former application provides the answer to regional timber supply questions in the economic long run and supplies insight on regional land allocations at a general level. The latter application focuses on local variations within the region and on specific features of the land allocational problem. Local variations consist of nongeneralizable differences in production and costs and management objectives; land allocational features are such things as timber opportunity costs and alternative recreational values. The French Pete case study of the next chapter is an example of this second level of application. The final chapter summarizes our conclusions.

We discuss the appeal of the Douglas-fir region for our problem before estimating the production function, associated costs, and prices necessary to find a value maximum, and, as derivatives, the long-run regional timber supply function and variable land production function. As stated at the outset (chapter 1), we use an engineering rather than a statistical approach for functional estimation because the engineering approach allows full introduction of current technologies as well as complete relaxation of institutional constraints in the economic long run (when all factors are variable). If we have reason to believe that either technical change or the relaxation of institutional constraints will proceed at a more rapid than historical rate, then the standard statistical analysis based on time series data underestimates timber supply.

The Douglas-fir Region

The area of Oregon and Washington west of the crest of the Cascade Mountains is known as the Douglas-fir region for its predominant timber species. It forms a single broad market for timber supply. The mountains on the east coincide with a change in species, and therefore a change in products; the Canadian and Californian borders also approximate changes in species and therefore products, on the north and south.

Both timber production and recreational uses of forestland are large parts of the regional life-style. The forest products industries are the largest employers in the region. Twenty-five percent of the nation's annual softwood harvest originates here. It supplies the largest share of any region in annual U.S. Forest Service harvests as well as substantial harvests from public lands managed by the State of Washington and the federal Bureau of Land Management. Environmental concerns about timber production and recreational uses of forestland are no less issues in the Douglas-fir region than they are nationally. Forestland reallocation in response to nonmarket values, however, is more of a possibility because of the large number of publicly owned acres.

Availability and quality of data also affected our choice of the Douglas-fir region. Timber production data are critical, given our intended concentration on timber production opportunities. In addition to the typical inventory data collected by the Forest Service for all regions, plentiful research data are available on the silvicultural practices applied within the region.[1]

[1] The bulk of research originates from the forestry schools at the University of Washington and Oregon State University and from the U.S. Forest Service's Pacific Northwest Forest and Range Experiment Station. The forest industries

Inventory data for the Douglas-fir region are more easily adapted to our purposes than are inventory data from other regions. Timberstand productivity data are collected by forest type (species mix) on a given land area, while annual harvest data are regional and are collected for each species separately. Therefore, wherever one species occurs in more than one forest type—which is the normal situation—it is exceedingly difficult to compare production with harvests from any given land area. We can avoid this problem with a simple model only in regions where a single species predominates.[2] An assumption of species uniformity is less severe a problem in the Douglas-fir region than it would be, for example, in the South where there are four major softwood species as well as many commercial acres of various hardwood species which "gum" up the production-supply transformation.[3]

Production

In this section we examine the underlying timber production processes, which are defined by the level and timing of silvicultural inputs. We examine five different processes, each *currently* observed in the region, because: (1) We have no prior information as to which is the least-cost process associated with a given stumpage price. (2) As prices and access change, we expect the least-

---

share some of their private research with the public, and some other university and state agencies (for example, Washington's Department of Natural Resources) conduct forestry research.

[2] The other important commercial species in the Douglas-fir region is hemlock. It grows in the very wet, high-productivity northern coastal sites and has become more important with the development of the export market to Japan. Several other species claim a small share of the market. Usually, they are high-elevation species (spruce) or slow-growing coastal species (cedar) of which a few old growth stands remain. It is quite possible that neither group will be actively managed in the commercial forests of the future.

[3] In spite of the difficulties inherent in the data available in other regions, Vaux first developed a timber supply model based on engineering rather than statistical functions in California, and Montgomery and others have since repeated the effort for Georgia. Henry J. Vaux, "How Much Land Do We Need for Timber Growing?" *Journal of Forestry* vol. 71, no. 7 (July 1973) pp. 399–403; Albert A. Montgomery, Vernon L. Robinson, and James D. Strange, "An Economic Model of Georgia's Long-Run Timber Market," Georgia Forest Research Council Report no. 34 (May 1975).

cost process to change. This is the direct implication of our earlier results ($dE/dp>0$ and $dE/dx<0$, where E is silvicultural effort, p is price, and x is access cost). (3) Production processes may also vary with land quality. With reference to this third point, we begin with an introduction to the land quality classification familiar to foresters. Subsequently, we identify the production processes and discuss their unique cost and output characteristics, which vary with land quality. Later sections apply this information to derive timber supply and land allocational conclusions.

Site Classification, Land Area, and Ownership

In order to develop a regional supply schedule and compare current and alternative forestland allocations, we need information about the number of acres in each land quality classification as well as their ownership distribution. It is intuitive that the least-cost timber production process varies with land quality. We will also find technical variations within production processes as land quality changes. Ownership determines land use objectives, therefore it also has an important impact on the efficiency of any given production process.

For general discussions, land is grouped into six different biological quality classes (site classes, hereafter) which are really measures of tree growth, an imperfect proxy for productive potential because it is not a full measure of available sunlight and nutrients. Site classes are arranged according to the productivity of fully stocked (that is, complete crown closure) natural timberstands at culmination of mean annual increment. Alternatively, land may be grouped by 100-year site indices where site indices measure the height at a given age of dominant and codominant trees (the 100 tallest trees per acre). Site class and site index possess an almost linear relationship.[4]

[4] The basic document for Douglas-fir is "The Yield of Douglas-Fir in the Pacific Northwest," by Richard E. McArdle, Walter H. Meyer, and Donald Bruce, USDA Technical Bulletin no. 201 (May 1961). The user must be careful to adjust for the difference between McArdle and standard U.S. Forest Service site classification. The McArdle classification is one roman numeral lower for each range of yields; that is, Forest Service Site Class I is McArdle II, and McArdle I is a super site. We use the Forest Service classification throughout.

Site Class	Site index (height in feet)	Yield (ft³ per annum)
V	0–75	20–50
IV	75–95	50–85
III	95–125	85–120
II	125–155	120–165
I	155–185	165–225
I+	185+	225+

Our analysis will suggest a timber production focus on land that is Site Class IV or better.

There is no easy system for modifying regional aggregates of these biological site classes for economic productivity. For our purposes, adjustment for economic productivity must be delayed, but not forgotten, until we discuss sensitivity to an accessibility parameter.

Normal yield tables have been prepared for each biological productivity class. They show the expected standing volume at ten-year intervals for fully stocked natural stands. Such stands are not "normal," however, in the usual dictionary sense of the word, because full stocking is not the rule in natural stands. We must later correct for an estimate of *natural* stocking density. Munger began preparing normal yield tables from Douglas-fir sample plots in 1909. His work was incorporated in McArdle's standard document. Staebler modified McArdle's work to obtain gross yield, or normal yield plus the mortality lost in the intervals between recorded measurements.[5] Gross yields are important because their added factor, mortality, is approximately that volume which can be recovered by thinning. Reukema and Bruce are in the process of expanding these tables to include expected yields resulting from various intensities of management.[6] The major weakness in each of these yield tables is the failure to account for stochastic effects arising from the seed source, soil nutrients, and weather. Sensi-

[5] George R. Staebler, "Gross Yield and Mortality Tables for Fully Stocked Stands of Douglas-Fir," USDA Forest Service Research Paper no. 14 (1955).

[6] More information is available from Donald L. Reukema and David Bruce, PNWFRES, U.S. Forest Service, Portland, Oregon.

tivity testing of our eventual conclusions may provide insight into the importance of stochastic effects.

Yield tables are prepared in several units of measure. Total cubic feet, including tip and stump, is the fullest measure of volume on the bole of the tree and the most satisfactory measure for our purposes because the trend has been toward full-volume utilization. There is no reason to expect it to change. There are already sawmills using trees too small to be included in the standard, or board foot, measure of volume, and pulp mills regularly use chips from the remains of dimension wood mills. Furthermore, we observe a considerable decline in regional capacity to saw large, old growth timber. Tables 5-3 through 5-7 in the subsequent part of this section summarize cubic foot yields expected with each production process.

In order to comment on regional timber supply and compare current and alternative forestland allocation, we will need to know the number of acres in each site class and for each ownership category: public, industrial, and nonindustrial private. The Forest Service collects this information. Sites I+ and I, however, are aggregated in their national reports.[7] The combined acreage can be separated according to proportional ownership shares reported earlier in more localized bulletins of the Forest Service's Pacific Northwest Forest and Range Experiment Station.[8] The result is:

Site Class

Ownership	IV	III	II	I	I+
		(thousand acres)			
Public	2,787	2,505	3,889	1,850	435
Industrial	801	1,193	2,338	2,136	599
Nonindustrial private	1,083	1,125	1,899	1,001	218

[7] USDA Forest Service, *The Outlook for Timber in the United States* (October 1973) appendix 1, table 5.

[8] Charles L. Bolsinger, "Timber Resources of the Puget Sound Area," USDA Forest Service Resource Bulletin PNW-36 (1971); Bolsinger, "The Timber Resources of the Olympic Peninsula," USDA Forest Service Resource Bulletin PNW-31 (1969); and Colin D. MacLean, "Timber Resources of Douglas County," USDA Forest Service Bulletin PNW-66 (1976). In addition, personal conversation with Charles Bolsinger was helpful.

These acreages should be regarded only as approximations. Wikstrom and Hutchison found that Forest Service data overestimated natural growth potential by 18 percent for one national forest in the region.[9] Curtis, Herman, and DeMars, on the other hand, found that growth potential for high elevation sites in the region was underestimated.[10] An educated guess might place the net effect in the direction of slight overestimation of natural growth potential. In addition, there will be adjustments in these acreages over time. Some forestland will be lost to roads and parks, some will change ownership category. Most probable shifts are (1) out of nonindustrial private into (a) industrial and (b) recreational ownerships, and (2) from public timberland to wilderness and multiple use setasides.

Certain shifts are implicit in the analysis. The changing costs and rates of return from site to site suggest that the inframarginal and extramarginal productive timberland boundaries will shift. In fact, if agricultural history is any indication, then, as forestry becomes a more crop-oriented technology and less a mining operation, concentration of production on the best sites will become more efficient. We can expect less management of the poor sites and improved competitive position for silviculture relative to agriculture on the best sites.

Timber Production Processes

In our analysis the production processes build upon one another, ranging from the least capital-intensive to the most capital-intensive silvicultural practices currently observed. The least intensive is the familiar (1) volunteer stands, or wild trees naturally grown. Each succeeding process adds one significant silvicultural practice: (2) planting, (3) thinning, and (4) fertilizing. That is, thinning includes planting, and fertilizing includes both planting and thinning. The fifth process continues the previous management practices with the exception of planting natural seeds or seedlings.

[9] J. H. Wikstrom and S. Blair Hutchinson, "Stratification of Forest Land for Timber Management Planning in Western National Forests," USDA Forest Service Research Paper INT-108 (1971).

[10] Robert O. Curtis, Francis R. Herman, and Donald J. DeMars, "Height Growth and Site Index for Fir in High Elevation Forests of the Oregon-Washington Cascades," *Forest Science* vol. 20, no. 4 (December 1974) pp. 307–317.

It requires (5) genetically improved seedlings. Improved seedlings may logically precede thinning and fertilizing in this sequence. We delay its consideration because of its newness as a production process—and because of the doubts some have about its viability. In all processes, the final harvest is clearcut, the standard practice for Douglas-fir.

The major characteristics of each process are its (1) regeneration lag, (2) stocking level, (3) production or yield and its timing, and (4) associated direct input costs and their timing. These characteristics vary among processes and often vary by site class of application within a given process since each site class responds differently to the various silvicultural treatments.

The magnitudes of response to each silvicultural treatment and the 1975 direct input costs were obtained from a large variety of Forest Service research notes and from responses to a questionnaire answered by nineteen professional foresters from the Douglas-fir region. The professional foresters were chosen so that a variety of backgrounds would be represented, including public (federal and state) and private, research (university, U.S. Forest Service, and industry) and industrial experience; geographic experience ranged from British Columbia to southern Oregon. They were asked to report their personal observations of local private costs rather than to share data which some might consider proprietary.

The questionnaire inquired as to both costs and degree of success of each of the various treatments. We will find that reported success rates were consistent with published results, but costs varied with personal experience: in particular, some respondents declined to answer questions for which they had no experience. Others pointed out that site quality fails to capture the full cost variation. A more thorough analysis would consider cost a function of slope, aspect, and soil type, as well as firm ownership, accounting principles, size,[11] and market location. This underlines the absence of error terms in the basic yield data. The questionnaire requested both the range of costs and the respondent's estimate of a regional average. The reported ranges were fairly uniform. The remainder of this section discusses each production process in detail. Direct

[11] There has been little examination of scale economies, an interesting aspect of timber production. The exception is Clark Row, "Probabilities of Financial Returns from Southern Pine Timber Growing" (Ph.D. dissertation, Tulane University, 1973), a comprehensive effort.

input costs are summarized for all timber production processes in table 5-8 and in the adjacent discussion at the conclusion of the section.

WILD TREES NATURALLY GROWN. The most basic timber production process consists of volunteer stands, or wild trees naturally grown. It assumes there is land and a seed source and that management has only custodial responsibilities before harvesting. The final productive result is whatever Mother Nature determines. Custodial responsibilities include general administration, some level of road maintenance, and fire, insect, and disease control. They are invariant with site class and age of stand. For example, brush-fires may occur on temporarily idle land—with an implicit stand age of zero. They are controlled, regardless of the lack of local damage, in order to prevent their spread to adjacent acres with vigorous timberstands. The estimate for custodial costs is $2 per acre per year.[12]

Regeneration lags and stocking density are the volunteer stand characteristics that are more difficult to estimate. Yield follows directly from our knowledge of them. Regeneration lags between natural rotations of Douglas-fir occur in the form of (1) idle land or (2) alder, which is often a pioneer species in Douglas-fir succession.[13] We ignore the alder problem, but, to the extent that the volunteer stand process proves efficient in the final analysis, the likelihood of alder succession implies an overestimate of softwood production.

Regeneration lags of the former variety vary throughout the region. They tend to be shorter in the North. In Douglas County, in southwestern Oregon, there are exceptional cases where the land has regrown only brush in three to four decades following harvest. Eventual regeneration of Douglas-fir in these cases will take somewhat longer yet. In spite of these variations, we might identify a range for the natural regeneration lag between zero and twenty-five years, with average lags per site generally as follows.[14]

[12] From a similar survey of current costs, the Washington State Department of Natural Resources found annual costs of $3 per acre. "Economic Analysis Phase II, Washington Forest Productivity Study," Olympia (1977).

[13] For an introduction to forest succession, see appendix A.

[14] Donald R. Gedney, PNWFRES, U.S. Forest Service, Portland, Oregon (personal communication, February 19, 1974) and Charles R. Bolsinger, PNWFRES (personal communication, January 11, 1974).

Site Class	Regeneration lag (years)
IV	16
III	14
II	12
I	10
I+	8

The lag is generally longer on poorer sites, because they are usually drier, and on some better sites where hardwoods and brush interfere more severely. The first cause predominates on a regionwide basis.

Stocking density is the most difficult characteristic to evaluate for this production process. Our intent is to estimate natural stocking levels, therefore we must exclude observations from industrial and nonindustrial private lands. Since industrial managers plant seedlings, we expect their land to be more heavily stocked than natural stock lands. Small private owners tend to harvest earlier and from better quality sites, thus leaving us with a poor sample of stocking for older age classes on poor sites. The major remaining ownership class is the public—and even using public land for estimating purposes has the disadvantages of including only a small sample of high-quality sites and some planted acres. We assume that the small sample of high-quality sites is sufficient for estimation, and that natural stocking is the rule for land stocked with age classes currently in the neighborhood of our expected optimal harvest times; that is, all public land planting has been recent. Our expectations are that stocking density increases as we move from poorer to better sites and from younger to older stands. Together these form what is known as the trend to normality,[15] "normality" being the fully stocked forest. Gedney and Fight reported the stocking class, site class, and age distributions for land in the National Forest System in the Douglas-fir region and their report is reassembled in table 5-1.[16] They reported timberstands in ten-

[15] McArdle found this trend to occur at a rate of 4 percent per annum for under- and overstocked stands between forty and eighty years old. McArdle, "The Yield of Douglas-Fir," p. 33.

[16] Donald R. Gedney and Roger D. Fight, "The Land Base for Management of Young Growth Forests in the Douglas-Fir Region," USDA Forest Service Research Paper PNW-159 (1973).

Table 5-1. Distribution of Naturally Stocked Acres

Stand age[a] (years)	Stocking class (%)	Midpoint (%)	IV–III	II	I–I+
				Site Class	
			(thousands of acres)		
35	70–100	85	17	2	0
	40–70	55	21	11	2
	10–40	25	21	9	0
45	70–100	85	28	6	0
	40–70	55	25	19	2
	10–40	25	40	4	0
55	70–100	85	40	13	8
	40–70	55	50	15	16
	10–40	25	43	4	0
65	70–100	85	51	15	10
	40–70	55	43	16	2
	10–40	25	47	11	2
75	70–100	85	39	9	6
	40–70	55	49	6	4
	10–40	25	38	0	2

Source: Adopted from D. Gedney and R. Fight, "The Land Base for Management of Young Growth Forests in the Douglas-fir Region," USDA Forest Service Research Paper PNW-159 (1973).

[a] The age of trees in the stand excluding regeneration lags.

year age increments between thirty-five and seventy-five years—which is the critical range for our optimal harvest timing. Notice that these are stand ages, the actual ages of stands exclusive of regeneration lag. (A few individual trees in any stand may be older.) They further separated stands into three stocking classes and three site classes. A 100 percent stocked stand is fully stocked, or "normal." A rule of thumb has it that the full growth potential of a site accrues to stands stocked 70 percent or better, therefore 70–100 percent is a logical stocking class. The other two classes are arbitrary. Another rule of thumb considers as nonstocked those sites with less than 10 percent stocking. The latter receive full consideration as part of the regeneration lag. Gedney and Fight combined their findings for Site Classes I+/I and III/IV.

Assuming the Gedney–Fight distribution resembles the natural distribution, we can calculate natural or volunteer stocking as a percent of full or normal stocking. Natural stocking varies by site class and age with the weighted average of per-acre stocking re-

Table 5-2. Natural Stocking by Site and Age

Stand age[a] (years)	Site Class (%)		
	IV–III	II	I–I+
35	53	54 (43)[b]	55
45	51[c]	57	55[c]
55	54	65	65
65	56	68 (58)[b]	72
75	56	73	75 (60)[b]

[a] Excludes regeneration lag.

[b] The number in parentheses is the result of the original calculation. It is replaced by the first number shown as a result of interpolation which accounts for a general pattern of relationships (the trend to normality) established by all entries in the table.

[c] Insignificant deviation from expectation.

ported in table 5-1. Identifying the stocking classes by their midpoints, for stands of a given age

$$\text{natural stocking percent} = \frac{\sum\limits_{i}(\text{midpoint})_i\,(\text{number of acres})_{ij}}{(\text{total acres in site})_j} \quad (5\text{-}1)$$

where i is the stocking class, say 70–100 percent; and j is the site class, say Site Classes III-IV. The results are recorded in table 5-2. For the most part, they are consistent with the trend to normality. For three exceptions, on better quality sites where the sample was smaller, we suggest an adjustment consistent with trends.

From this information and knowledge of yield on fully stocked stands, it is an easy step to calculate natural or volunteer stand yield. The latter is readily obtained in the form of the McArdle yield table for trees of greater than 1½ inches in diameter at breast height (dbh).[17] Volunteer stand yield in any given year is the normal yield volume adjusted downward for the less than normal stocking that we observe in natural stands. McArdle shows yield in *ten*-year increments beginning with age 20, therefore we must interpolate to get *five*-year comparisons with the natural stocking table 5-2. The result is table 5-3, yield by site and age for volunteer stands. The entry for dbh at each site and age is expected average dbh in a normal stand reported by McArdle. It will be useful when we discuss prices. Regeneration lag is still not a part of the reported age, but must be added later. The regeneration lags associated with each site are repeated at the bottom of table 5-3.

[17] See table 5-4 or McArdle, "The Yield of Douglas-Fir."

Table 5-3. Yield by Site and Age for Volunteer Stands
(yield per acre in cubic feet, dbh greater than 1½ inches)

					Site Class					
	IV		III		II		I		I+	
Age		vol/		vol/		vol/		vol/		vol/
(years)	dbh	acre	dbh	acre	dbh	acre	dbh	acre	dbh	acre
35		a	5	1,545	7	2,309	8	2,932	11	3,369
40		a	6	1,836	7	2,908	9	3,775	12	4,337
45		a	6	2,127	8	3,506	11	4,617	14	5,295
50	5	1,489	7	2,503	9	4,312	12	5,510	15	6,328
55	6	1,712	8	2,878	10	5,119	13	6,403	17	7,361
60	6	1,919	9	3,219	11	5,764	14	7,435	18	8,530
65	7	2,125	9	3,559	12	6,409	15	8,467	20	9,720
70	7	2,328	10	3,812	13	7,129	16	9,273	21	10,644
75	8	2,430	10	4,066	14	7,848	17	10,080	22	11,569
t_r in years [b]		16		14		12		10		8

[a] Insignificant.

[b] t_r = regeneration lag, the period during which land is vacant between harvesting one stand and the appearance of new growth. Thus, on Site Class IV land when trees are thirty-five years old, it has actually been 35 plus 16 or fifty-one years since the previous harvest.

PLANTING. The remaining timber production processes require succeedingly intensive *plantation* management. The objective of the planting process is to obtain fully stocked stands. Full stocking requires (1) planting to fill the gaps where natural regeneration fails to occur within a given time and (2) control of competing vegetation.

If there is any justification for planting, then it is not cost efficient to delay it and thereby allow the land to lie idle or allow establishment of competing vegetation. Since it is impossible to foresee the eventual location of gaps in natural reforestation, we assume the planting effort is immediate and complete. A usual goal is to plant two-year-old nursery stock within one year of the preceding harvest; thus the effective regeneration lag is minus one for all sites.

However, all planting is not successful the first time. In order to obtain fully stocked stands, a portion of each site must be replanted. Assuming our nursery stock is of the bare-root variety, a survival rate of 83 percent, invariant with respect to site, is good.[18]

[18] Peyton W. Owston and William I. Stein, "First Year Performance of Douglas-Fir and Noble Fir Outplanted in Large Containers," USDA Forest Service Research Note PNW-174 (1972); and Jerry R. Guzweiler and Jack K. Winjum, "Performance of Containerized Seedlings in Recent Forest Regeneration Trials in

This implies a 17 percent replanting effort within, say, five years of the initial restocking. But survival does vary by site; it decreases on poorer, drier sites. Considering the heavy concentration of land in the Douglas-fir region among the better site classes, the following distribution represents a mean failure rate of approximately 20 percent:

Site Class	Planting failure (%)
IV	35
III	30
II	25
I	20
I+	10

We assume planting failure has no significant impact on regeneration lag or stand age.

Initial planting costs are approximately $75 per acre, invariant with site. Replacement planting costs are a multiple of initial planting costs and the initial planting failure rate.

Planting costs are a function of cost per seedling, spacing (trees per acre), and planting difficulty. Spacing poses a problem. Our initial planting cost estimate is based on 600 *seedlings* per acre, while the model of managed Douglas-fir yields developed by Reukema and Bruce assumes 402 *survivors* at the first commercial thinning. The former number is close to current best industry practice, and alternative yield tables are not available to us. As a result, we may either overestimate planting costs or underestimate early harvest volume.

Control of competing vegetation remains an issue, particularly on higher quality sites. Competing vegetation, like the Douglas-fir, grows better on good sites than on poor, therefore the good sites

Oregon and Washington," in Richard W. Tinus, William I. Stein, and William E. Balmer, eds., *Proceedings of the North American Containerized Forest Tree Seedling Symposium,* Great Plains Agricultural Council Publication no. 68 (Denver, 1974). Respondents to our cost questionnaire suggested this average was too high for low-quality sites and too low for high-quality sites. Our adjustments follow their advice. They are somewhat more optimistic than MacLean's estimates for Douglas County. C. MacLean, "Timber Resources of Douglas County."

require more attention. This suggests a tradeoff between greater volume growth and higher costs as the better quality sites are brought into production. It is possible, therefore, that sites of intermediate biological potential have the greatest economic potential.

One control of competing vegetation is site preparation, which precedes planting and includes any treatment that destroys competing grasses, brush, and alder and increases the likelihood of successful planting. In the Douglas-fir region, its approximate requirement by site class is

Site Class	Acres treated (%)
IV	5
III	10
II	20
I	30
I+	40

The approximate cost of site preparation is $62 per acre, adjusted by the portion of acres requiring treatment.

A second control of competing vegetation is weeding or hardwood control after the new stand establishment, say at age five. It too varies by site quality:

Site Class	Acres treated (%)
IV	5
III	20
II	50
I	75
I+	90

Together, site preparation and hardwood control overcome the alder conversion problem which remained in the volunteer stand process. The approximate cost of weeding or hardwood control is $12 per acre, adjusted by the portion of acres requiring treatment.

With these treatments, it is possible to introduce and maintain a fully stocked timberstand. McArdle prepared the yield table for

Table 5-4. Yield by Site and Age for Fully Stocked Natural Stands

(in cubic feet per acre and dbh of average tree harvested)

					Site Class					
	IV		III		II		I		I+	
Age (years)	dbh	vol/ acre	dbh	vol/ acre	dbh	vol/ acre	dbh	vol/ acre	dbh	vol/ acre
20	a	a	a	a	a	a	5	1,550	6	1,830
30	a	a	4	2,270	6	3,300	7	4,110	9	4,750
40	4	2,110	6	3,560	7	5,250	9	6,550	12	7,500
50	5	2,840	7	4,780	9	7,050	12	8,840	15	10,150
60	6	3,500	9	5,880	11	8,700	14	10,860	18	12,500
70	7	4,090	10	6,830	13	10,150	16	12,660	21	14,500
80	8	4,580	11	7,690	14	11,350	18	14,220	23	16,350
90	9	5,000	12	8,400	16	12,390	20	15,540	26	17,880
100	9	5,350	13	9,000	17	13,270	21	16,610	28	19,140
t_r in years[b]		−1		−1		−1		−1		−1

Source: R. McArdle, W. Meyer, and D. Bruce, "The Yield of Douglas-fir in the Pacific Northwest," USDA Technical Bulletin no. 201 (1961).

[a] Insignificant.

[b] t_r = regeneration lag, the period during which land is vacant between harvesting one stand and the appearance of new growth. Thus, on Site Class IV land when trees are twenty years old, it has actually been 20 minus 1 or nineteen years since the previous harvest.

fully stocked *natural* stands, our table 5-4. His table is, however, a slight underestimate of *plantation* yield because of the better spacing, therefore fuller exploitation of the site's biological potential, which occurs in plantations. Once again, the ages in table 5-4 are stand ages at harvest exclusive of regeneration lags—which are shown at the bottom of the table. The regeneration lags are identical since planting was assumed for all sites.

THINNING. This production process adds precommercial and commercial thinning to the planting process. If a timberstand is planted too densely in order to ensure full stocking after establishment, then, in some parts of the stand, survival will be greater than necessary; density will be too great and growth of individual trees will be stunted. On these parts of the stand, early thinning (called precommercial) of the unmerchantable stand controls stocking. Its approximate cost is $40 per acre.

Later commercial thinnings gather the timber volume that would otherwise stagnate or die. This allows concentration of the site's biological potential in a remaining stand composed of those trees with the most desirable growth characteristics. Stands are initially planted with a larger number of stems than are expected in the final harvest—not only because seedling survival is not 100 percent but also because early growth of those trees in the final harvest fails to utilize the site's full potential. Denser planting and commercial thinnings of the merchantable stand capture the additional potential. Commercial thinning costs vary with the volume removed at the rate of approximately $32.50 per cunit (100 cubic feet).

Estimates of yields recovered from thinnings originate from the Reukema–Bruce managed-yield model.[19] The model is driven by an equation for gross growth increments of normal yields. Gross growth is a function of age and site index. Neither the timing of precommercial nor commercial thinning is in any sense optimized. Rather, the intent is to simulate observed behavior.

The Reukema–Bruce model, as we apply it, assumes precommercial thinning (PCT) for spacing control at age two for all sites. While age two is early for observed PCTs, Reukema and Bruce justify it as an attempt to simulate plantation stocking. The impact of PCT is an upward adjustment in the site index and a slight reduction in stand age when it reaches merchantable diameter.

The initial commercial thinning requires a merchantable stand diameter of 8 inches. Thinning occurs from below, that is, smaller diameter trees are removed and larger diameter trees remain, on the theory that the latter are better competitors. The minimum diameter of merchantable thinnings is 6 inches. Succeeding commercial thinnings are made for every 15 feet of height growth. Thus the age of the stand at any commercial thinning varies by site. The thinning rule of the model is to reduce the stand to a recommended basal area related to merchantable diameter or to two-thirds the basal area before thinning, whichever leaves more volume.[20] The intent is to allow a sufficient interval for revenues to exceed costs

[19] Donald J. DeMars, an associate of Reukema and Bruce, provided the necessary assistance in applying their model to meet our requirements.

[20] Basal area is a proxy for volume. It is the sum, for an acre of timber, of the horizontal cross-sectional areas of individual trees measured at breast height (4.5 feet). An acre of land of given site quality can support only some maximum basal area and annual increment in basal area, just as it can support only some maximum volume and annual increment in volume.

for each thinning, yet frequent enough thinnings to allow vigorous growth until the final harvest. The industry rule for commercial thinnings is that revenues exceed costs despite the possibility that it pays for costs to exceed revenues from a given thinning if the discounted value of the increment to later harvests is great enough. This rule reflects the industry's concern with annual cash flows.

The number of trees assumed per acre (402), the large minimum merchantable diameter requirement, and the length of time required for basal area increments to level off are important assumptions.[21] With more trees and a smaller merchantable diameter, basal area increments level off earlier, implying earlier and more frequent commercial thinnings and, perhaps, more volume recovered. Of course the increased costs of more frequent thinnings may offset any gain.

Table 5-5 shows the full yield volumes and average diameters for the thinning process. Stands can be either thinned or fully harvested at the ages shown. The ages vary by site. If the stands are thinned, the first volume (CT for commercial thinning) is removed, and the difference between the two volumes remains to add new growth. If fully harvested, the stand is clearcut of the second volume shown (F for final harvest) with each date. Harvest ages can vary from twenty to one hundred years, as in the planting process. The exact ages vary as a function of the thinning rule. The regeneration lag remains unchanged from the planting process.

FERTILIZING. The fertilizing process continues the inputs discussed for the planting and thinning processes. It adds 200 pounds of nitrogen per acre (most forest fertilization in the Douglas-fir region is in the form of urea, although some thought is given to adding phosphates and potassium) immediately *following* each commercial thinning. The intent is to concentrate the full impact of the fertilizer on the remaining, preferred growing stock.

Fertilization costs increased substantially with the recent change in energy costs because nitrogenous fertilizer production requires large energy inputs. Therefore, our estimate of $60 per acre for 200 pounds of nitrogen is taken from only the most recent

[21] Full printouts of assumptions and results of this model are too lengthy for this manuscript. Further detail can be obtained from the author or from Reukema, Bruce, or DeMars.

Table 5-5. Thinning and Final Harvest Yield by Site and Age for Fully Stocked Stands

(in cubic feet per acre and dbh of average tree harvested)

	Site Class									
	IV		III		II		I		I+	
Age (years)	dbh	vol/acre	dbh	vol/acre	dbh	vol/acre	dbh	vol/acre	dbh	vol/acre
22 CT									8	1,106
F									8	3,328
26 CT							8	1,203	9	962
F							8	3,620	10	3,911
30 CT									10	743
F									12	4,643
31 CT					8	1,258	9	1,012		
F					8	3,783	10	4,143		
35 CT									12	855
F									15	5,970
37 CT							10	907		
F							12	5,139		
38 CT			8	1,263	9	1,103				
F			8	3,796	10	4,397				
40 CT									14	810
F									17	7,101
43 CT							12	808		
F							15	6,136		
46 CT					10	925				
F					12	5,291				
49 CT			9	1,209						
F			10	4,608						
51 CT	8	1,227					14	1,001		
F	8	3,681					17	7,687		
54 CT									18	1,156
F									23	10,411
56 CT					12	992				
F					15	6,634				
61 CT							17	1,147		
F							21	9,358		
62 CT			11	1,026						
F			13	5,555						
63 CT									21	1,197
F									26	12,112
70 CT					15	1,240				
F					18	8,428				
72 CT	9	1,312								
F	10	4,725								

Table continues on next page

Table 5-5. continued

	Site Class									
	IV		III		II		I		I+	
Age (years)	dbh	vol/ acre	dbh	vol/ acre	dbh	vol/ acre	dbh	vol/ acre	dbh	vol/ acre
74 CT							19	1,335	24	1,332
F							24	11,278	30	14,047
82 CT			13	1,277						
F			16	7,308						
89 CT					18	1,435			27	1,617
F					23	10,366			34	16,446
91 CT							23	1,518		
F							28	13,363		
100 F	13	5,756	19	8,087	25	10,510	31	13,448	37	17,229
t_r in years[a]	−1		−1		−1		−1		−1	

CT = Commercial thinning yield.

F = Final harvest yield.

[a] t_r = regeneration lag, the period during which land is vacant between harvesting one stand and the appearance of new growth. Thus, on Site Class IV land when trees are twenty years old, it has actually been 20 minus 1 or nineteen years since the previous harvest.

experience. Those questionnaire respondents who did not indicate that their cost estimates were for 1975 or later were ignored.

Relative growth response per fertilizer application varies inversely with the site quality since we expect that one reason poorer sites are poorer is their nitrogen deficiency. Absolute growth response remains greater for the better quality sites.

Site Class	Growth response (%)
IV	25
III	20
II	15
I	10
I+	5

Growth increments following fertilization are temporary. Present estimates are that response lasts at least ten years, although the duration is probably longer on poorer sites. (Thus we expect greater delays between thinnings and fertilizer applications on poorer sites.) As many as five applications may be possible before the increment in net returns diminishes to zero.[22]

The Reukema–Bruce model again sets our expected yields. The only difference is that gross increment is now a function of age, site index, and *fertilization*. The effect of fertilization on volume growth is indirect through site index and diameter. It is consistent with the growth responses shown above. Table 5-6 shows commercial thinning and final harvest results for this process. Stand ages at commercial thinnings and final harvest vary from those of the thinning process (table 5-5) because fertilization causes the 15-foot height increments that dictate thinning to occur more rapidly. Regeneration lags are unchanged.

GENETICALLY IMPROVED SEEDLINGS. This process continues all the activities of the preceding processes except that it replaces natural seedlings with genetically improved ones.

We assume three-year-old, genetically improved, containerized nursery stock instead of the natural, bare-root stock used in preceding processes. Three-year-old stock is not normal, yet not unheard of. By the third year, seedlings are well on their way to overcoming all potential competition. If seedlings are planted in the first year succeeding a final harvest, regeneration lag is minus two. The extra year removed from rotation length provides a large discounted value bonus.

Containers extend the planting season and increase early growth as well as the likelihood of seedling survival. Ninety percent appears to be a reasonable mean survival rate, although reported observations have been mixed.[23] If we assume a 7 percent survival rate improvement on natural, bare-root stock success (90

---

[22] Robert O. Curtis, Donald L. Reukema, Roy R. Silen, Roger Fight, and Robert M. Romancier, "Intensive Management of Coastal Douglas Fir," *Loggers Handbook* vol. 33 (1973); S. P. Gessel, T. N. Stoate, and K. J. Turnbull, "The Growth Behavior of Douglas Fir," College of Forest Resources Contribution no. 7, University of Washington, Seattle (1969); and Richard E. Miller and Richard L. Williamson, "Dominant Douglas-Fir Respond to Fertilizing and Thinning," USDA Forest Service Research Note PNW-216 (1974).

[23] See the references cited in footnote 17. Questionnaire respondents suggested variance by seedling size as well as site quality. Containerized seedlings are larger than bare-root stock of the same age.

Table 5-6. Thinning and Final Harvest Yield by Site and Age for Fertilized, Fully Stocked Stands

(in cubic feet per acre and dbh of average tree harvested)

Age (years)	IV dbh	IV vol/acre	III dbh	III vol/acre	II dbh	II vol/acre	I dbh	I vol/acre	I+ dbh	I+ vol/acre
									Site Class	
22 CT									8	1,106
F									8	3,328
26 CT							8	1,203	9	992
F							8	3,620	10	3,970
30 CT									10	792
F									12	4,781
31 CT					8	1,258			9	1,073
F					8	3,783			10	4,258
34 CT									12	737
F									14	5,779
36 CT							10	857		
F							12	5,079		
38 CT			8	1,263	9	1,199				
F			8	3,796	10	4,576				
39 CT									14	878
F									17	7,196
42 CT							12	911		
F							15	6,369		
45 CT					11	924			16	992
F					13	5,373			20	8,743
48 CT			9	1,244						
F			10	4,666						
49 CT							14	978		
F							17	7,770		
51 CT	8	1,227								
F	8	3,681								
52 CT									18	1,074
F									23	10,360
54 CT					12	1,023				
F					15	6,788				
57 CT							17	1,021		
F							21	9,200		
60 CT			11	1,061					21	1,134
F			13	5,657					27	12,017
65 CT					15	1,096				
F					19	8,257				
68 CT							19	1,260		
F							24	11,115		
70 CT	9	1,305							24	1,296
F	10	4,708							29	13,961

Table 5-6. continued

	Site Class									
	IV		III		II		I		I+	
Age (years)	dbh	vol/ acre	dbh	vol/ acre	dbh	vol/ acre	dbh	vol/ acre	dbh	vol/ acre
77 CT			13	1,202						
F			16	7,231						
82 CT					18	1,428				
F					22	10,363				
83 CT							22	1,483	27	1,497
F							28	13,255	33	16,162
100 F	14	6,086	20	8,883	26	11,761	32	15,032	37	18,570
t_r in years[a]	−1		−1		−1		−1		−1	

CT = Commercial thinning yield.

F = Final harvest yield.

[a] t_r = regeneration lag, the period during which land is vacant between harvesting one stand and the appearance of new growth. Thus, on Site Class IV land when trees are twenty years old, it has actually been 20 minus 1 or nineteen years since the previous harvest.

Site Class	Planting failure (%)
IV	28
III	23
II	18
I	13
I+	5

percent containerized minus 83 percent bare root equals 7 percent), then the following failure rates apply by site class:

Improved seedlings cost approximately $85 per acre for the initial planting. Replacement costs must be adjusted by the initial failure rate. We might expect improved seedlings to increase planting costs substantially above the $75 per acre estimate for unimproved stock. This is doubtful, however, because there is no substantial difference in nursery treatment between natural and improved seed or seed stock. Genetically improved stock might even reduce overall reforestation expenses if wide-spaced improved stock replaces otherwise more nursery-intensive natural stock. Wide-spaced stock is more expensive but has a better survival rate.[24]

[24] David Cox, Industrial Forestry Association, Portland, Oregon (personal communication, July 2, 1976).

Finally, the cost of seed stock or seedlings itself is small compared with the labor costs of reforestation.

Genetic improvement in forestry is in its infancy. There is a limited supply of improved seedlings today, and this restricts us from anticipating adoption of this production process on all land. As applied today, genetic improvement only means *progeny selection,* not *hybridization.* Seeds are usually chosen from taller and faster growing parent stock. Expected volume growth increments range from greater than 10 to 45 percent,[25] with no evidence of decrease in the specific gravity of wood fiber.[26] If we use 20 percent, a conservative estimate, and apply it in the Reukema–Bruce managed-yield model, the result is table 5-7. A single qualification is the concern that trees of a given genetic structure may have a maximum growth capacity.[27] To incorporate this possibility—remember, forest genetics is in its infancy—the model sets an upper bound on growth. Fertilization of genetically improved trees on Site Class I+ exceeds the upper bound, so we withheld the more expensive activity, fertilization, from this site class. Stand ages at commercial thinning and final harvest shift once again because the 15-foot growth increments occur faster for improved stock.

Costs

Table 5-8 provides a summary of the 1975 direct input cost estimates previously explained for each timber production process. The first column records costs per acre or per 1,000 board feet (Mbf). The middle columns record costs adjusted for success

[25] Richard L. Porterfield, "Predicted and Potential Gains from Tree Improvement," School of Forest Resources Technical Report no. 52, North Carolina State University, Raleigh (1974); statement by George R. Staebler in *"Clearcutting" Practices on National Timberlands,* Hearings before the Subcommittee on Public Lands of the Committee on Interior and Insular Affairs, U.S. Senate, 92 Cong., 1 sess. on Management Practices on the Public Lands, Part I, April 5 and 6, 1971 (Washington, GPO, 1971) pp. 241–252; Bruce J. Zobel, "Increasing Productivity of Forest Lands Through Better Trees" (Berkeley, University of California School of Forestry and Conservation, S. J. Hall Lectureship, 1974); and A. H. Vyse and D. E. Ketcheson, "The Cost of Raising and Planting Containerized Trees in Canada," in Tinus and others, eds., North American Containerized Forest Tree Seedling Symposium, pp. 402–411.

[26] Zobel, "Increasing Productivity."

[27] It may be that maximum yields of trees, like corn and grains, will be obtained by finding stock genetically adapted to using fertilizer on any site.

Table 5-7. Thinning and Final Harvest Yield by Site and Age for Fertilized, Fully Stocked, Improved Stands

(in cubic feet per acre and dbh of average tree harvested)

Age (years)	IV dbh	IV vol/acre	III dbh	III vol/acre	II dbh	II vol/acre	I dbh	I vol/acre	I+ dbh	I+ vol/acre
						Site Class				
19 CT									8	1,019
F									8	3,069
23 CT							8	1,165	9	1,096
F							8	3,508	10	4,052
26 CT									10	645
F									12	4,499
27 CT					8	1,167	9	1,004		
F					8	3,503	10	4,049		
29 CT									12	612
F									14	5,388
31 CT							10	778		
F							12	4,802		
32 CT					9	975				
F					10	4,072				
33 CT									13	796
F									17	6,801
34 CT			8	1,267						
F			8	3,809						
36 CT							12	900		
F							15	6,186		
37 CT									15	773
F									19	7,970
38 CT					10	974				
F					12	5,217				
41 CT							14	847		
F							17	7,345		
42 CT			9	1,200					17	932
F			10	4,597					22	9,552
44 CT					12	852				
F					15	6,229				
45 CT	8	1,243								
F	8	3,729								
47 CT							16	951		
F							20	8,808		
48 CT									20	1,068
F									25	11,289
51 CT			11	1,019						
F			13	5,566						

Table continues on next page

Table 5-7. continued

					Site Class					
	IV		III		II		I		I+	
Age		vol/		vol/		vol/		vol/		vol/
(years)	dbh	acre	dbh	acre	dbh	acre	dbh	acre	dbh	acre
52 CT					14	1,042				
F					18	7,811				
55 CT							19	1,175	22	1,174
F							23	10,682	28	13,121
59 CT	9	1,253								
F	10	4,661								
62 CT			12	1,036	17	1,166			25	1,096
F			16	6,876	21	9,675			31	14,631
64 CT							21	1,205		
F							26	12,374		
72 CT									27	1,457
F									34	17,031
75 CT					20	1,313	24	1,328		
F					24	11,326	30	14,291		
79 CT	11	1,224	15	1,342						
F	13	5,926	19	8,815						
84 CT									31	1,585
F									38	19,313
90 CT							27	1,592		
F							34	16,638		
93 CT					23	1,551				
F					28	13,518				
99 CT									34	1,758
F									42	21,806
100 F	16	6,834	23	10,462	32	13,502	37	17,233	44	20,299
t_r in years[a]		−2		−2		−2		−2		−2

CT = Commercial thinning yield.

F = Final harvest yield.

[a] t_r = regeneration lag, the period during which land is vacant between harvesting one stand and the appearance of new growth. Thus, on Site Class IV land when trees are twenty years old, it has actually been 20 minus 2 or eighteen years since the previous harvest.

rates by site class. For example, 5 percent of Site Class IV acres require preparation at $62 per acre, or the average Site Class IV acre requires (0.05 × $62.00) $3.10 worth of site preparation. The final column records the year each cost occurs. Occurrence is adjusted for regeneration lag. Therefore, to compare costs with their impacts as demonstrated by yield tables 5-3 through 5-7, the regeneration lag must be added to the harvest timing of the latter five

Table 5-8. Costs of Growing Timber—Exclusive of Capital Costs
(in 1975 dollars and by year of occurrence)

Costs per unit	IV	III	II	I	I+	Year
			Site Class			
Annual costs $2/acre	←———————		2.00	——————→		All
Site preparation $62/acre	3.10	6.20	12.40	18.60	24.80	1
Planting						
Natural $75/acre	←———————		75.00	——————→		1
~ 17–20% failure	26.25	22.50	18.75	15.00	7.50	5
Improved $85/acre	←———————		85.00	——————→		1
~ 13% failure	23.80	19.55	15.30	11.05	4.25	5
Weeding/hardwood control $12/acre	0.60	2.40	6.00	9.00	10.80	5
Thinning Precommercial $40/acre	←———————		40.00	——————→		3
Commercial $50/Mbf	←———————		32.50/cunit	——————→		According to timing on yield table plus t_r
Fertilization $60/acre	←———————		60.00	——————→		Each commercial thinning
Sale administration $7.50 Mbf	←———————		5.00/cunit	——————→		Each commercial thinning
$3.75 Mbf	←———————		2.50/cunit	——————→		Final harvest

tables. Finally, recall that these are the years in which costs occur only *if* they are relevant to the particular production process under discussion.

It may be useful to note that annual custodial costs and the eventual cost of timber sale administration are the only costs relevant to all processes. We commented earlier on custodial costs. Sale administration is necessary for every commercial thinning as well as for final harvests. Final harvest administration is less expensive than thinning administration because clearcuts are easier to administer than partial cuts. (We list sale administration costs for both the more common board foot and the cunit measures.)

To this point we have ignored capital costs—which accumulate at the annual rate r in the profit-maximizing equation of chapter 3. They have a large impact on the magnitude of total costs for an investment as long lasting as a timber rotation—at least thirty years. Unlike direct input costs, capital costs are invariant with the production process; rather, they are a function of ownership alternatives. We expect different capital costs to apply for public, industrial, and nonindustrial private ownerships because each class of owners may have different alternative forestland uses:

(1) Federal ownerships are required to show that proposed investments promise returns consistent with a rate specified by the Office of Management and Budget.[28] This rate is our pragmatic choice for all public ownerships—although, in reality, it does not apply to nonfederal public ownerships and, where it does apply, both the rate itself and its method of calculation are controversial.[29]

(2) Nordhaus found *before-tax,* real corporate yields for all industries averaging about 10 percent in the early 1970s.[30] Industrial timberland owners, however, receive a capital gains tax incentive. Therefore, assuming a 50 percent marginal tax bracket, this all-industry average is equivalent to 7½ percent for industrial timberlands.

(3) Finally, for nonindustrial private ownerships, the best alternative land use in western Washington and Oregon is probably for Christmas tree production. The *before-tax,* real rate of return on this investment approximates 6 percent.

There is yet an alternative forestland use which we have not evaluated: common property amenity uses that prohibit timber production altogether; for example, recreation of various intensities and forms available to the public without exclusion. If the real value of this use grows at a rate faster than that for the real value of commodity uses such as timber production, then either the minimum commodity capital cost must compensate with an upward adjustment, or reallocation of land to amenity uses becomes so-

[28] U.S. Office of Management and Budget, "Discount Rate to be Used in Evaluating Deferred Costs and Benefits," Circular A-94 (1973).

[29] See chapter 2 for a discussion of public agency calculation of the rate of return on timber investments.

[30] William D. Nordhaus, "The Falling Share of Profits" *Brookings Papers on Economics Activity* (Washington, D.C., Brookings Institution, 1974) pp. 167–217. See table 5.

cially optimal over time. We can only justify the increasing amenity value where there is both an absence of satisfactory substitutes and a potential for irreversibility or for permanent change in the land form.[31] These conditions may be met on the external margin of economic timberland—higher elevations, steeper slopes, rocky outcrops, shallower soils; in general, land of poorer biological potential, but of the usual character of mountain parks and scenic vistas. Not all poor timberland is of park quality, but there may be a tendency for it to be so. Certainly, greater potential for irreversibility exists where timber production is more environmentally risky, that is, on the poor sites.

In another case involving undeveloped land, Krutilla justified a real amenity value growth rate of between 1 and 3 percent per annum.[32] Taking his results, we adopt rates of 3, 2, and 1 percent for Site Classes IV, III, and II, respectively. The assumption is that Site Classes I and I+ fail to satisfy the irreversibility criterion, while Site Classes II–IV are progressively better qualified for amenity uses as a general rule. That is, as site quality decreases, the amenity-valued characteristics of forestland increase.

Public land managers have a responsibility to adjust for non-market amenity values. Private land managers have no such responsibility. But for private land managers, amenity valuation is affirmed by market transactions, that is, by the increasing removal of forestland from timber production in favor of hunting retreats, second homes, etc. The capital cost adjustment on private land serves in lieu of a better estimate of this effect.

We can incorporate the rate of increasing amenity valuation with the cost of capital so that final capital costs equal the market capital cost plus the real growth rate of amenity values. The summary capital costs arranged by ownership and site quality follow.

---

[31] For full theoretical justification see V. Kerry Smith, *Technical Change, Relative Prices and Environmental Resource Evaluation* (Baltimore, Johns Hopkins University Press for Resources for the Future, 1974).

[32] Krutilla assumed growing real incomes over time. One to three percent is the estimated range of difference between income elasticities of demand for amenity and commodity uses. In Krutilla's case, Hell's Canyon, the amenity uses were those associated with wilderness preservation and the commodity use was hydropower. John V. Krutilla and Anthony Fisher, *The Economics of Natural Environments* (Baltimore, Johns Hopkins University Press for Resources for the Future, 1975) pp. 128–130.

| | *Site Class* | | | | |
Ownership	IV	III	II	I	I+
Public	13%	12%	11%	10%	10%
Industrial	10%	9%	8%	7%	7%
Nonindustrial					
private	9%	8%	7%	6%	6%

Prices

The yield and direct cost information contained in tables 5-3 through 5-8, plus our knowledge of capital costs, are insufficient for evaluation of the long-run timber supply schedule. In chapters 3 and 4 we learned that the efficient level of timber production is a function of its expected price as well as its marginal costs. Given our cost and yield information, we might still search for the efficient level of annual harvests for each of several prices and then use the series of price-harvest combinations to trace out a supply schedule— except that the supply price for stumpage must yet be normalized for access. It is difficult to say anything about the expected market equilibrating price without knowing more about the expected demand price and technical change. We can, however, obtain some insight by examining (1) the current market price response to qualitative differences and (2) the long-term secular trend in market prices.

Access

Stumpage costs recorded in the market derive from mill demand net of extraction costs or access. Identical timber sales, therefore, may sell at different prices as access to the sales varies. The formulation of chapter 3, however, isolates the impact of access such that timber sales identical in quality of timber and timing of sale bring the same market price regardless of access.

To reconcile what occurs in the market with our formulation, we need to know more about access. Because our interest is in stumpage, not log prices, we are not interested in harvest costs themselves, but only in the part that varies as a result of accessibility. Assuming necessary roads have been built and trucks are already owned by the logger, then access costs are a function of (1) hauling distance and (2) ease of logging the sale site, that is, ease of felling, bucking, and skidding. Mills are located at lower elevations on more level ground and tend to be near the better quality sites. Hauling costs increase as logging moves from the mill to more distant and generally poorer sites and across steeper slopes, which require more road miles per acre. Ease of logging decreases (access costs increase) as site quality decreases, implying less volume recovered per unit of effort, and as elevations increase and slopes become steeper, thereby requiring more roads and more miles traveled. In general (1) and (2) tend to reinforce each other as site quality decreases with elevation and slope.

In the short run, market stumpage prices vary greatly and access costs absorb a large share of this variance. This is reasonable because in the short run more timber cannot be grown. The only possible response to short-run demand-induced increases in stumpage is for the logger to bid on previously marginal timber, that is, timber with poorer access to the mill. Access is the only variable cost in the short run. In the long run, all production costs are variable and our analysis applies: Access costs remain a determinant, but not the sole determinant, of the degree of silvicultural management (or, in the terms of our previous analysis, $dE/dx<0$ in the long run where E is the level of silvicultural effort and x is the access cost).

Access costs in the Douglas-fir region range up to $36 per cunit. Production is concentrated on the good sites. The geometric nature of circles is such that area of the working circle is concentrated away from the mill. Assuming that regional site quality distribution holds for each working circle and site quality is uniformly distributed within each working circle, from best sites next to the mill to poorer sites at the working circle perimeter, then the following average allocation of access costs per harvestable cunit might be made:

Site Class	Cost per cunit ($)
IV	36
III	33
II	24
I	18
I+	10

The assumptions that regional site quality distribution holds for each working circle and that site quality is uniformly distributed within each working circle are obviously heroic regardless of any trends we can identify. Therefore we will test our eventual annual harvest conclusions for sensitivity to variation in access costs.

Quality

Diameter is a proxy for quality. The larger the diameter, the greater the portion of wood fiber in the long clear bole of the tree. Darr examined the price–diameter relationship for Douglas-fir and found that diameter up to 20 inches is an important determinant of price variation. He hypothesized that this reflects scale economies in logging, as well as changes in timber quality. He also found that the importance of diameter decreases with time as mills adopt lower cost processes for small diameter timber.[33] The latter effect is one we might expect, but one which we cannot estimate. As a result, use of Darr's observations overstates the future price differential between small and large diameter timber by a small but undetermined amount. Furthermore, Darr's observations are imperfect for our use to the extent that (1) tastes will change and (2) our eventual projected annual harvests suggest a different-than-current product (quality of timber) mix. Nevertheless, it would be a greater error to ignore qualitative differences and Darr's price–diameter relationship has the right sign. Where p_1 is the price of small-diameter stumpage, the price–diameter relationship Darr observed approximates

$$p(\text{dbh}) = \begin{cases} p_1 & \text{dbh} < 10 \\ p_1 + [p_1(\text{dbh} - 10)/10] & 10 \leq \text{dbh} < 20 \quad (5\text{-}2) \\ 2p_1 & \text{dbh} \geq 20 \end{cases}$$

That is, price increases by one-tenth for each inch of diameter in excess of ten but less than twenty.

Secular Trend

The real market prices of most basic resources, including the factors of timber production, have either remained constant or de-

---

[33] David R. Darr, "Stumpage Price—Does It Vary by Tree Diameter?" *Forest Products Journal* vol. 23, no. 10 (October 1973) pp. 58–60.

creased over time. *Stumpage* prices may have been an exception, but there is no lengthy time series data with which to examine their trend. We do know, however, that *lumber* price is the single exception among those resources with lengthy time series data.[34] This exception may be explained by a slower rate of technical change in timber production or wood processing industries relative to all other industries[35] and by the long slow adjustment of the natural inventory. The existence today of some of our original old growth inventory suggests the latter is true.[36] There have been many attempts in the past 100 years to ensure future supply by controlling current inventory.

We expect that part of the relative price rise which can be attributed to inventory adjustment to be positive but falling, asymptotically approaching zero as the optimal long-run inventory level approaches. The other part of the relative price increase, that part due to relative technical change, continues to adjust according to the current rate of technical change. The summation of these effects on relative stumpage prices is unknown to us. We expect it to decrease over time, but it will probably continue to be positive and significantly different from zero for at least the period of our focus—the single timber rotation of the economic long run.

[34] Harold J. Barnett and Chandler Morse, *Scarcity and Growth* (Baltimore, Johns Hopkins University Press for Resources for the Future, 1963), and Vernon W. Ruttan and James C. Callahan, "Resource Inputs and Output Growth," *Forest Science* vol. 8, no. 1 (March 1962) pp. 68-82, independently examined price series on primary resources, both renewable and nonrenewable. Both found the *only* resources, renewable or nonrenewable, in the U.S. market with an increasing relative price since 1800 was lumber. See also Paul G. Bradley, "Increasing Scarcity: The Case of Energy Resources," *American Economic Review* vol. 63, no. 2 (May 1973) pp. 119–125; Sherry H. Olson, *The Depletion Myth: A History of Railroad Use of Timber* (Cambridge, Harvard University Press, 1971); and Robert B. Phelps, "The Demand and Price Situation for Forest Products 1974–75," U.S. Department of Agriculture Miscellaneous Publication no. 1315 (1975) p. 18; Robert Manthy, *Natural Resource Commodities—A Century of Statistics* (Baltimore, Johns Hopkins University Press for Resources for the Future, 1978); and V. Kerry Smith, "Measuring Natural Resources Scarcity" *Journal of Environmental Economics and Management* (June 1978) pp. 150–171.

[35] Vernon L. Robinson, "An Estimate of Technical Progress in the Lumber and Wood Products Industry," *Forest Science* vol. 21, no. 2 (June 1975) pp. 149–154.

[36] Catherine A. Hoffmann, "An Evaluation of the Structural Changes in the Forest Product Industries and Their Implications for Public Forest Management Policies" (Ph.D. dissertation, University of Washington, 1969). Hoffmann demonstrates that, as conscious public policy has slowed the rate of old growth inventory adjustment, it has simultaneously short-changed public welfare.

Several persons have examined the relative stumpage price change problem. Their observations vary from a 1.5 to a 3.4 percent increase annually according to starting points of their time series—although each lacks something in conviction because each time series was necessarily short.[37] We adopt an intermediate annual rate of 2.5 percent, but expect to examine our eventual annual harvest conclusions for sensitivity to this rate.

A 2.5 percent rate of annual stumpage price increase is consistent with the planning expectations of industrial timberland owners. It conflicts, however, with the common economic assumption (for analyses such as ours) of constant long-term prices—an assumption which on its own grounds is both highly subjective and probably incorrect in our case. Rising relative stumpage prices imply increasing scarcity. Indeed, rising relative prices cause us to question the concept of renewability as it applies to timber. There can be no doubt that timber is biologically renewable. Nevertheless, where rotations are exceedingly long and when relative prices are rising, we ponder over the conflict between renewability and scarcity. How can we reconcile the advantages of renewability with the social disadvantage of a rising relative price?

Supply

We have completed our survey of production, cost, and price information. In this section we intend to apply this information to develop the long-run regional timber supply schedule. Our approach is to first examine single-acre production as a function of expected prices and then aggregate across all acres in the region to obtain regional supply. The subsequent section will discuss policy implications of our supply schedule and associate it with forestland allocation.

We can derive supply curves for each of the five sites and three ownerships. Each supply curve is the locus of maximum annual harvests offered for successively higher expected relative stumpage prices. Stumpage prices continue to be adjusted for uni-

[37] See, for example, Clark Row, "Probabilities of Financial Returns," and the stumpage price series in the annual Forest Service publication, "The Demand and Price Situation for Forest Products," particularly the 1973 volume.

form accessibility. We must alter the profit-maximizing equation Eq. (3-8)

$$V^6 = \max_{T,E} [pQ(T,E)e^{-rT} - wE]/(1 - e^{-rT})$$

to a form which fits our data; that is, a form which allows for secular price increases, price variations with diameter, multiple harvests, silvicultural inputs subsequent to planting, and distinction among site classes and ownerships. What appears to be a complex problem in the calculus of variations must be simplified to accept discrete data points. It must also disregard optimizing intermediate harvest schedules because our yield tables do not allow such manipulation.

Price is an exogenously fixed function of timber quality or diameter, which is a function of harvest age. We shall return to this function in a moment. Price expectations increase over time at the rate ρ. Since price affects rotation age, second and subsequent rotations are of different length than the first rotation and the profit-maximizing equation takes a complex, extended form. Harvests Q and factor costs C may occur at any time in the T_n year rotation. Harvest and cost levels vary with the silvicultural process E (which is our operational measure of effort) and site quality S. Access costs x also vary with site quality. Capital costs r vary with site and ownership. The new form of the profit-maximizing equation is

$$
\begin{aligned}
V^7 = \max_{T_n,E} \Bigg\{ & \sum_{n=1}^{\infty} p_n \left[\sum_{k=1}^{T_n} \theta_k Q(k,E,S) \exp(\rho-r)k \right] \\
& \exp(\rho-r) \sum_{i=1}^{n} T_i \\
& - x(S) \sum_{n=1}^{\infty} \left[\sum_{k=1}^{T_n} \theta_k Q(k,E,S) \exp(-r)k \right] \\
& \exp\left(-r \sum_{i=1}^{n} T_i\right) \\
& - \left[\sum_{k=1}^{T_n} C(k,E,S) \exp(-r)k \right] \exp\left(-r \sum_{i=0}^{n-1} T_i\right) \Bigg\}
\end{aligned}
$$

(5-3)

In this equation θ is an operator which instructs us to use the commercial thinning volume from our yield tables for intermediate harvest years and the full volume of the remaining stand in the final harvest year T_n. It instructs us to disregard all years in the production period $k = 1, 2, \ldots, T_n$ for which the yield tables fail to project harvests.

Thus expected prices, site quality, and ownership are exogenous. The silvicultural process and final harvest date are decision variables. Given site and ownership and expected prices, there is one silvicultural process and one final harvest date which together maximize net return to the landowner V^7. We can obtain this value only by searching all E and all T_n.[38] If this value is positive, timber production is a profitable use of the land; if it is zero, the land is marginal for timber production; and if the land attracts a negative value as timberland, it is best allocated to nontimber uses—*for given expected prices and ownership.*

We can derive a single-acre long-run supply curve for any combination of site and ownership. First choose an expected price

$$p_n = \sum_k^{T_n} p_k \theta_k Q(k,E) \Big/ \sum_k^{T_n} \theta_k Q(k,E) \tag{5-4}$$

where θ remains the operator instructing choice between commercial and final harvest volumes. Choose this price such that, for any given harvest year, it is the *average* price of all intermediate and final harvests *weighted* by their proportionate components of various diameters. Together, this price and the site, silvicultural process, and ownership combination determine a series of V values and harvest levels, one for each alternative rotation length. The harvest

---

[38] The second and subsequent rotations have small impact on the maximum V in our application. They demonstrate no impact on the optimal length of the first rotation or the optimal silvicultural process. These results can be explained by the large impact of discounting on second and subsequent rotations and by the discrete nature of our harvest age and silvicultural process observations. The results allow us to simplify our search process, maximizing Eq. (5-3) over a single rotation and only checking alternatives in the neighborhood of our optima for greater multiple rotation V values.

level associated with *maximum* V converts to the optimal long-run annual harvest level Q^*/T^*,

$$Q^*/T^* = \sum_{k=1}^{T^*} \theta_k Q(k,E^*)/T^* \qquad (5\text{-}5)$$

which is the annualized sum of intermediate and final harvests.

$(p_n, Q^*/T^*)$ is a point on the supply curve. If we repeat the process for a vector of alternative expected prices, we obtain a series of points which together define the annual supply for a *given site, silvicultural process, and ownership.* By repeating the entire process for all silvicultural alternatives (for a given site and ownership), and by choosing the alternative with greatest V for each weighted price, we obtain the long-run supply curve *for that site.*

As an illustration, see figure 5-1, which describes supply for a single acre of public ownership, Site Class I. Silvicultural processes are shown independently. At an expected price of zero, none are profitable. Above $25 per cunit, volunteer stands or wild-tree management becomes profitable. At succeedingly higher prices, wild-tree management remains profitable. Indeed, it becomes more profitable, but (as the vertical dashed line demonstrates) higher prices have no effect on optimal harvest volume for this process. They do not alter the optimal wild tree rotation age. Higher prices do cause other processes to become more profitable, however. As the price rises, first less, then more intensive processes return a positive net value V. At $25 per cunit, wild-tree management is profitable. By $50, both wild tree and the planting process obtain positive returns, but highest land value shifts to the latter; its maximum V is greater. At $60, it shifts again—to genetically improved seeds. At $47, thinning, fertilizing, and genetic improvement all provide a positive return to land ownership, but planting makes the greatest return. The solid line in figure 5-1 coincides with maximum land values and traces the supply curve for a single acre of Site Class I in public ownership.

This example demonstrates two interesting characteristics which reappear in other sites and ownerships: First, either planting or genetic improvement processes dominate the thinning and fertilization processes, depending on the price level. It is apparent that, beyond minimum custodial management, early planting (whether natural or improved stock), therefore reduction of the regeneration

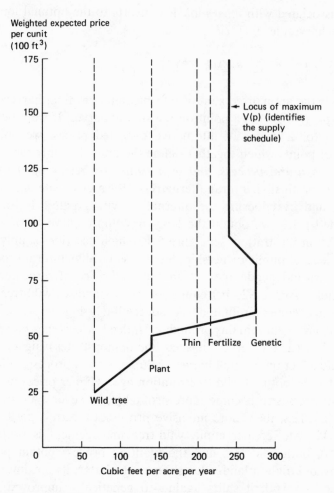

Figure 5-1. Timber supply: Public ownership, one acre, Site Class I.

lag, is the most effective of investments. This result causes us to wonder (1) at what reduction in costs would thinning and fertilization stand on their own and (2) what results would derive from genetically improved seedlings which were not later thinned and fertilized. The genetic process is last in our sequence of silvicultural processes only because it is the newest, least-certain timber growing technology. As it becomes more dependable and more widely applied we expect to see a change in the sequence of implementing silvicultural processes to planting–genetic–thinning–fertilizing.

Genetically improved seedlings themselves would become a profitable investment at slightly lower stumpage prices. The supply curve in our single-acre example would shift outward in the $50–60 range, but remain unchanged thereafter.

Second, the fixed land area supply curve may bend backward. We predicted this in chapter 4 and it occurs in our example when the price rises from $80 to $90 per cunit. The genetic improvement process is most profitable at both prices, but it is more profitable at a higher price. At the higher price, maximum net value occurs for a shorter rotation; therefore, average annual harvests are less. (It is only coincidental that rotations, therefore annual harvests for other silvicultural processes, do not change within the reported price range.) This unusual result occurs because (1) the price increase raises annual land rental costs relatively more than it raises the present value of receipts, thereby causing shorter rotations and reduced harvests and (2) the partial nature of the model excludes substitution from accompanying price increases, i.e., substitution in the form of timber from other land.

Aggregate Supply

To obtain aggregate regional supply, we (1) multiply the annual harvest level at each price times the number of acres in the site, (2) then repeat the operation for each site and accumulate to obtain the supply schedule for each ownership. (3) Finally, we accumulate across ownerships to obtain the regional supply schedule.

Our results appear in table 5-9 and figure 5-2. In table 5-9 the annual harvest volume in cunits of each succeeding expected stumpage price level is added cumulatively to harvest volumes associated with lower price levels. That is, to obtain the long-run harvest level associated with any given price level, simply sum all entries in column two for that and lower prices in column one. Negative entries reflect a backward bend in the single-acre supply curve for that site class and ownership. Notice that the backward bend disappears as the analysis is generalized to allow variation in the number of acres used as prices rise. The supply schedule is lumpy because we tested for prices in intervals of $10 per cunit. In a more detailed application, price levels, input variability, and

Table 5-9. Timber Supply Schedule: Douglas-fir Region

Expected stumpage price (1975 $)	Increment in annual harvest (million cunits)	Ownership	Site Class	Silvi-cultural intensity	Acres (thousands)
50	1.3112	Public	I+	Genetic	435
	2.6219	Public	I	Plant	1,850
	1.9105	Public	II	Wild	3,889
	2.1907	Industry	I+	Genetic	599
	3.5874	Industry	I	Plant	2,136
	2.6605	Industry	II	Plant	2,338
	0.9338	Industry	III	Plant	1,193
	0.8191	Nonindustrial private	I+	Genetic	218
	3.1749	Nonindustrial private	I	Genetic	1,001
	2.5563	Nonindustrial private	II	Plant	1,899
	0.8806	Nonindustrial private	III	Plant	1,125
	22.6469				16,683
60	2.3295	Public	I	Genetic	
	2.4149	Public	II	Plant	
	−0.0888	Industry	I+	Genetic	
	2.6396	Industry	I	Genetic	
	2.2885	Industry	II	Genetic	
	1.8813	Nonindustrial private	II	Genetic	
	1.0332	Nonindustrial private	III	Genetic	
	35.1451				16,683
70	3.8067	Public	II	Genetic	
	0.8497	Industry	III	Genetic	
	39.8015				16,683
80	−1.1313	Public	II	Genetic	
	0.9927	Nonindustrial private	IV	Genetic	1,083
	39.6629				17,766
90	−0.5155	Public	I	Genetic	
	1.9608	Public	III	Plant	
	−0.1038	Nonindustrial private	I	Genetic	
	40.0044				17,766

Table 5-9. continued

Expected stumpage price (1975 $)	Increment in annual harvest (million cunits)	Ownership	Site Class	Silvicultural intensity	Acres (thousands)
110	1.0055	Public	III	Genetic	2,505
	0.7343	Industry	IV	Genetic	801
	−0.0218	Nonindustrial private	I+	Genetic	
	41.7224				21,072
250	2.5548	Public	IV	Genetic	2,787
	44.2772				23,879

harvest levels would be smoother and, in the limit, continuous. Columns three, four, and five show the ownership, site class, and level of silvicultural intensity associated with each efficient price-harvest relationship. Column six associates the number of acres in each ownership and site class combination with the stumpage price at which they first become profitable for timber production. Figure 5-2 reproduces the supply schedules for each ownership class. We obtain the regional supply schedule by adding these horizontally.

The results support the findings of our basic production and supply formulation in chapters 3 and 4. Some site class, ownership, and silvicultural combinations become profitable at very low expected prices. This just demonstrates that trees can grow with very little management. For greater price expectations, the efficient level of silvicultural intensity and number of profitable timber-producing acres both increase. (The expansion of timber-producing land would have been even more emphatic had we considered conversion of agricultural land in response to greater price expectations.) Together, the silvicultural and acreage impacts of greater price expectations suggest the fallacies of (1) managing all sites with equal intensity and (2) worst-first policies, which encourage silvicultural inputs on poor timberstands and poor sites before turning to more productive areas. In fact, it may be good practice to intensify on good sites long before poorer sites receive even minimal attention. Note the sequence of efficient silvicultural practices for

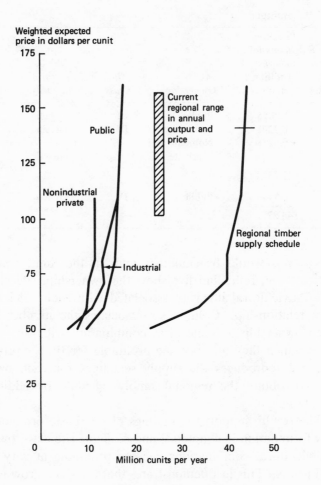

Figure 5-2. Timber supply: Douglas-fir region.

Site Classes II, III, and IV in public ownership. For the poorest sites, the least intensive silvicultural practices may never be efficient. Note Site Class IV in any ownership. For it, the wild-tree and planting processes are not efficient at lower prices. At price levels for which they are profitable, the genetic process is optimal.

For comparison with our supply projection in table 5-9 and figure 5-2, the current (1975) annual regional production and price range is 24 to 26 million cunits of all species for $90 to $150 per cunit. Our analysis suggests production so much in excess of current annual harvest levels that the question emphatically seized upon is, "What is there about the analysis that leads to such very different results than currently obtained?" Various reruns of the analysis, using total costs increased as much as 30 percent per year, still suggest annual harvests at least comparable with current levels at comparable prices; therefore, the basic explanation must be more fundamental. Our greater projected harvest levels are a function of the assumptions of (1) increased biomass utilization and (2) widespread conversion from volunteer stands to more intensive silvicultural processes. The expected level of biomass utilization is a matter of judgment. With normal technical change, our projection is not out of the question. A separate run of our analysis, allowing only volunteer stands or the wild-tree production process, leads to annual harvest and price levels approximating those current. This is a good check on our analysis and confirms our explanation for the projected change in timber supply. The change to more intensive silviculture is already apparent to on-the-ground observers. Its impact on prices and harvests has not yet been felt because intensively treated stands are still in the ground. They have yet to be harvested.

Public and nonindustrial private ownerships may be slow to adopt intensive practices; the former, because of environmental constraints and recreational land use objectives; the latter, because owner objectives are less frequently maximization of timber values and because the owner's comparative advantage may lie elsewhere (for example, agriculture). Our regional timber supply projections, nevertheless, are nearly as impressive when the more intensive silvicultural processes are excluded from these ownerships. If fertilization and improved seedlings are excluded, then, at a stumpage price of $140 per cunit, regional annual harvests remain in excess of 36 million cunits—still 10 million in excess of current harvests at comparable prices.

As a concluding reminder, we attempted to err on the side of production underestimates during our discussion of silvicultural processes. To the extent we were successful, the entire regional supply schedule is an underestimate and should be shifted to the right. We also focused on one productive margin, ignoring the opportunity for conversion of agricultural lands to timber production as stumpage price expectations rise. This also suggests a shift to the right for the regional supply schedule, a shift which becomes

**Table 5-10. Timber Supply Sensitivity to the Rate of Relative
          Stumpage Price Increase**

Expected stumpage price (1975)	Annual harvest (million cunits) for given rate of price increase		
	1.5	*2.5*	*3.5*
50	13.94	22.65	39.22
75	29.91	38.67	47.51
100	36.49	40.01	47.38
125	39.44	41.72	48.37
150	41.18	41.72	48.75

more emphatic with higher price levels. Thus, we have confidence
in the production levels associated with each expected price level,
but mean to draw no conclusions about the supply price elasticity.

   Sensitivity

   We turn now to the timber supply implications of shifts in
various parametric values. The assumption of rising relative stumpage prices is most unusual in long-term economic analyses like this
one. The usual expectation is that higher prices eventually induce
sufficient investment and substitution to discourage further price
increases. Nevertheless, an assumption of constant relative prices
for our period of analysis would be highly questionable in light of
both historical observations and current industrial expectations to
the contrary. Historical observations suggest that the actual rate
of price increase has varied with the time periods from which the
observations were taken. Accordingly, we recognize our estimate
of 2.5 percent annually as just that, an estimate. It is appropriate
that we consider the impacts on timber supply of both lesser and
greater rates of change, say from 1.5 to 3.5 percent annually. The
resulting aggregate regional supply schedules are displayed in table
5-10 and figure 5-3. The supply forthcoming with a 2.5 percent
annual price increase is retained in table 5-10 for reference.

   We observe that higher rates of price change uniformly attract
greater annual harvests. This conforms with our conceptual statement in chapter 4, condition (4-7). We also observe that at lower
prices harvests are relatively more sensitive to changes in the price

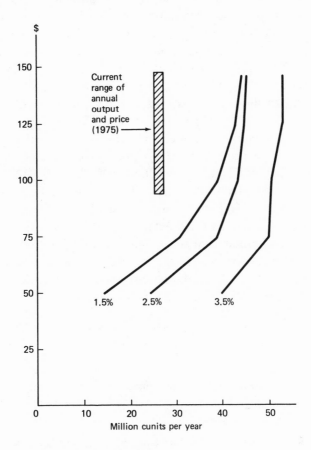

**Figure 5-3. Timber supply sensitivity to the expected
rate of relative stumpage price change.**

level, while at higher prices harvests are relatively more sensitive
to changes in the rate of price increase. This suggests that accurate
prediction of the rate of price increase becomes more important
with the passage of time.

At price levels comparable to current observations (current
prices adjusted for the upward price trend), projected harvests are
substantially in excess of current harvests. This is true regardless
of the rate of price change. Apparently our projected large expansion of annual harvests would hold for even smaller rates of price
change than those examined.

Let us now turn to the sensitivity of annual harvest levels to changes in factor costs. Annual harvest levels associated with any given expected stumpage price are most sensitive to a change in the cost of capital. An increase in the cost of capital of one percentage point has the approximate effect of a 10 percent increase in the general cost level. Given that the *public* cost of capital is institutionalized, private capital costs are the more likely to change. An increase of two to three percentage points in the private cost of capital has the equivalent effect of shifting industrial and nonindustrial *per acre* production levels until they are coincident with previous public and industry production levels, respectively. Such an increase has a greater impact on the minimum efficient price for lower quality sites (minimum price at which the site can be profitably managed for timber), greater impact on harvest volume on better sites, and greater impact on industrial timberland, in general, than on nonindustrial private timberlands. That is, a two to three percentage point increase in the private cost of capital has the following general effects per acre by site and ownership:

	Site Class	
Ownership	IV–III	II–I–I+
Industry	Increase minimum efficient price $25–$50, insignificant effect on harvest volume	Insignificant price effect, decrease harvest 20–60 ft³/acre/yr
Nonindustrial private	Increase minimum efficient price $0–$25, insignificant effect on harvest volume	Insignificant price effect, decrease harvest 10–20 ft³/acre/yr

In the aggregate, a two to three percentage point increase in the private cost of capital shifts the regional supply schedule left, decreasing the previous harvest level by one-tenth to one-sixth, depending on price. Production remains in excess of 10 million cunits greater than current annual harvests at comparable prices.

Changes in other factor costs have lesser impacts; most interesting are planting and fertilizing costs. A 20 percent increase in planting costs causes no noticeable shift away from silvicultural processes emphasizing either planting or genetic improvement. (The only significant impact is on poorer quality public lands on which profitable timber production is delayed, awaiting somewhat higher prices.) This further underlines our suspicions of the efficiency of durable (planting) investments.

The long-run level of fertilizer costs is uncertain because of the large energy input in nitrogenous fertilizers. Adding one third to fertilizer costs seldom affects their profitability. In the other direction, subtracting one third from fertilizer costs never makes fertilization more efficient than the genetic process. Rather, it expands the price and site quality ranges and the ownership classes over which the addition of fertilization is more profitable than just thinning and planting. The suggestion that fertilization is justifiable for a wide range of costs compares favorably with empirical observations on private lands.

In general, given an expected stumpage price level, any cost decrease or substantial rate of price increase causes small increases in either silvicultural intensity or rotation length within a silvicultural process. Both cases imply increased harvest levels and increased site values. When costs are low, there is greater impact on harvest levels, particularly on good sites. When costs are high, there is greater impact on site value. Given lower capital costs on private timber investments and higher on public investments, private harvest levels but public timberland values (opportunity costs) are more sensitive to other input cost adjustments.

This causes us to inquire after the change in rotation accompanying a change in management intensity. Shifting from volunteer stands to the planting process usually decreases rotation (including regeneration lag), but shifting to the genetic process increases rotation. A harvest level increase occurs in each case. Recall our expectation that as the introduction of improved seed becomes more widespread, the price-sensitive sequence of implementing production processes will become planting–genetic–thinning–fertilizing. This sequence results in a uniformly positive management/rotation relation. (And with this knowledge we can demonstrate a trend toward the coincidence of biological and economic solutions for harvest timing as discussed in appendix B.)

It remains for us to examine the sensitivity of our results to varying extraction costs. Our analysis substantiates the judgment of chapter 3 that, as difficulty of access increases, optimal rotation ages increase and optimal levels of silvicultural intensity decrease. These results are invariably accompanied by a decrease in the *annual* harvest level. Higher extraction costs have their most notable impacts on low-valued land, that is, on marginal sites.

We have assumed that biological site quality decreases as difficulty of access increases, but we know this is a generalization, not a universal truth. We expect to observe working circle boundaries which both reach out to take in a few acres of less accessible, high-quality sites and draw in to avoid more accessible, low-quality sites. We might inquire as to extraction cost and stumpage price extremes—issues of particular relevance for public land managers since the perimeter of efficient timberland is often composed of public lands. (Western public forestland is generally what was left after private owners took their pick.) Since the remaining old growth timberstands tend to be the least accessible even on public land (more accessible sites were harvested first) as well as a battleground for the timber industry and conservationists, the importance of this question is heightened.

First, we can set land value V equal to zero, and for the maximum extraction costs of $36 per cunit search for the minimum stumpage price at which timber production becomes profitable on each site class. The following *minimum* expected stumpage prices per cunit (normalized by the 2.5 percent annual rate of increase) are required to include *public* land in the working circle. They compare with current prices in the range of $90 to $150 per cunit.

	Site Class				
$x = \$36$	IV	III	II	I	I+
Minimum weighted price	$274	$88	$52	$31	$27

Site Class IV is unprofitable timberland at anything approaching current prices. This result is all the more emphatic when we recognize that genetics is the profitable silvicultural process on Site Class IV at a stumpage price of $274 per cunit. The usual practice is more likely to be either the volunteer stand or planting processes, and these do not become profitable until stumpage prices reach $970 and $290, respectively!

This analysis tells us only to exclude Site Class IV from timber production when it is on the margin. What if access were less an issue, for example, if the site is adjacent to the mill (or if we contemplate building a new mill on an adjacent site)? Access costs are zero and the minimum profitable stumpage prices are

	Site Class				
$x = \$0$	IV	III	II	I	I+
Minimum efficient price	\$234	\$71	\$40	\$20	\$15

Once again, genetics is the profitable process on Site Class IV. The wild-tree and planting processes on Site Class IV require minimum prices of \$960 and \$276, respectively. Given that current prices are in the range of \$90 to \$150 per cunit, we can confidently generalize that timber production on Site Class IV public land in the Douglas-fir region is inefficient.

Policy Implications

Our estimation of long-run regional timber supply, in the absence of any change in overall national public policy, is complete. Before we draw any policy implications, however, we must (1) say something about demand, and then (2) determine the feasibility of any long-run projection level. That is, is the current standing inventory sufficient for conversion period production between now and the economic long run, one rotation or thirty to fifty years from the present?

To evaluate the demand–supply equilibrium and its price, harvest level, and land use implications, we first need to know something about demand. The required knowledge is implicit in the initial price and price trend assumed by each producer. Thus, throughout our analysis we have made the implicit assumption that the equilibrium price level is rising from its current level at the rate of 2.5 percent annually. In the remainder of this section we inquire as to the reasonableness of this rate and the implied long-run equilibrium.

Because our focus is on the economic long run, we need not examine optimal inventory conversion. We only need to inquire whether the current inventory is sufficient to provide all short-run consumption as the equilibrium price rises at a rate of 2.5 percent annually from its current base. Following our determination in chapter 4, Eq. (4-12), sufficient inventory I, if properly distributed among classes, is

$$I = \sum_i A_i Q_i^* (\$140)/2 = 765.1 \text{ MM cunits} \tag{5-6}$$

This compares with an actual current regional inventory of 1,101.4 million cunits, including only those trees greater than 5 inches dbh, but also including standing volume on Site Class V—a site class so low in quality that it failed to meet efficiency criteria on any ownership and at any price below $350 per cunit. Thus, in the 1,101.4 million cunits of uncertain age, some inventory which will eventually be marketed is overlooked because it is currently too small for measurement, but some inventory from unprofitable timberland is added.

As a generous check on the effects of the unknown age distribution and of Site Class V inventories (whose own magnitude is unknown), we might exclude the *entire* U.S. Forest Service inventory from all sites. About half of all Site Class V land, including many high-volume old growth stands, is managed by the Forest Service. It is, however, only 4 percent of Forest Service timberland in the Douglas-fir region. Therefore, exclusion of the entire Forest Service inventory grossly overcompensates for the exclusion of the Site Class V inventories. It also corrects for the unknown age distribution because stagnant age classes are the only ones which really increase the 765.1 million cunit requirement. Private ownerships have already harvested their very old stands. Where such stands remain, they are generally on public land. Thus the estimate of private inventories is a very conservative estimate for total available inventory. This estimate, 746.6 million cunits, is nearly sufficient by itself—recall from chapter 4 that our sufficiency condition assumes an *immediate* increase to the long-run consumption level, an unlikely occurrence which further supports a finding of sufficient conversion period inventory to restrict the equilibrium price from rising at a rate of greater than 2.5 percent annually.

Long-run Equilibrium

Timber depletion has been an off-and-on issue in the world at least since the time of Solomon and the cedars of Lebanon, and in North America since 1546 when the Viceroy of Mexico called attention to short fuelwood reserves. In the United States, it was a justification for the creation of the Forest Service[39] and has been a continued theme in projections of the Forest Service,[40] presidential commissions,[41] and private researchers.[42] The Douglas-fir region has been the specific subject of several of these reports.[43]

[39] Good references on timber famine and U.S. public land policy are Karen Mask, "Perspectives on Timber Shortages" (unpublished M.S. thesis, University of Washington, 1975) and the classic Benjamin H. Hibbard, *A History of the Public Land Policies* (Madison, University of Wisconsin, 1965) chapters 19–22, 26. Greeley credits Gifford Pinchot, early Chief of the Forest Service, as the originator of the phrase "timber famine." Whether Greeley is correct is uncertain, but he does convincingly demonstrate both Pinchot's and the Forest Service's awareness of the issue. William B. Greeley, *Forests and Men* (Garden City, N.Y., Doubleday, 1951). (Greeley eventually became Chief of the Forest Service himself.)

[40] USDA Forest Service, *The Timber Supply of the United States* (1909); *Timber Depletion, Lumber Prices, Lumber Exports, and Concentration of Timber Ownership* (1910), commonly known as the Clapper report; *A National Plan for American Forestry* (1933), commonly known as the Copeland Report; *Forests and National Prosperity* (1948), also known as the Reappraisal; *Timber Resources for America's Future* (1958); *Timber Trends in the United States* (1965); *The Outlook for Timber in the United States* (October 1973). These reports uniformly underestimated growth and increases in wood utilization. See Marion Clawson, "Forests in the Long Sweep of American History," *Science* vol. 204, no. 4398 (June 15, 1979) pp. 1168–1174.

[41] President's Materials Policy Commission, *Resources for Freedom* (1952); Commission on Population Growth and the American Future, *Population, Resources, and the Environment* vols. II, III (1972); Edward Cliff, *Timber: The Renewable Material*, National Commission on Materials Policy (August 1972).

[42] For example, Stanford Research Institute, *America's Demand for Wood, 1929–75;* Hans Landsberg, Leonard Fischman, and Joseph Fisher, *Resources in America's Future* (Baltimore, Johns Hopkins University Press for Resources for the Future, 1962); Donella H. Meadows, Dennis L. Meadows, Jørgen Randers and William W. Behrens III, *The Limits to Growth* (New York, Universe Books, 1972).

[43] USDA Forest Service, "Timber Trends in Western Oregon and Western Washington" (October 1963); see also William Deurr in the *Congressional Record,* daily ed. January 17, 1966, pp. 374–388, which was originally intended to be part of the manuscript, USDA Forest Service, "Douglas Fir Supply Study" (1960); Donald R. Gedney, Daniel D. Oswald, and Roger D. Fight, "Two Projections of Timber Supply in the Pacific Coast States," USDA Forest Service (1975); John H. Beuter, K. Norman Johnson, and H. Lynn Scheurman, "Timber for Oregon's Tomorrow," Research Bulletin no. 19 (Corvallis, Oregon State University School

In spite of these fears, we have never run out of timber, and contemporary analysts know that it is unlikely we ever will.[44] As reduced volumes of timber become available, prices adjust upward, inducing (1) some consumers to leave the market altogether, (2) some consumers to substitute other products, and (3) additional investment in timber production. Thus, "Will we run out of timber?" is not a useful question. It is useful to consider, however, the supply and demand equilibrating price as a measure of shortage. Thus, expected changes in the equilibrium price or expected shortfall or excess of consumption relative to production are useful topics of discussion. Producers, consumers, and policy makers can act in a meaningful way on conclusions originating from such discussion.

We consider demand and the demand–supply equilibrium given an upward trend in current prices continuing at the annual rate of 2.5 percent for the next thirty to fifty years. If supply exceeds demand at this price, then the projected rate of price increase is too great. If demand exceeds supply, then either prices will rise at a rate greater than 2.5 percent, or some public policy intervention is required. It is difficult to predict which is the case but we can contrast our projection with knowledge of the current equilibrium quantity and price shown in figures 5-2 and 5-3—approximately 25 million cunits at $140 per cunit. Our long-run supply projection is considerably in excess of this for a wide range of factor costs. It suggests a 68 percent increase in consumption if the expected price trend is accurate.

This is a very large shift for this number of years. Therefore we consider the alternative explanation that supply exceeds demand at our prices. Let us first reflect on why this might be so, and then consider the market and policy implications.

---

of Forestry, 1976); and State of Washington Department of Natural Resources, "Forestry Productivity Study" (Olympia, Washington, 1975); and Robert E. Wolf, "The Douglas Fir Region Timber Supply Situation," Library of Congress, Congressional Research Service (May 1975).

[44] See Robert U. Ayres, *Technological Forecasting and Long Range Planning* (New York, McGraw-Hill, 1969) pp. 18–21, 94–117, for a review of forecasting problems. See also John A. Zivnuska, "The 1964 Timber Trends Study in Perspective," *Proceedings* (Society of American Foresters, 1964) pp. 84–88; Henry J. Vaux and John A. Zivnuska, "Forest Production Goals: A Critical Analysis," *Land Economics* vol. 28, no. 4 (November 1952) pp. 318–324; G. R. Hall, "Comments on an Estimate of Capital Needed in Forestry" *Journal of Forestry* vol. 63, no. 11 (November 1965) pp. 678–682.

Our supply projection might be too enthusiastic if we overlooked a cost of production. Recall from chapter 1 that this possibility is a weakness of the engineering approach. The overestimate might also be caused by a too rapid introduction of currently known technologies, thereby leading us to project more intensive silviculture and higher levels of wood utilization than may actually occur in thirty to fifty years. We assumed that efficient current technologies will be introduced as rapidly as the old stand is harvested throughout the conversion period. Conservative landowners may be slower to invest and intensive silvicultural practices may never be introduced on the public lands. Finally, our supply projection will be an overestimate so long as institutional barriers to efficiency remain. Notable among these are the foresters' preferences for allowable cut harvest models and maximizing mean annual increment (see chapter 2).

If the preceding arguments suggest that the supply projection is an overestimate, recall the counter arguments explicit in our conservative production estimates and the denial of predictable general advances in technology. Furthermore, note that as stumpage prices rise relative to agricultural prices, there will be some introduction of timber production on formerly agricultural land and an attendant shift in supply. Any supply overestimate in our analysis is countered by disregarding this shift in land use.

On balance, however, there is a strong suggestion of a supply overestimate. If the entire 68 percent implicit increment in demand for timber from the Douglas-fir region cannot either be (1) absorbed by long-run demand expansion or (2) substituted for production decreases elsewhere in the world, then we can assume either (3) Douglas-fir region producers will not make the full adjustment to efficient production processes or (4) the upward price trend will be not nearly so great. Apparently those firms expecting a 2.5 percent annual price rise are literally banking on expectations of inefficient production behavior by others and perhaps by themselves.

Public policy has traditionally played a large role in the timber market through incentives to the construction industry and for private home ownership as well as through the sale of public timber. Our analysis suggests that public policy might more appropriately focus on barriers to production efficiency. Barriers such as those discussed in chapter 2 may be most easily recognized on public lands.

Table 5-11. Land Use

(stumpage price is $140 per cunit)

	Economic	Current (1970)[a]
Industry		
Acreage (millions of acres)	7.067	7.222
Site classes	I+ to IV	I+ to V
Annual product	15.786 MM cunits	9.07 MM cunits
Nonindustrial private		
Acreage (millions of acres)	5.326	5.526
Site classes	I+ to IV	I+ to V
Annual product	11.212 MM cunits	2.81 MM cunits
Public		
Acreage (millions of acres)	8.679	11.878
Site classes	I+ to III	I+ to V
Annual product	15.814 MM cunits	9.07 MM cunits
Residual acreage (millions of acres)		
Industry	0.155	0
Nonindustrial private	0.200	0
Public	4.601	1.402
(Total)	(4.956)	(1.402)

[a] USDA Forest Service, "Appendix I," *The Outlook for Timber in the United States,* Forest Resource Report no. 20, October 1973.

Forestland Allocation

This discussion is in two parts: timberland and nontimber or recreational forestland. Abstracting from multiple use, efficient forestland allocation is judged by the profitability of the land in timber production. Land is efficiently allocated to recreational uses wherever recreational values cover their own costs and the land is unprofitable for timber, as well as wherever net recreational values can be shown to exceed net timber values.

TIMBERLAND. Given our demand price assumption, long-run annual production of 42 million cunits can profitably originate from 21,072,000 acres. Table 5-11 shows this result by ownership class and compares it with current timberland use. As expected, most industrial and nonindustrial private land is profitable in its use for timber production. The relatively few (355,000) acres of Site Class V land which fall outside efficiency boundaries may still be justified as timberland by private owners who intend to mine the currently standing timber. These acres may also be justified as timberland where they occur in isolated pockets surrounded by better timberland. It may be easier to include such acres in the larger, profitable plot than it is to manage around them.

Public timberland is another matter. Profitable output is 60 percent greater than current output and on 27 percent fewer acres, those in Site Classes IV and V. (Site Class V on public land fails to be profitable timberland until stumpage prices exceed $500!) The currently inefficient 27 percent is a sufficiently large portion that it cannot be explained as occasional acres surrounded by better land. It suggests considerable inefficiency in current public land management.

Mining the existing timber resource on these acres cannot always be justified either. Where regeneration is not justified, access costs may exceed the value of standing timber. Elsewhere, social costs (for example, aesthetic values or downstream effects of soil erosion created by timber management) which are properly internalized in public management, together with access costs, may exceed the value of standing timber. Furthermore, public law (the Multiple Use–Sustained Yield Act, the Knutson–Vandenberg Act, and the National Forest Management Act) precludes mining timber on federal land.

Withdrawal of the land that is inefficient for timber production promises additional favorable impacts on loggers and mill operators as well as on landowners. A smaller and more geographically concentrated capital base—that is, fewer roads, trucks, etc.—is needed per cunit produced. Because mills are closer to the productive land, we may, at the same time, expect greater efficiency in wood fiber recovery. The implication is that there will be greater returns to capital as well as greater returns to landowners for withdrawal from inefficient timberland. We can imagine extreme cases where entire isolated communities may currently be maintained on inefficient public timberland. Here, the cost of social services (roads, hospitals, schools, etc.) would be less and the quality might be greater if inefficient timber production were abandoned and new timber-based communities were allowed to develop closer to or as part of existing population centers.

The conclusion is that fewer acres than are currently managed are justified for timber production on efficiency grounds. The vast majority (92 percent) of these doubtful acres are in public owner-ship. Since we suspect an efficient public harvest expansion is possible without these acres, we deduce that production on the good sites must currently be paying for inefficient public manage-ment on poor sites. Apparently greater financial and volume returns can be obtained from managing fewer acres of public land.

RECREATIONAL FORESTLAND. Because best current practices are not followed everywhere in the region, our analysis suggests an even greater efficiency in timberland management than is current. Fewer acres than we suggest are currently profitable timber producers, and more acres should be residual to timber production as currently practiced. If, in the long run, (1) more efficient timber management processes are not applied, or (2) demand fails to expand to 43 million cunits at a stumpage price equal to $140 per cunit plus the current rate of price increase, or (3) general advances in technology continue the trend to intensive silviculture on good sites, then the efficient timberland perimeter will shift yet further. Even more acres will be residual to profitable timber production.

There are currently 1.4 million acres in the Douglas-fir region which meet the 20 ft^3 per acre per annum (Site Class V or better) timber production criterion, yet are deferred from timber harvesting. These acres include public forestland managed by various local, state, and federal agencies. The largest segments are state parks, national parks, and U.S. Forest Service Wilderness areas and areas currently under official study for addition to the Wilderness System (the productive-reserved and the productive-deferred components discussed in chapter 2). These acres do not include all public land roadless areas because some are not under official study; nor do they include all Wilderness areas, all National Park land, etc., because much of this land cannot meet the 20 ft^3 criterion.

To these 1.4 million acres we can add 3.2 million acres of public forestland (Site Classes IV and V) and, perhaps, 0.4 million acres of private land at zero cost in terms of forgone timber oppor-tunity. This is enough to *triple* the amount of forestland in the Douglas-fir region on which timber harvesting is currently restricted. To put these results in some perspective, consider the restricted land in North Cascades, Mount Rainier, and Olympic national parks; add a considerable amount for Forest Service Wilderness areas and for state parks; then *triple* the sum. To the extent that current timber production inefficiencies continue to exist, they make timber production more expensive and less profitable, and we can increase this acreage even further. Obviously, efficient timber production is a strong argument for wilderness.

It may be that many of these acres possess characteristics preferred by recreationists: high elevation, scenic outcroppings, seclusion. It may also be that they are among the fragile, steep, and shallow-soiled sites which cause environmental problems when managed for timber. If, however, recreationists are allowed to use only these residual timber sites, they will rightfully object that there are also recreational values uniquely attached to good timber acres and that we are ignoring those values. For example, those who appreciate wildlife can point out that there is no substitute for some of the wildlife habitat on better timberland.

Abstracting from multiple use, our response to this argument is that any good timber acreage which is more valuable for recreational uses or which has large environmental costs should also be withdrawn from timber production. (Our timber supply results must be adjusted for each withdrawal of this class of land.) It is not within the scope of this chapter to generalize about how many such acres exist. We can, however, identify the timber value, that is the value of the timber opportunity, which must be exceeded by recreational values or environmental costs in order to justify removing the land from timber production. It is the site value of the land, the V in our Eq. (5-3). For public timberland within the Douglas-fir region in general, and for a stumpage price equal to $140 per cunit plus the rate of price increase, the timber opportunity value per acre is as follows:

Public timberland opportunity cost	Site Class			
	III	II	I	I+
Site value	$125	$500	$1,000	$1,500
Site value (excluding intensive processes)	$100	$300	$600	$700

Current public agency practice is to delay harvest timing and avoid efficient applications of certain silvicultural processes. Such practice restricts both the value of the timber opportunity and previous estimates of timber production opportunities. If the only managerial constraint were a rejection of the fertilizing and genetic improvement processes, then the second set of timber opportunity values becomes appropriate. The difference between the two values for an acre of a given site class is the social cost of the constraint. This cost becomes very large on the better sites. Regardless of managerial constraints, acres of Site Classes IV and V have positive timber opportunity values only in exceedingly unusual circumstances.[45] (The values shown above are high compared with timberland prices in the Douglas-fir region today—which only substantiates our conviction that long-run timber management efficiency is not the current rule. Our estimate of the efficient number of acres to allocate to recreational uses is, accordingly, conservative and our estimate of the minimum recreational or environmental value necessary to overcome the timber opportunity is high.)

These timber opportunity values are comparable to an *annual* timber opportunity, or economic rent, of the cost of capital times the associated site value. Ten percent is the capital cost required by the Office of Management and Budget for federal agency investments. Thus, if a wildlife manager, for example, can demonstrate that the annual net value of a generalized acre of Site Class II devoted to wildlife habitat is in excess of $50 (0.10 $\times$ $500), then there is sufficient justification for excluding timber production from that acre. If he expects the wildlife population to eventually migrate and no longer regularly use this acre, then the wildlife manager will eventually return the acre to timber management. Meanwhile, harvests may be postponed, and silvicultural opportunities may be forgone, but the standing timber will grow in volume and in value. The temporary delay in timber management has a timber opportunity cost composed of two elements: the land rent and the discounted growth in value of the standing timber crop. The latter is a benefit, or negative cost of delay, such that if the Site Class II acre is stocked with vigorous young timber, its timber opportunity cost may be considerably less than $50 per year.

Aside from the fact that recreational forestland and environmental protection may be substantially increased in the Douglas-fir

---

[45] If managerial constraints delay harvest until culmination of mean annual board foot increment, then even Site Class III has zero timber opportunity value.

region without any reduction in timber production, there are two implicit conclusions to be drawn from this section. First, environmentalists and recreationists do not compete with the interests of the poor who desire better housing. At least with respect to the Douglas-fir region, both groups can improve their situations if timberland managers take a longer view of efficiency criteria.[46] Second, environmentalists and recreationists who object to more intensive forestry should carefully evaluate the implicit tradeoff. More intensive forestry, where justified by economic efficiency, may mean less environmental damage—because riskier timber sites are often less profitable—and more recreational acreage. This is no argument against considering the aesthetic and environmental costs of intensification.[47] Rather, it is encouragement to consider real alternatives in land use.

Summary

Long-run (years 2000–2020) timber supply is an important policy issue and a multitude of policies have been recommended to cope with the perceived problem of a timber shortage. We have argued for an examination of unconstrained, efficient, timber management as an indicator of expected timber supply in the absence of statutory policy intervention.

In the long run, the capital investment and managerial constraints placed on production are fully adjustable. These adjustments may be particularly significant in timber production where the economic long run is thirty to fifty years and the conditions of production are changing rapidly and perhaps inconsistently with previous experience. Therefore, long-run timber supply may be considerably different from what we might expect from the most sophisticated statistical projection of historic trends.

As an alternative, we recommend a long-run supply projection based on our estimate of best current (1975) practice. All timber

[46] This is a regularly heard view. Dorothy Duke, representative of The National Council of Negro Women, is notable among those who express it.

[47] An economic analysis of the costs of forest monoculture could yield interesting results. To my knowledge no one has tackled the problem in spite of considerable political attention on clearcutting, a specific segment of the monoculture issue.

managers may not implement best 1975 practice by the years 2000 to 2020, but they have the opportunity to do so, and some will even make improvements on best 1975 practices as additional technologies become available. Therefore, our projection represents a conservative estimate of what timber supply can be—an estimate from which we can usefully consider public policy options.

In chapter 2 we explained the deviations from efficiency found in the current general model of forest management. In chapters 3 and 4 we developed the conceptual model for determining efficient levels of timber production and supply. In this chapter, we demonstrated application of this model for a region where timber supply is an important issue, the Douglas-fir region of Washington and Oregon. Our empirical observations of best current practice distinguish among factor costs and timber yields for six land classes, five levels of silvicultural effort, and three ownership categories. The data are equal to the task at hand and good to a first approximation.

Applying these data, we developed a single-acre supply schedule as a function of silvicultural and capital costs and expected stumpage prices. In effect, we found that for any given expected price, certain silvicultural practices are efficient, and result in the efficient annual harvest level. Therefore, when we looked at a vector of expected prices, we were able to produce a single-acre supply curve. By doing the same thing for each class of acres and each ownership category and then aggregating across all acres and categories, we were able to produce the long-run, regional timber supply schedule. Abstracting from multiple uses, we were also able to say something about the efficient use of land for timber.

Our results support the findings of our basic production and supply model. As prices rise, the level of silvicultural intensity and number of profitable timber-producing acres both increase. As land quality decreases, the level of silvicultural intensity decreases. Tests for sensitivity to changes in access costs demonstrate a direct relation between access and harvest timing and an inverse relation between access and silvicultural effort. Access is a most important variable for public lands—which tend to be less desirably located than private lands. (When land was originally claimed by settlers, the settlers naturally chose the best land. Public land includes the remainder plus any private land which reverted in lieu of tax payments.) The important points to be learned from these observations are that (1) it is not efficient to manage all acres, even within a single ownership, at the same level of intensity and (2) access can be an important variable, particularly for public lands.

In order to pursue the implications our analysis has for timber shortage and land allocation, we need to know something about the long-run demand price. We made this implicit in our analysis. Current annual harvest and price ranges for the region are 24 to 26 million cunits of all species for $90 to $150 per cunit. At $140 per cunit plus the rate of price increase, potential annual long-run harvests are 42 million cunits. (We found sufficient standing inventory to make this long-run solution feasible.) The 68 percent increase in harvest is due to changes in technology and shifts from volume maximization to efficiency criteria in production and very likely overstates expected consumption at this price. In fact, the projected harvest level is so great that we expect either (1) it will cause reduction in the expected market-clearing price or (2) market pressures and the profit motive will be unsuccessful in attracting some producers to efficient production technologies. Or, to put it another way, the 68 percent increase is not a projection of what will occur, but of what can occur. Even without technological advances or price increases, timber producers apparently have the ability to respond to expected increases in demand without additional investment incentives originating from public policy.

Moreover, even if the lack of opportunity for multiple uses and nonpriced resource services is a sufficient argument to exclude all but the least intensive timber management from *public* ownerships, regional long-run annual harvests would still exceed 36 million cunits—a 44 percent increase from the present level. In any case, efficient management is apparently a more important policy issue than a timber shortage *per se*.

This is particularly true for the public lands where both expenditure of public funds and land allocation are issues which demand careful scrutiny. Site Class V is inefficient timberland for all ownerships at current prices below $250 per cunit. The same is true for publicly owned land of Site Class IV. Even if timberstands on these sites are a gift of nature, road maintenance, access, fire and insect protection, and sale preparation costs are often too great to permit profitable harvesting. The large number of acres

(3.5 million) allocated to timber, but which are nevertheless unprofitable for timber production under the most efficient technologies, occur mostly in public ownership (3.2 million). Those in private ownership are few enough to be viewed as occasional poor sites surrounded by better sites. It might be more costly to "fence out" these occasional poorer sites than to manage them as integral parts of larger land units.

There are too many poor quality *public* acres used for timber production to rationalize on such grounds, however. Their removal from timber production would result in a net saving to the public treasury and the public timber budget. Under the best circumstances, it costs more to produce timber on these lands than is returned in revenue from timber. Their best allocation is to a deferred decision category until either (1) timber prices change to make them productive or (2) their value as permanent nontimber reserves is demonstrated. Lands in the deferred category would be open to any use which does not cause irreversible impact—essentially they would constitute *de facto* (not statutory) wilderness areas. With additional evidence that they have positive value in a wilderness classification, statutory allocation is appropriate. These inefficient public timberlands are sufficient to expand the forested acreage in national forest wilderness and state and national parks in the region by 229 percent, or to approximately three times their current acreage.

There are two final qualifiers on our analysis: (1) This case study was chosen only as an illustration of an analytical method for questions of long-run policy relevance. While we have considerable confidence in the general harvest level and land allocation results for the Douglas-fir region, they do not apply for other regions with different species, silvicultural practices, access problems, prices, and costs. The emphatic nature of our findings, however, suggests that similar tests should be made for other regions. (2) Moreover, the results must be carefully applied even within the Douglas-fir region. For example, we are confident that our harvest levels are conservative, but due to our effort to be conservative—particularly for higher expected prices—we have no confidence in our ability to project supply price elasticity. Furthermore, even before localized harvest and land allocation conclusions can be drawn for areas within the region, locally specific data must be developed. This is one intent of chapter 6.

6
French Pete: A Case Study

This chapter illustrates the application of the model of chapters 3 and 4 to a specific site, the French Pete Creek drainage.[1] Chapter 5 demonstrated the model's application in a broad region. In that case we were able to draw some general conclusions about timber supply and land allocation, but we know those conclusions are subject to modification according to site-specific biological production functions and more localized market conditions. Moreover, on public lands, they are also subject to a variety of timber management constraints (discussed in chapter 2) as well as modification for multiple use values where the latter are efficient.

This chapter begins with some background on the French Pete case. Thereafter it discusses, in succeeding sections, standing timber values and the value of long-term management of the land. Each case is considered both with and without the public timber management constraints known as "even flow," "sustained yield," and "culmination of mean annual increment." Dispersed recreation is an important and competing use of French Pete. In both the standing timber and the long-term management cases we can draw conclusions about the necessary value of the recreation opportunity in order to justify preemption of timber for recreational use on efficiency grounds.

[1] This chapter benefits from advice and assistance in data collection by several persons who are more familiar with French Pete than I am: in particular Lewis Manhart, Robert Burns, and Zane Smith, all once with the Willamette National Forest and Dr. Richard Noyes of the Coalition to Save French Pete.

French Pete is a complex case. The conclusions regarding efficient land allocation and timber harvest are not clear. We will find that they rest on one's view of the legal constraints on public timber management. It is our contention that, in French Pete, these constraints impose large social welfare costs. In their presence, timber harvests are severely restricted while recreational land uses and wilderness preserves become increasingly attractive.

Background

The French Pete Creek drainage is composed of about 19,200 acres in the Willamette National Forest along the Cascade Range in central western Oregon. Among all recently controversial *de facto* wilderness areas in the country, it probably has the greatest timber values per acre. The Forest Service had been working, since early 1968, at determining the best use of the 18,600 roadless acres in the drainage. Congressional action in 1977 finally made it part of the Wilderness System. There are approximately 700 million board feet (MMbf), or more than one million cunits,[2] of standing timber —mostly mature timber from 100 to 400 years of age. The allowable harvest (see chapter 2) under the approved timber management plan (1971) is about 2.9 million board feet annually. Naturally, loggers and nearby mill owners see French Pete as prime timberland. Recreationists and environmentalists, on the other hand, counter that French Pete is one of three remaining roadless valleys 10 miles or more in length in western Oregon. It is of wilderness quality and was once part of the adjacent Three Sisters Wilderness. Recreationists have difficulty deciding whether they prefer wilderness or backcountry status, but unite in opposing harvest of the standing timber. (Backcountry camping is a recreational experience that is intermediate between developed campsites next to roads and truly isolated wilderness. That is, backcountry suggests short hikes and secluded tent platforms.)

The preference of Forest Service professionals in most such cases is to maintain management options. They would avoid the

[2] The board foot measure is in wider current use than the cubic foot measure. The trend is to cubic feet but the board foot remains a more convenient measure of old growth.

extreme of allocating French Pete predominantly to any single use. Nature, however, provides a difficulty. The steep terrain and existing road structure in neighboring areas dictate that any timber management roads be on the poorer sites at higher elevations. Logging would be done by high leads from landings adjacent to these roads to the good timber sites at lower elevations. Therefore, timber and recreational uses of French Pete cannot easily be separated among lower and higher elevations. Recreational users must be exposed to the usual visual disamenities of clearcuts *plus* the timber roads and the actual harvest operations themselves.

Standing Timber Values

French Pete presents us with the new problem of allocating existing timber inventories. Up to this point, our perspective on forestland allocation has focused on the value of idle land that would be permanently devoted to timber production. This ignores the value of existing standing timber. *Management of standing timber until it is ready for harvest may be profitable even where continued timber management is inefficient. This is known as the "timber mining" case* because extraction, or short-run management and harvesting, is profitable, while regeneration and even custodial long-run management for timber is unprofitable.

The most important timber mining cases involve old growth timber, timber which is ready for harvest and for which no further management is necessary. Old growth volumes per acre are often greater than the volumes of managed stands, therefore the potential revenues from old growth harvests are also greater. The large expected revenues must be balanced, however, against sale administration costs and the potentially larger costs associated with access to old growth stands.

Access means roads. The benefits of roads, once built, accrue to both the current and future rotations. Therefore the initial capital costs of road building are properly allocated to both the old growth harvest and to subsequent rotations as well. However, depreciation of roads at a reasonable rate, together with the long time periods between harvests, diminishes substantially the present value of their benefits to subsequent rotations. Therefore, a reasonable rule is to allocate initial capital costs for road building to old growth harvests and to charge subsequent rotations with only the periodic road operation, maintenance, and repair costs. Applying this rule, the value of an old growth stand equals the potential revenue from sale of the old growth timber minus the cost of building the access road and the smaller cost of administering timber sales.

At current (1976) stumpage prices of $230 Mbf in the Eugene–Springfield, Oregon area, French Pete's 700 MMbf of standing timber inventory is worth $161 million. Since all but one small corner of French Pete is currently roadless, a large initial outlay must be made to construct the permanent roads necessary to harvest the current stand and to manage and harvest future stands. Timber access alternatives were the subject of a recent Willamette National Forest study.[3] The most extensive road system considered requires 47 miles of permanent roads. Other alternatives require fewer miles of road, but logging methods which are, on the whole, more expensive (that is, multispan skyline, balloon, or helicopter logging). The 47 miles can be constructed at less than $200,000 per mile, or less than $9.4 million total. Sale administration costs are in the neighborhood of $6 per Mbf, or $4.2 million total. This suggests a net old growth timber value approximating $147 million.

It may, however, take up to five years to complete such a harvest. Sale administration costs are spread over the entire period along with timber sales themselves. Expected future stumpage prices increase at the real rate of 2.5 percent per year, but future harvest values must be discounted at the real annual rate of 10 percent required by the U.S. Office of Management and Budget. Finally, consider that the basic roads must be built in order to gain even limited access to the very first harvests, therefore the full road-building costs occur in the first year. The present net worth of the five-year flow is, then,

$$\frac{\$161 \text{ MM} - \$4.2 \text{ MM}}{5 \text{ years}} \sum_{t=1}^{5} (1.075)^{-t}$$

$$- \$9.4 \text{ MM} = \$116 \text{ MM} \qquad (6\text{-}1)$$

Thus, $116–147 million is an estimate of the value of the standing timber, the one-time revenue loss associated with removing

[3] Willamette National Forest, "Access Alternatives for Timber Management Purposes; French Pete Drainage" (Eugene, Oregon, October 1973).

French Pete from timber production and incorporating it into the statutory Wilderness System. At a 10 percent social capital cost, this is the same as an annual rental payment of $11.6–14.7 million in perpetuity.

We can examine the net wilderness value necessary to justify forgoing these revenues. Wilderness is thought to possess a number of values ranging from various kinds of dispersed recreation (e.g., camping, hunting, fishing) to gene pool preservation, and may include grazing for domestic livestock. The arguments for preserving French Pete focused on its recreational values alone, however.

The District Ranger estimates its total recreational use at 2,000–3,000 visits per year. Few visitors stay more than one day; some only stay a few hours in the lower end of the drainage away from the bulk of the good timber sites.[4] Nevertheless, recall that the timber harvesting activity affects recreational use throughout the drainage. (French Pete is indivisible for timber harvests and recreation.) Therefore, in order to justify forgoing timber revenues, the net recreational value must fall in the improbable range of $3,870 ($11.6 million/3,000) to $7,350 ($14.7 million/2,000) per visit. In contrast, the Water Resources Council values dispersed recreational use at $9 per visit.[5] Published econometric research suggests values in the range of $6 to $23 per visit.[6] Even the expectation that recreational use will increase over time fails to reduce the French Pete values to a probable range.[7]

The 1976 National Forest Management Act, however, imposes statutory limitations on harvest of the standing timber inventory for the ostensible purpose of guaranteeing long-term timber supply and ensuring the economic stability of local communities dependent on

[4] Robert Burns, personal communication, December 23, 1976. Notice that our data are in the form of unrestricted duration visits, instead of the more common "visitor day." The standard visitor day statistic is unavailable.

[5] Water Resources Council, "Water and Related Land Resources: Estimates of Principles and Standards for Planning," *Federal Register* vol. 38, no. 174, part III (1973).

[6] John F. Dwyer, John R. Kelly, and Michael D. Bowes, "Improved Procedures for Valuations of the Contribution of Recreation to National Economic Development" (Urbana-Champagne, University of Illinois Water Resources Center Research Report no. 128, Sept. 1977) includes a survey of this research.

[7] An interesting alternative develops, however, if $11.6–14.7 million is in excess of recreationist willingness to pay year after year, but is not in excess of the last-chance recreational value of a single-year harvest delay. We could then justify harvest delay while recreationists concentrate the recreational use of French Pete into a single year.

public timber harvest flows. As applied, this law causes the Forest Service to plan even annual harvest flows for periods as great as 400 years. Since the age of the standing inventory exceeds the age of financial maturity for managed forests, standing inventory volumes and current harvest levels would exceed future harvest levels. Therefore an even harvest flow can occur only if current harvests are curtailed and the excess over sustainable levels is effectively extended over the up-to-400 year planning period. This policy, known as "even flow," acts as a severe constraint on efficient management of the standing timber inventory.

We can estimate the efficiency costs of the even-flow constraint as well as the necessary recreational use values if it is applied. The efficiency costs equal the difference between timber revenue flows with and without the constraint. From Eq. (6-1) we know that the present net worth of the five-year flow without the constraint is $116 million. From the 1971 timber management plan, we know that planned even-flow harvests are 2.9 MMbf annually. At this rate the 700 MMbf will take 241 years to harvest. Following the form of Eq. (6-1), the present net worth of the 241-year flow is:

$$\frac{\$161 \text{ MM} - \$4.2 \text{ MM}}{241 \text{ years}} \sum_{t=1}^{241} (1.075)^{-t} - \$9.4 \text{ MM} < 0 \qquad (6\text{-}2)$$

This ignores the small periodic road maintenance cost. Its inclusion would result in an even more negative present net worth. We conclude that the even-flow constraint absorbs the entire efficiency-derived net revenue obtained from harvesting the standing timber. Thus, with a policy of even flow, it is probable that it is more efficient to allocate French Pete to recreational uses because net recreational use values only need be positive.

Long-term Management

In view of these values, social welfare may best be served by altering the even-flow policy and harvesting the standing timber inventory according to efficiency criteria. Federal law, however, introduces additional constraints. It also requires that timber harvesting be accompanied by continued timber growth on the same land. Timber mining on federal lands is prohibited by the 1960

Multiple Use–Sustained Yield Act, the 1976 National Forest Management Act, the reforestation requirements of the 1930 Knutson–Vandenberg Act, and by public concern for sustainable timber flows and reforestation.[8] Therefore, we must reject the option of mining French Pete's standing timber inventory (even in the absence of even flow) and focus on permanent, sustainable management alternatives. The standing timber values can only be realized if harvesting is consistent with the chosen permanent management alternative. Accordingly, we turn our attention to growing timber and its alternatives for permanent management of French Pete. We examine these alternatives in the order of their increasing input levels and their decreasing flexibility to adjust to changing future values.

The 1977 state of French Pete was roadless forestland, or *de facto* wilderness. This is consistent with the least intensive, or "custodial," management. Even custodial management is not costless, however. It requires a minimum expenditure for administration and forest protection (i.e., from fires, insects, and diseases) for the ostensible purposes of protecting future on-site values as well as currently high-valued adjacent land uses. Wilderness recreation may be justified under custodial management—even where its direct benefits fail to cover its direct costs—because the costs of excluding recreational users exceed the minimum clean-up and safety costs of wilderness recreational management. Otherwise, active use and more intensive management is restricted until some future time when use values change.

The second alternative is *statutory* Wilderness designation and management. It is justified on efficiency grounds where wilderness values exceed their own maintenance costs and no higher valued use of the land exists. We assume no change in the observed level of use (2,000–3,000 visits per year) between custodial management and economically justifiable statutory wilderness management.

Growing timber is the final management alternative. It is justified where net timber values are positive and in excess of the reasonable range for wilderness recreation values. Our analysis focuses

---

[8] For example, see "Reforestation Arouses Congress," *Public Lands News* vol. 3, no. 3 (February 9, 1978) p. 7. The argument against timber mining is not based on economics. Economics can justify timber mining if the external costs (downstream and aesthetic) as well as the harvest costs are paid by the timber miner. To put it another way, by virtue of continued emphatic support for sustained yield and reforestation, the public may have decided external costs are too high to permit timber mining.

on these timber values. They require some detailed modification of our chapter 5 production functions to reflect local land productivity characteristics, as well as examination of local market conditions.

Finally, there is an important harvest timing constraint on public timber management which we have yet to examine. Subsequent to finding the efficient, unconstrained, permanent management alternative, we can examine the impact of this constraint on our findings.

Site Quality and Land Area

The site class distribution of timberland within the French Pete Creek drainage is:

Site Class	Biological potential (cubic feet per annum)	Acres
V	20–50	995
IV	50–85	4,054
III	85–120	6,654
II	120–165	4,438

The two best Site Classes, I and I+, are absent. Site Classes II and III are Douglas-fir sites. Site Classes IV and V are predominantly true fir sites. They are higher elevation or north-facing sites, often steep and rocky. These Site Class IV lands are considered good growing sites in spite of their unstable soils. Site Class V is so far from being economic in the general regional case that we can dismiss it from further consideration.

Production

As in the Douglas-fir regional case, we consider five alternative timber production processes. Once more, we present them in order of increasing complexity. The major characteristics of each are its (1) regeneration lag, (2) stocking, (3) yield, and (4) associated direct input costs. The general opinion is that, given the site class, French Pete is of better than average regional quality for timber production.[9] Therefore, for any given site class, we might expect

---

[9] Some uncertainty attaches to this conclusion. I suspect my correspondents meant that it is better than the average west slope Cascade land. This may still

shorter regeneration lags and better stocking than the regional average for natural stands. Better quality should also imply increased natural competition from undesirable plants. By overlooking this point, we attach an upward bias to timber values and a conservative bias to recreational land allocation.

WILD TREES NATURALLY GROWN. In accordance with professional opinion, the regeneration lag on each site is shortened to less than half the regional average.

Site Class	Regeneration lag
IV	7 years
III	5 years
II	5 years

Evaluation of natural stocking is more difficult. Current standing inventory (including Site Class V land) is approximately 700 million board feet of sawtimber. Trees in the stand average in the neighborhood of 115 to 150 years old. Consulting McArdle yield tables,[10] we find this inventory normal for 125-year-old stands of site index 110—Site Class IV. Since the average site in the drainage (including Site Class V) is in Site Class III, we know the difference between full and actual stocking is at least the equivalent of the normal volume difference between two adjacent site classes. "At least" because the trend to normality over time tells us that the younger stands that will be the rule for future rotations demonstrate an even greater volume difference than observed in the current old growth stand.

A check on this stocking conclusion was made by asking locally experienced foresters how much better stocked French Pete and the Willamette National Forest are than the regional average. Con-

---

be poorer than the regional average if the region is defined to include the entire Douglas-fir region (as in chapter 5), including the highly productive coastal fog belt forestland. Giving the benefit of the doubt to French Pete productivity may lead to a generous estimate for timber values and a conservative bias for recreational land allocation.

10 The basic document for Douglas-fir is "The Yield of Douglas-Fir in the Pacific Northwest," by Richard E. McArdle, Walter H. Meyer, and Donald Bruce, USDA Technical Bulletin no. 201 (May 1961). As per standard practice, sites are classified by growth of species currently on the site in spite of the fact that other native species may grow faster.

Table 6-1.   Yield by Site and Age for Wild Stands Naturally Grown, Douglas-fir in French Pete Creek Drainage

(in ft^3/acre and dbh greater than 1½ inch)

Age (years)	Site Class					
	IV		III		II	
	dbh	vol/acre	dbh	vol/acre	dbh	vol/acre
35	a	a	5	1,860	7	2,770
40	a	a	6	2,200	7	3,480
45	a	a	6	2,550	8	4,200
50	5	1,790	7	3,000	9	5,055
55	6	2,100	8	3,450	10	5,910
60	6	2,300	9	3,870	11	6,615
65	7	2,550	9	4,270	12	7,320
70	7	2,800	10	4,570	13	8,110
75	8	2,920	10	4,850	14	8,900

t$_r$ in years [b]

[a] Insignificant.

[b] Regeneration lag, the period during which land is vacant between the harvest of one stand and the appearance of new growth. Thus, on Site Class IV land when trees are thirty-five years old, it has actually been 35 plus 7 or 42 years since the previous harvest.

sensus puts it at ten percentage points. Adjusting average regional stocking (table 5-2) and the resulting estimates of wild tree yields accordingly gives us table 6-1, wild tree yields (in cubic feet) for French Pete. These yields are consistent with those suggested in the previous paragraph.

PLANTING.   Planting is done to obtain and maintain fully stocked natural stands. It includes site preparation before planting as well as the planting itself. Hardwood control and weeding may be added to improve survival and early growth.

Site preparation begins with clean-up of the previous final harvest. Following final harvests, the Forest Service piles unutilized material (PLIM), woody material too small for the logger to profitably remove. This is done on all acres to create openings for planting, as well as to reduce the threat of subsequent fire and to make the harvested acre more pleasing to the eye. PLIM varies in cost with the amount of defect materials in the old stand and with the market for chips. Vigorous second growth stands better represent permanent timber management than the older growth, which dominates current harvests. They have less defect and, therefore, require reduced PLIM expenditures. We use the low cost of $100 per acre from the Willamette-wide range of $90–1,000 for our permanent timber management alternative.

.   Site preparation itself varies locally within the Willamette National Forest, with perhaps 20–30 percent of all acres requiring some preparation. Site preparation often includes some burning but, in the Willamette River basin, this adds to already difficult air pollution problems. Therefore timing is important and costs are high, ranging from $34 to $200 per acre and averaging $145 per acre (more than double the regionwide average). The following treatment distribution, ten percentage points greater than the regional average for each site, is assumed.

Site Class	Acres treated (%)
IV	10
III	20
II	30

It is Forest Service policy to reestablish stands within five years of final harvests. In the Willamette National Forest this is difficult to achieve only on the hot, dry sites which are, as a consequence of their hotness and dryness, of poorer quality. On these sites a third attempt at stand reestablishment is occasionally required in the five-to-ten-year period following the previous harvest. Otherwise planting success is better than the regional average, with 90 percent survival not unusual.

Site Class	Planting failure (%)
IV	20
III	10
II	10

We optimistically assume at most that two reestablishment efforts are required. Planting costs fall in the range of $90–170 per acre for a forestwide average of $144. Cost of the second reestablishment effort in the fifth year is a function of per acre costs and the failure rate.

Better than average quality sites should imply more biological competition for the young growth and more frequent hardwood control/weeding. This activity, however, receives only limited attention in the Willamette National Forest and even less attention will be given over time as its occurrence is better anticipated and met as part of site preparation. Where needed, it is currently applied in the seventh or eighth year of the stand—the seventh year in our model.

Site Class	Acres treated (%)
IV	0
III	5
II	20

The combined results of PLIM, site preparation, planting, and hardwood control/weeding are fully stocked natural stands with the yields estimated in table 6-4.

THINNING, FERTILIZING, AND GENETICS. There is little basis on which to predict variation from the regionwide estimates for these three processes. The extent to which any of them is now followed in the Willamette National Forest is minor, but the intention is to expand applications of each.

Only 470 to 500 seedlings are planted per acre. This is fewer than the industry considers best practice, but it allows precommercial thinnings (PCT) to be postponed until the twelfth to eighteenth year (year fifteen in our model). Currently, commercial thinnings are being made in 80–110-year-old stands, but age at first commercial thinning is decreasing over time. Willamette National Forest costs average $140 per acre for each PCT and $58 per cunit for commercial thinnings.

Fertilization is rare, but where it occurs it matches the regionwide model of 200 pounds of nitrogen per acre for $58 per acre. Planting of selective seedlings has yet to begin, but the first step of selecting parent stock has been completed. The seedlings themselves delay for want of a good seed crop year. We assume a $10 per acre difference in natural and improved planting costs, as well as continuation of the natural stock planting success rate. There is no reason to believe that once implemented, these various treatments should alter regionwide expectations summarized in the managed yield tables 5-5, 5-6, and 5-7.

Costs and Prices

In our discussion of timber production processes, we have assessed all direct input costs except the annual road maintenance and sale administration costs common to all processes. Access costs, capital costs, and the various price relationships applicable to the French Pete market also remain to be examined. The annual administration and protection costs charged to timber management in our regional analysis are inappropriate here. Recall that these constitute custodial management and are, therefore, unchanging with the decision to upgrade management intensity from custodial to any level of timber management.

If timber management is the efficient use of French Pete, then the initial capital outlay for roads can be charged to harvests of the standing timber inventory. Road maintenance can be postponed until commercial thinning or final harvests. This is one advantage to the (often objected to) high quality and expensive Forest Service roads. Intermediate stand treatments, such as precommercial thinning and fertilizing, require, at most, light use of roads and can get by with unmaintained roads. Charging road maintenance costs to eventual harvests is like adding approximately $1 per cunit to the regional average for timber sale administration. (Our sale administration estimate compares conservatively with actual Forest Service costs.)

Direct input costs are summarized in table 6-2. On the whole, they are considerably in excess of the regional average (summarized in table 5-8). This may imply any or all of the following: (1) The Forest Service, specifically the Willamette National Forest, pays a price for environmental awareness. The Willamette is more careful, therefore it expends more than local private landowners for many of its timber management activities. (2) The Willamette is wasteful. (3) Access is more important than we suspected. The Willamette is not an isolated national forest but its forestland is,

Table 6-2.   Estimated Costs of Growing Timber—French Pete Creek Drainage

(in 1976 dollars and by year of occurrence)

	Site Class			
Cost per unit	IV	III	II	Year
Piling unutilized				
material $90–1,000/acre	100	100	100	1
Site preparation				
$34–200/acre	14.50	29.00	43.50	1
Planting				
Unimproved $90–170/acre	←———— 144 ————→			1
Failure	28.80	14.40	14.40	5
Improved (genetic)	←———— 154 ————→			1
Failure	30.80	15.40	15.40	5
Weeding/hardwood control	0	2.50	10.00	7
Thinning				
Precommercial $140/acre	←———— 140 ————→			15
Commercial	←———— 58/cunit ———→		According to timing on yield table plus t_r	
Fertilization $58/acre	←———— 58 ————→		Each commercial thinning	
Sale administration				
incl. $1/cunit for roads	←———— 6/cunit ———→		Each commercial thinning	
$5–8/Mbf	←———— 3.50/cunit ——→		Final harvest	

nevertheless, less accessible than the average acre in the region. This may affect not only stumpage bids but also site preparation, planting, and precommercial thinning costs.

Access costs are easily assessed. French Pete is approximately 65 miles from Eugene–Springfield, the local milling center. Sixty-five miles is an average haul for Willamette National Forest timber sales. The latter have an average haul credit of $11 per cunit. Therefore, $11 per cunit can be added to French Pete road maintenance costs to obtain access costs.

Capital costs and the price relationships remain unchanged from the regional averages: The rate of stumpage price increase is 2.5 percent per annum. The price/diameter relationship continues as in Eq. (5-1). The social cost of capital is 10 percent minus a 2 percent adjustment for the rate of increase in amenity values. This accounts for expected increasing recreational use. The uniform amenity value adjustment is at variance with our regionwide assumption in chapter 5. It depends upon recognition of French Pete as a *single* management unit for amenity valuation.

Table 6-3. Perpetual Timber Management Values

Price timber becomes efficient ($/cunit)	Production process	Site Class	Annual harvest (thousand cunits)	Site value ($/acre)	Rotation ages (years)
50	Wild	II	3.073	20	40 (35)
50	Wild	III	3.094	11	40 (35)
125	Wild	IV	1.273	2	57 (50)
175	Genetic	II	5.030	145	29 (31)
250	Genetic	III	4.785	119	29 (31)

Perpetual Timber Management

If we can first establish the perpetual timber production values derived as in chapter 5 except with local cost and yield data, then we can estimate the value of French Pete as timberland and the value of the timber opportunity forgone if statutory Wilderness designation is the preferred land allocation. Thereafter, with the introduction of recreational use information, we can consider the efficiency of alternative land allocations, as well as whether restrictions on growing timber imply additional welfare loss in French Pete.

Table 6-3 summarizes our conclusions about profitable timber growing operations. Some production is profitable for stumpage prices as low as $50 per cunit (plus a 2.5 percent relative annual increase). More is profitable for higher prices. Reading down table 6-3, we find the profitable additions to the timber management program associated with higher prices. Reading across, we find the production process, site class, incremental annual harvest, site value, and optimal rotation age associated with each given price. For example, at $175 per cunit, genetically selected seedlings become efficient on Site Class II, 5.030 thousand cunits are added to the annual harvest (for a total of $5.030 + 3.073 = 8.103$ thousand cunits on all Site Class II acres), a single acre of Site Class II is worth $145 for timber production, and there is a full timber rotation every twenty-nine years. (Trees on such acres are thirty-one years old at harvest.[11])

One of our purposes in this chapter was to demonstrate that the regional averages of chapter 5 were just that, averages. They

[11] Site Class V becomes a profitable timber producer at $250 per cunit, which is considerably in excess of current market prices.

Table 6-4.   The Value of French Pete for Perpetual Timber Management at Current Stumpage Prices

		Price $=$125 *per cunit*		
Site Class	IV	III	II	
Site value	$12	$52	$67	
Acres	4,054	6,654	4,438	15,146
Total value	$48,648	$346,008	$341,726	$736,382
		Price $=$ $150 *per cunit*		
Site Class	IV	III	II	
Site value	$14	$62	$92	
Acres	4,054	6,654	4,438	15,146
Total value	$56,756	$412,548	$408,296	$877,600

can be applied more locally only with care. Contrasting table 6-3 with the public entries in table 5-9 bears out this warning. The least intensive level of timber management becomes profitable at lower prices on French Pete than regionwide—mostly due to the absence of annual costs. More intensive silvicultural practices only become profitable on French Pete at higher prices than the regional average. These practices are much more expensive on French Pete. Compare, for example, planting, PCT, and commercial thinning costs in tables 5-8 and 6-2.

Current (1976) market prices fall in the range of $125–150 per cunit. Table 6-4 shows the value of the timber opportunity or site value for stumpage prices at the boundaries of this range. Multiplying the timber opportunity value by the number of acres in the site class and aggregating across all acres provides an estimate of the value forgone when the timber growing opportunity is removed from French Pete.

Timber growing is not justified on all 18,600 roadless acres of French Pete, but it may be justified on the 15,146 acres of Site Class IV or better. Assuming a market price of $150 per cunit, the net social value of the timber opportunity is $877,600. It, or its equivalent annual rental payment of $87,760 (that is, the social cost of capital, 0.10, times the site value of the land), sets an upper limit on value of the timber growing opportunity. These positive values assure that timber growing is more efficient than custodial management, but leave us uncertain as to whether it is preferable to statutory Wilderness designation with recreational benefits in excess of their costs. Recalling an annual wilderness recreation use rate of 2,000–3,000 visits, increasing at an annual rate of 2 percent, the value of the forgone timber opportunity is $29.25–43.88 per visit. Timber growing is the efficient long-term management alternative in the still very likely event that net recreation values fail to exceed this range.

The Harvest Timing Constraint

Current Forest Service practice does not permit the efficient rotations which led us to the above calculations. Instead, the preference is for rotations aimed at biological maximization of sawtimber measured, natural stand, volume (hereafter "volume maximization").[12] The intention is not to appease recreational and environmental interests but to grow a special product (sawtimber) and to avoid eventual harvest "falldown." (Recall chapter 2.) Indeed, we earlier suggested that recreational and environmental interests might prefer shorter rotations and intensive management if these mean that critical areas can be protected and more land made available for recreation. Therefore, let us examine the opportunity returns of forgone timber production when rotations are constrained to (1) 100 years, which is not an unusual rotation for Forest Service management of Douglas-fir, and (2) eighty years, a short rotation for Douglas-fir in the management unit including French Pete, but a good approximation for the volume-maximizing age.

At current stumpage prices of $150 per cunit (plus a 2.5 percent relative annual increase), the net benefits of timber growing are negative for rotations of 100 years or longer. Either *de facto* or statutory Wilderness is the constrained social preference for French Pete.

For eighty-year rotations, the following timber opportunities obtain:

Site Class	IV	III	II	
Site value	$1	$2	$4	
Acres	4,054	6,654	4,438	15,146
Total value	$4,054	$13,308	$8,876	$26,236

12 The National Forest Management Act of 1976 requires volume maximization, but says nothing about either the preferred volume measure or natural stands. Different volume measures and managed stands each yield larger volumes at shorter rotations than the sawtimber measure preferred by the Forest Service.

Permanent timber values are positive and growing timber is the preferable management alternative unless net recreation use values exceed the range of $0.87–1.31, a real possibility.

When taken all together, the various constraints on timber management lead us to a range of doubt regarding its efficiency. Certainly wilderness recreation values exceed the negative value of 100-year rotations and it is not unreasonable that they exceed the value derived from eighty-year rotations.

Where single-use timber growing shows doubtful economic promise, multiple use is sometimes advanced as an argument for timber management on public lands.[13] If timber management is not justified by itself, however, it does not automatically follow that combining timber with other forest uses is automatically justified. Rather, the incremental multiple use benefits must exceed their own

[13] There is a lengthy body of literature on this topic. "Multiple use" probably originated in William B. Greeley, "Report of the Chief" (U.S. Forest Service, c. 1928) and, in the academic literature, in Frederick A. Waugh, "Reconciliation of Land Uses," *Journal of Land and Public Utility Economics* vol. 12, no. 1 (February 1936). For historical and analytical surveys, see George R. Hall, "The Myth and Reality of Multiple Use Forestry," *Natural Resources Journal* vol. 3, no. 4 (October 1963) pp. 276–290; Richard Behan, "The Succotash Syndrome, or Multiple Use: A Heartfelt Approach to Land Management," *Natural Resources Journal* vol. 7, no. 4 (October 1967) pp. 473–485; and Stephen S. Strand, "An Evaluation of Effective Multiple Use Management" (Master of Forestry thesis, University of Michigan, 1971).

The economic theory of multiple outputs is well known. See most intermediate price theory textbooks, for example, James M. Henderson and Richard E. Quandt, *Microeconomic Theory* (New York, McGraw-Hill, 1958) pp. 67–72, or L. J. Lau, "Profit Functions of Technologies with Multiple Inputs and Outputs," *Review of Economics and Statistics* vol. 54, no. 3 (August 1972) pp. 281–289; also Sigfried V. Ciriacy-Wantrup, *Resource Conservation* (Berkeley, California Agricultural Experiment Station, 1952). This theory has long been applied by water resource economists: John V. Krutilla and Otto Eckstein, *Multiple Purpose River Development* (Baltimore, Johns Hopkins University Press for Resources for the Future, 1958); and Arthur Maass, Maynard M. Hufschmidt, Robert Dorfman, Harold A. Thomas, Jr., Stephen A. Marglin, and Gordon M. Fair, *Design of Water-Resource Systems* (Cambridge, Mass., Harvard University Press, 1962). It was conceptually demonstrated to foresters by G. Robinson Gregory, "An Economic Approach to Multiple Use," *Forest Science* vol. 1, no. 1 (March 1965) pp. 6–13; and Michael D. Bowes and John V. Krutilla, "Cost Allocation in Efficient Multiple Use Forest Land Management: A Comment" *Journal of Forestry* vol. 77, no. 7 (July 1979) pp. 419–420. The few discussions by timber, wildlife, watershed, and range managers have tended to be site specific and production oriented. The outstanding example is the water, timber, and grazing production analysis at the U.S. Forest Service's Beaver Creek, Arizona, experiment project.

direct costs, plus any costs they impose on timber management, by enough to make the combined value of timber and multiple uses not just positive, but in excess of alternative management values. For eighty-year timber rotations, any judgment of the constrained efficient allocation of French Pete may hinge on these multiple use values. Therefore, final allocation is beyond our scope.

We conclude that statutory constraints on public timber management, as applied, lead to large welfare losses. In their absence French Pete is valuable timberland. There can be no doubt that timber values outweigh all others. In the presence of these constraints, however, the efficient allocation of French Pete may be to wilderness recreation—forgoing at least $116,000,000 of standing timber plus an annual net income stream of $87,760.

Summary and Anticipated Objections

This chapter discusses the rules for making local public forestland allocation decisions and demonstrates application of these rules in the case of the French Pete Creek drainage of the Willamette National Forest in western Oregon, a self-contained roadless area that has been the subject of recent controversy between timber and wilderness recreational interests. This case serves as a model for public land allocation involving these two often conflicting uses.

The foundation for our allocational rules is the efficient timber production analysis of chapter 3 and the conceptual application of opportunity costs from chapter 4. In chapter 5 we illustrated application of our analysis to obtain general insights on broad regional timber supply and forestland allocation questions. Our interest in this chapter is to show how the analyses can be applied to more specialized questions. For French Pete, as for many controversial public forestlands, this means consideration of short-run management opportunities for the existing timberstand as well as continued timber growing or wilderness recreational use of the forestland.

Timber mining is prohibited on federal land, therefore harvesting the existing timberstand and thereafter allocating the land to recreational uses is not permitted. Allocation of federal land to timber production rests entirely on the continued timber growing opportunity and its relationship to recreational values. The welfare loss associated with this rule, that is, the forgone timber value of the existing stand, may be large—approximately $141 million in French Pete if harvesting this stand is restricted forever because growing timber proves to be an unjustifiable management alternative in our final analysis.

Growing timber is justifiable on economic efficiency grounds if the net timber benefits are positive and exceed net wilderness recreation benefits. Recreation management is justified in the opposite case. Where neither timber nor recreation is justified, the remaining alternative land allocation is to custodial management—which is like a deferred decision status—until values change. We modified our previous data for the local production and market conditions, and examined efficient long-term allocation of French Pete in two cases: an unconstrained case and a case constrained by the Forest Service requirement of sawtimber rotations. (Our data are imperfect, but sufficient for our analysis. Data imperfections should not cause us to lose sight of the fact that a correct method of analysis, together with conservatively applied data, can convincingly solve many applied economic problems.) Our conclusions are summarized in table 6-5. Because our recreational data were incomplete, these conclusions are presented in terms of timber opportunities and the value of a recreation visit necessary to exceed the timber opportunity forgone.

At current stumpage prices on the local market of $150 per cunit (annually increasing at a 2.5 percent relative rate), the unconstrained annual value of perpetual timber production is large and positive. Recreational values per visit must exceed $29 per visit (assuming 3,000 visitors to French Pete annually and visitation growing at a 2 percent annual rate) in order to justify wilderness allocation; therefore timber growing is the most likely efficient management alternative. In the *constrained* case, the annual value of perpetual timber production is smaller, but still positive. Statutory Wilderness may be efficient for net recreational values in excess of only $0.87 per visit. In some current applications, rotations are constrained to even longer periods, timber growing values are negative and either statutory Wilderness or custodial management is the constrained efficient management alternative, depending on whether recreational values exceed their costs.

Table 6-5.   Annual Value of the Timber Opportunity, and Recreational Values Necessary to Justify Allocation of French Pete to Recreation

	Timber production case	
	Unconstrained	*Constrained* (80-year rotation)
Annual value of timber opportunity	$87,760	$2,624
Wilderness recreation value		
2,000 visitors per year	> $43.88 per visit	> $1.31 per visit
3,000 visitors per year	> $29.25 per visit	> $0.87 per visit

Because we do not know the actual value of a French Pete visit, final conclusions about constrained efficient allocation of French Pete are difficult to draw. *It is apparent, however, that the old growth rule, the even-flow constraint, and the sawtimber rotation constraint impose heavy social costs on federal land timber management. Administrative rules for the latter two can be questioned as they are apparently more restrictive than the law itself. In their presence, recreational use under custodial management is a serious possibility and statutory Wilderness status may very well be an economically efficient allocation.* The social welfare gains from disposing of these constraints, however, and managing the timber by efficiency criteria should be clear.

We chose French Pete from among many controversial roadless federal lands because of its large standing inventory and high quality (among roadless areas) sites. Therefore, a more usual roadless area might have lower old growth and lower perpetual timber growing values.[14] The impacts of the timber mining rule for old growth especially, but also the sawtimber rotation constraint may still be heavy in these more usual cases. Perpetual timber growing values, however, are probably very low—given lower quality sites. Constrained efficiency in timber production may be a strong argument for reserving many currently roadless sites for Wilderness.

---

[14] For an example of such a case, see William F. Hyde, "The Social Failures of Public Timber Management in the Rockies," in John Baden and Richard Stroup, eds., *The Environmental Costs of Government Action Expansion* (proceedings of a Liberty Fund conference in Big Sky, Montana, September 1978).

Some may object to these conclusions because they fail to consider the beneficial impacts that timber management creates for the local community. Two reminders are in order in anticipation of this objection: (1) Beneficial secondary impacts occur as part of all investments—including timber, recreation, and all alternative uses of any public agency budget. Part of any argument about the beneficial secondary impacts of public timber management must be a demonstration that these impacts are greater than would occur with alternative investments (in short, the secondary opportunity costs). (2) It is not in anyone's interest to maintain inefficiency in perpetuity. If timber management is inefficient, but closing the operation will cause social hardship, then, in order to ease the community's transition, *temporary* inefficiency *may* be socially desirable. Or it may be more efficient to buy out the local mill owners and to compensate the local population for necessary job retraining and physical mobility.

In general, community stability is a fuzzy concept in the forestry literature. The theory itself needs to be developed, or better, applied from economic theory, beginning with labor as a factor of production. Opportunity costs for labor are just as fundamental in such a discussion as were opportunity costs for land in the body of this chapter. Finally, sociologists may have a lot to tell us about the kinds of communities which ought to be stabilized, developed, encouraged, or whatever. This is already more than sufficient comment on this subject for our purposes. It should be apparent that (1) forest management and community impacts is a topic requiring careful analysis and (2) there is no easy intuitive reason why unspecified community impacts should alter conclusions about allocation of the forestland within French Pete.

7
Summary, Conclusions, Policy Implications

Forest management is among the most controversial of environmental and resource management issues. Concern over timber supply has been an important national issue throughout the past decade. It is particularly important in the coastal Pacific Northwest (the Douglas-fir region) where there is fear of a severe shortage for the next thirty to fifty years. Environmental and dispersed recreational values compete with timber both nationally and in the Pacific Northwest. There is a comparable level of concern that these values as well as timber supply receive just consideration in forest management decisions. We have attempted to examine forest management from the perspective of market efficiency. Our conclusions strongly suggest a rare Pareto gain; that is, increased timber production as well as expanded provision for environmental and dispersed recreational values would accompany a conversion from current management criteria to market efficiency.

Efficiency criteria justify expanding production until the benefits of the last unit of output just equal its factor costs. The industry has changed, and previously efficient rates for harvesting the natural inventory of timber are no longer appropriate. The geographical focus of the industry is now relatively fixed. Instead of harvesting natural stands and moving on, the industry now remains in one place and grows timber with intentional silvicultural inputs. The private sector is moving toward efficient rates to guide silvicultural management, and market incentives are likely to reinforce this trend. The public, an important sector in the timber industry, owning as it does one-quarter of national production and one-third of Douglas-fir regional production, remains reluctant to embrace this trend. Long-run tendencies of the public sector, however, are less clear.

If there is a private sector trend toward efficient silvicultural management, and it is *recent,* then projections of *historical* production trends, while useful in the short run, are unsatisfactory for the economic long run of thirty to fifty years when all productive factors are variable. Projections based on industrial conversion to efficient technologies may be more reliable. In any case, if market pressures become truly severe, and warrant public policy intervention, then they should also provide strong incentives for efficiency in the private sector. Thus we can argue that long-run projections based on efficiency are a baseline from which to examine the necessity of additional public intervention in private markets.

Efficiency-based projections for *public* sector timber production are, perhaps, less justifiable. There is some doubt that the public sector will ever be efficient in the usual economic sense. It has little incentive. Nevertheless, efficiency is a useful benchmark against which to judge public sector performance. Efficiency results can be compared with those obtained under current management criteria. The difference between the two represents the public costs of the latter.

Analytical Approach

Initially we examined traditional timber management criteria. Subsequently we determined the characteristics of efficient timber management and applied them in a case study of the Douglas-fir region. We also examined a more site-specific case within the region in order to demonstrate the generality of our data and conclusions, as well as the social costs of management constraints on public lands.

Generalizing about current timber management practice is difficult given the variety of landowners—public or private, large or small, dependent on a timber income, or holding forestland for other purposes. Nevertheless, public agencies and many industrial land managers have followed broadly similar practices in the past. These traditional practices resemble natural stand, sawtimber measure, volume maximization over time (hereafter, "volume maximization"). Perhaps a reasonable argument can be made that volume maximization was consistent with rational behavior under historical biological and economic conditions. The shift away from volume maximization by private landowners is evidence that it is no longer financially rational.

The public agencies continue to follow a constrained volume maximization rule. Unlike the private sector, the U.S. Forest Service, our public agency model, may argue that the public law and provisions for nonpriced resource services require that they follow this rule. This legal argument has some grounds. The National Forest Management Act of 1976 forbids harvest ages less than culmination of mean annual increment (CMAI), which is the volume maximizing age. The Forest Service administratively extends this harvest age requirement, ostensibly to protect against uncertainty. NFMA does not, however, require this extension, and it does not require that CMAI be calculated in sawtimber measure—which begins at 11½ inches in tree diameter at breast height. Other volume measures that capture growth increments on smaller trees would allow Douglas-fir harvests as much as twenty years earlier than culmination of mean annual sawtimber increment, or at close to their optimal financial harvest age.

In addition, NFMA constrains decennial harvest flows to a level that can be perpetuated and the Multiple Use–Sustained Yield Act of 1960 and various other laws restrict timber mining or harvesting without regrowing timber on the same land. These latter two statutory policies have perhaps severe impacts on harvests of the existing stock of mature timber, but they place no restrictions on efficient long-run management, that is, management over the entire timber growing cycle. With constant or increasing relative stumpage prices, wherever it is efficient to grow timber, it will also be efficient to harvest and regrow. Annual harvest levels will be steady, or even increasing with technical change, and the laws' perpetual yield requirements will be met.

Nor do observations of Forest Service land allocations uniformly support the contention that nonpriced resource services are better provided under the volume maximization rule. The Forest Service is responsible for large amounts of economically submarginal timberland. The volume maximization rule permits combining this land with valuable timberland until both segments together show a joint profit. Thus, harvests are sometimes carried out where timber values are actually negative—and regardless of competing nonpriced resource values. The marginal land and cost accounting clauses of the NFMA restrict continuation of such procedures and actually encourage efficient management rules. Therefore, I believe a sound argument can be made that historically reasonable Forest Service administrative policies are today more restrictive than the law. The law is not the important constraint on long-run efficient management, agency administrative policy is. (There is some evidence, however, that the agency is changing in response to NFMA.)

With these observations of changing timber management criteria in mind, we might contrast the expected patterns of resource use and harvest levels under volume maximization and market efficiency criteria. The basic volume maximization model emphasizes even harvest volume flows over time and is generally unresponsive to prices, factor costs, and the discount rate. As applied, it often results in uniform management across all productive land classes. Economic efficiency, on the other hand, is responsive to prices, factor costs, and the discount rate. In the short run our attention focuses on current harvest levels. When there is a large standing volume of valuable mature timber, the discount rate alone makes this year's harvests more valuable than next year's and, therefore, encourages larger harvests of the mature stock now and smaller harvests in the future. Large harvests eventually exert downward pressure on stumpage prices, thereby preventing full harvest of this stock in the first year.

In the long run, volume maximization directs limited attention to prices and factor costs. It compares annual receipts with annual costs for the entire management unit, thereby tying receipts on one acre to costs on another and justifying investment if the annual net flow is positive. This results in disregard for carrying costs accumulating between the time of investment and the time of harvest on each acre. It results in levels of investment in land that are greater than is efficient, as well as capital and labor transfers from good land to poor land.

An alert investor recognizes, however, that he can have his receipts from one acre without reinvesting on another. Instead, he can invest wherever he expects the greatest returns, either within or outside forestry. He disinvests on the poorer acres until his expected incremental returns just equal his incremental costs. If he feels constrained to maximize volume on his remaining timberlands, then he still maintains long rotations or overinvests in capital relative to labor and land. When he relaxes this constraint, he alters his investment to efficient long-run levels—where expected returns on the last dollar invested in land, labor, and capital are equal and profit is at a maximum. In comparison with volume maximization, efficient harvest levels are smaller on poor land, but greater—due to increased investment—on good land. The *a priori* net difference in aggregate harvest levels is indeterminant.

We examined the characteristics of efficiency more carefully in chapter 3, using the standard Faustmann model modified for important local variations as our point of departure. The efficient landowner maximizes rent, his expected net return from selling stumpage after payment of all labor, capital, and managerial expenses accumulated while growing it. He maximizes rent by (1) increasing timber management (silvicultural) intensity until the present value of the last unit of silvicultural effort just equals its factor cost and (2) extending the rotation age until the revenue gains from further harvest delay (the relative value appreciation plus the value of incremental growth) just offset the revenues forgone (the delayed harvest receipts adjusted for delayed new crop silvicultural costs).

For a given acre there is only one efficient level of silvicultural intensity and one efficient rotation age, therefore one efficient harvest level—the rent maximizing level. This level varies from acre to acre with ownership and with land quality and location. It also varies with the expected price level and its rate of change. Therefore, on any acre, the efficient level of silvicultural intensity, the efficient rotation age, and the efficient harvest level each vary with these parameters. All land is not managed uniformly, and at some locational boundary the entire rent is dissipated in access costs. Beyond this boundary, land has no value for timber harvests or long-run timber management. (The reader is referred to chapters 3 and 4 for full determination of the efficient production characteristics.)

Empirical Application and Conclusions

The private sector trend to efficient silvicultural management criteria, together with a recent trend from harvesting naturally grown timber to a more cultivation-oriented production technology, suggests that expected long-run production estimates based on long historical trends are irrelevant. Our alternative was to derive production estimates by applying efficiency criteria to functions on the frontier of current technical observations. This approach creates overenthusiastic projections if it disregards risk and uncertainty by setting guiding rates of return too low and if some producers fail to implement efficient technologies. On the other hand, it creates conservative projections to the extent it disregards the new technologies of the next thirty to fifty years. We introduced additional conservative bias into our timber harvest projections by disregarding timber expansion to agricultural land and by hedging production levels associated with current technologies.

The Douglas-fir Region

We chose the Douglas-fir region to demonstrate our approach because the necessary data are readily available and because it is an active region for questions of timber management policy. Our data are not perfect, but they are good to a first approximation and equal to the task at hand.

We identified five general technical production processes for coastal Douglas-fir in order of their silvicultural intensity: (1) natural production, which is synonymous with the absolute minimum level of silvicultural effort; (2) planting natural seedlings to ensure full stocking, followed by the minimum level of protection until the harvest year; (3) planting with periodic thinning; (4) planting followed by periodic thinning and fertilizing; and (5) planting select seedlings, followed by periodic thinning and fertilizing. Each technical process is distinctive for each of six site classes where site class is an indicator of biological productivity.

Harvest levels associated with each technical process and site class are based on yield tables developed through U.S. Forest Service research. They vary with rotation length. Factor costs, levels, and timing associated with each process and site class were estimated from surveys of recent literature and local experts. The cost of capital, or guiding rate of return, was obtained from recent experience in the private sector (7½ percent for industrial and 6 percent for nonindustrial private ownerships) and federal agency requirements (10 percent) for the public sector.

In addition, competing amenity values imply an increasing forestland opportunity cost. Land transfers from productive timberland to hunting clubs and second home developments demonstrate these values for private land. Expanding parks and Wilderness reserves demonstrate them for public land. Krutilla estimated the rate of increase in such values in earlier research. Since amenity values compete with timber production, this rate is the same as an increasing rate of general timber production costs and it can be introduced in the Faustmann equation as an increase in the cost of capital (from zero to 3 percent, depending on the site class, with poorer site classes being charged higher rates because they may be more attractive for amenity values).

In the economic long run, production is also a function of expected output prices. Stumpage prices vary with diameter as a measure of quality and temporally at an historic annual rate of 2.5 percent. This historic rate has long been the experience of U.S. forestry and experienced observers expect it to continue for the thirty- to fifty-year period of our analysis.

We determined long-run production levels from this collection of information and the modified Faustmann equation. Searching all rotation lengths and technical processes, we found the maximum single-acre land rent for each site class and ownership. By repeating the search for all other site classes and ownerships, we identified the different maximum land rents and, therefore, the different efficient technical processes, harvest ages, and harvest levels for each site class and ownership.

Our empirical production results bear out our *a priori* expectations. It is not efficient to manage all land identically. Silvicultural intensity increases with site quality and with decreasing difficulty of access. Rotation ages increase with more difficult access. In general, efficient per-acre harvest levels exceed currently observed harvest levels on the better sites, while they are exceeded by current levels on the poorer sites. Even minimal long-run management and harvest on the poorest sites cannot be justified on efficiency grounds, regardless of currently observed harvests.

Where productive time is as important as it is in forestry, the cost of capital (the cost of holding standing inventory) in effect becomes a summary expression for all factor costs. Therefore, it is not surprising that harvest levels are more sensitive to changes in the cost of capital than to changes in any single productive activity such as fertilizing or thinning. Where the cost of capital ranges upward to 10 percent, as in our case, a one percentage point change is approximately equivalent to a 10 percent increase in the general level of all factor costs. Harvest levels are most variable on high quality industrial lands where decreases of up to 10 percent per acre are associated with a one percentage point increase in the cost of capital.

By varying expected stumpage prices, we can compare the impacts of different price levels on silvicultural intensity and rotation length. At low expected prices, the best sites are efficient timber producers. Poorer sites become efficient at higher prices. Rotations decrease with higher price expectations for each given site and production process.

We can trace out the entry of technical production processes for any given site and ownership. Natural production is efficient at low prices. Natural production returns larger land rents at higher prices, but first the planting, then the improved seedling processes, return even greater rents. Apparently the improved seedling process is always more efficient than either thinning or fertilizing following natural seedling establishment. This finding is at variance with current observations, perhaps because it involves the most recently developed production process, which has yet to be implemented everywhere and which in fact cannot be implemented everywhere until the beginning of new rotations. Meanwhile, thinning and fertilizing existing natural stands is efficient short-run practice. The sequence from natural trees to improved seedlings holds even with a 20 percent change in planting costs. It changes only when the poorest land becomes efficient at the highest expected stumpage prices. On this land the improved seedling process is the first to return a positive rent.

The most interesting results of our empirical test have to do with efficient land allocation. Land is efficiently allocated to long-run timber production only where the land rent is positive. There is little change in the observed private land allocation at current regional stumpage prices of $140 per cunit, normalized over the long run for an expected 2.5 percent annual increase and a 1 to 3 percent annual increase in competing amenity values. Public land allocation, however, is an altogether different matter.

Of 12,748,000 acres of private timberland in the region, only 355,000 are inefficient for long-run timber management. Current management on these acres may be explained as (1) harvesting existing mature timber stands where no long-run management is contemplated, (2) management of isolated acres surrounded by better sites—managing to exclude the isolated poor sites would be more expensive than including them, or (3) inefficiency. In the third case, landowners have not made the conversion from traditional to efficiency criteria and receipts from their better lands subsidize management on the few poor acres.

Of 11,878,000 acres of public timberland in the region, 4,601,000 (Site Classes IV and V) are inefficient for long-run timber management. This result is insensitive to the range of access costs. It is also insensitive to greater stumpage price expectations. Nearly three million (Site Class IV) of these poorer public acres become efficient timber producers at stumpage prices of $250 per cunit, normalized, but this price is an unlikely 79 percent greater than current expectations. At this price efficient technology requires improved seedlings. Many public ownerships, however, currently refrain from using both improved seedlings and fertilizers, in which case these acres become efficient timber producers only at the impossible stumpage price of $970 per cunit, normalized. The remaining 1,814,000 acres (Site Class V) of currently managed public timberland are not efficient at any foreseeable prices.

We can also determine the long-run regional supply from our production information and the modified Faustmann equation. The first step is to aggregate harvest levels at given expected stumpage prices across all site classes and ownerships. By subsequently changing stumpage prices and repeating the aggregation process, we can trace out the locus of the expected price-harvest relation, that is, the efficient long-run timber supply function. The reader is referred to chapter 5 for the function itself. We will recall here only our supply conclusions for current prices, normalized, and their implications for a timber shortage in thirty to fifty years.

At current stumpage prices of $140 per cunit, normalized, projected long-run regional timber supply is 44 million cunits annually, 68 percent greater than the currently observed level of 24–26 million cunits annually. There is apparently sufficient currently standing timber to permit conversion to the higher long-run annual harvest level. The projected harvest level is sensitive to changes in the expected rate of stumpage price increase, but not so sensitive as to call into question the overwhelming difference from currently observed levels. For a 1.5 percent rate of annual stumpage price increase, projected harvests are 41 million cunits annually. For a 3.5 percent rate, projected harvests are 49 million cunits annually.

An argument can be made that public and nonindustrial private landowners will be slow to introduce the more intensive silvicultural processes: Public managers call their reluctance protection against the perceived uncertain yields of these production processes. Nonindustrial private owners may be slower only because the comparative advantage for their managerial effort lies elsewhere, perhaps in agriculture. In any case, restricting public and nonindustrial private lands to the natural, planting, and thinning silvicultural processes, while allowing the full range of known technologies on industrial lands, calls forth a 36-million cunit annual harvest projection, still 44 percent greater than the current level.

We conclude that a timber shortage is unlikely at price trends we commonly experience. The market provides all the incentives private landowners require to prevent it. In fact, if prevailing stumpage prices, normalized, and conditions of market-efficient timber management prevail, then we project a radical increase in timber harvests. Since a radical harvest increase is unlikely, this suggests that either (1) the shift to efficient timber management criteria will be less than complete, even for industrial timberland owners, (2) harvests will be so great as to exert substantial downward pressure on stumpage prices, causing a further decrease in the amount of land efficiently allocated to timber production, or (3) there will be some combination of remaining inefficiency and downward price movement. In any case, public policy intervention to prevent a timber shortage in the Douglas-fir region is unnecessary.

French Pete

We also examined a locally specific case study in order to establish the generality of our previous empirical technical observations and production conclusions. We chose the French Pete Creek drainage, a 19,200-acre segment of U.S. Forest Service land within the Douglas-fir region. The allocation of this land was the subject of controversy between timber and environmental interests until Congress selected it for the Wilderness System in 1977. We examined the timber values involved, including the costs of public constraints on efficient timber management, and their implications for the land allocation decision.

We found some local variation in factor costs and input levels associated with each silvicultural production process. The Forest Service can justify costs of minimal measures of forest protection and administration as requirements on all public land for the ostensible purposes of protecting adjacent lands and future values. Accordingly, these costs are not incremental to timber management, and we did not charge them against any silvicultural process. Occasionally, other factor costs are slightly higher than the regional average. French Pete timberland is generally thought to be better than the regional average, therefore it is not surprising that input level requirements associated with each silvicultural process and its fixed yield schedule are below the regional average. In general, this evidence just supports a conclusion that there is some variance around our previously recorded regional means. The regional data can only be applied to select sites with judicious care.

Our local data still support the *a priori* expectations of the efficiency model; that is, it is not efficient to manage all timberland identically. At given expected stumpage prices, silvicultural intensity declines and rotation ages increase as we move from better to poorer sites, etc. If timber management does not need to bear the annual protection and administration costs, French Pete becomes efficient for timber management at lower expected stumpage prices. Site Class IV is notable in that it becomes efficient at $125 per cunit, normalized, in comparison with its regional average efficient price of $250 per cunit.

Efficiency overestimates current public land rents obtained from traditional timber management criteria and without all known technical advantages. Therefore, efficiency-derived conclusions, like ours, place an upper bound on currently efficient land allocations to timber *management*. Our efficiency rents are long run, however. Judgments of the *short-run* efficiency of *harvesting* standing timber are another matter.

French Pete possesses a large volume of standing mature timber which, after deduction for road-building costs necessary for access to it, was worth $116 million in the 1976 market. The "even-flow" constraint restricts harvests, and this value, to a level which can be perpetuated. As even flow is applied by the Forest Service, it severely delays the harvest of mature timber. The planned delay on French Pete is sufficient to fully depreciate the net value of standing timber. Thus, the even-flow constraint, as applied, imposes a large cost in terms of forgone public revenues. In its presence wilderness recreation may be preferable to timber allocation for French Pete.

Regardless of the even-flow constraint, the sustained yield and reforestation requirements of several public laws may, however, tie timber harvesting to regrowth and continued management. Thus, harvesting French Pete's mature timber may hinge on the long-run efficiency of the land for permanent timber management. Our original analysis was designed to investigate this. At expected stumpage prices of $150 per cunit, normalized (comparable to prevailing prices in the local market), the value of the French Pete Creek drainage for efficient long-run timber management is $877,600. Some additional recreational value may occur jointly with this timber value. Minimum *competing* recreational values must still exceed the unlikely value of $29.25 per visit in order to override the efficiency of timber management.

Efficient timber management is, however, constrained to a rotation age equal to culmination of mean annual sawtimber increment. For Douglas-fir this is approximately eighty years, although it is sometimes extended beyond 100 years. For 100-year rotations, French Pete loses all value for long-run timber management, and allocation to competing recreational uses is the constrained efficient solution. For eighty-year rotations, French Pete has a constrained efficient long-run timber value of $26,236 for the entire drainage. Minimum competing recreational values of $0.87 per visit offset the timber value. This is well within the range of reasonable values for competing recreation. Final constrained efficient allocation of French Pete hinges on the level of noncompeting recreational values.

When taken together, the various constraints on public timber management lead us to a range of doubt regarding its efficiency in French Pete. The even-flow, reforestation, and harvest age constraints impose large costs on public management and are important items for public policy review. In their presence, allocation of public forestland to competing recreational uses may be the economically efficient solution.

Policy Implications

To this point we have discussed a method for both evaluating efficient performance and projecting long-run supply for an industry which is breaking with past technical and behavioral patterns. We applied the method to timber production in the Douglas-fir region of Oregon and Washington. Our conclusion is that a timber shortage within thirty to fifty years is unlikely if we are willing to accept historical price trends. An industry responsive only to market incentives, and without additional public policy assistance, is able to produce at greater annual harvest levels than ever previously experienced.

Our analysis does point to another important problem, however. This problem is economically efficient management of public forestland—and it ought to be a priority public policy issue. The land management inefficiencies of public agencies, in particular the U.S. Forest Service, are such that in the Douglas-fir region larger annual harvests can be had from a smaller timberland base—and probably with a smaller agency timber production budget.

We projected that harvests from all public lands could be increased by 74 percent, from 9,070,000 to 15,814,000 cunits annually at currently expected prices. As we expect that such an increase would have a downward impact on stumpage prices, the final long-run harvest level would be somewhat less, but still substantially above current levels. The smaller timberland base implies more remaining land to meet the competing demands of dispersed recreation and environmental interests and, thereby, reduction of the intense industry–environmental conflict. Our estimate is that 4.6 million public acres currently managed for timber are inefficient for that purpose when we consider the accumulating costs of timber management over the full growing period. Even more acres are unprofitable under the strict management constraints which exist now. And more acres yet will be inefficient in thirty to fifty years if our large projected harvest levels have the expected downward price effect and, therefore, exert downward influence on the use of productive factors such as timberland. Nevertheless, even the 4.6 million acres are sufficient to expand forestland in the state and national parks and Forest Service Wilderness areas of the region by 229 percent, or to more than three times its current level.[1]

Marginal Lands and Production Hazards

We might direct some thought to timber, recreation, and environmental values with respect to lands like these 4.6 million acres. So far we have focused on the financial aspect of efficient timber production, but there is additional good reason for restricting timber production on the unprofitable acres. Undoubtedly the greatest conflicts with commercial timber uses of forestland arise from recreational uses. On one extreme, dispersed or wilderness-type recreational experiences preclude any timber management operations, while, on the other extreme, higher density recreational uses can occur jointly with timber, but even they interfere with planting, thinning, harvesting, and other active management activities. The acres most desirable for recreation are probably those which either show greatest physical and biological diversity or possess unusual characteristics. Rocky outcrops and scenic vistas, alpine meadows, lake and stream boundaries, and isolated sites might all qualify. A convenient characteristic of each of these is that, with the exception of lake and stream boundaries, they are rarely very productive timber sites. Productive timber sites are usually on flatter, less physically diverse land where the soil is deeper and access is easier. Commercial timberland may border streams and lakes, but it does not lie in the bogs at lake edge or on the gravelly edges of streams. Furthermore, the best commercial species are not high-elevation trees. Thus, we conclude that as land quality decreases for commercial timber purposes, it generally (although neither uniformly nor inevitably) increases for recreational purposes; some "natural" complementarity exists, or at least competition is muted.

---

[1] Technically, the 4.6 million acres are "commercial forestland," or acres capable of producing in excess of 20 ft^3 per acre per year of naturally grown timber. Forestland in state and national parks and Forest Service Wilderness areas also include poorer forestland and even nonforestland. Therefore, this is not the same as increasing all park land and Wilderness reserves by 229 percent.

A similar relation exists between those acres which need greatest environmental protection and those which are the best commercial timber acres. Environmental hazards are greatest on the most fragile sites—probably the high-elevation sites and the steep slopes. The greatest environmental hazard of commercial timber production is the soil erosion problem caused by felling, skidding, and road building. This is reduced considerably if logging is kept off the steep slopes and out of the shallow-soiled high elevations.

These relationships strengthen our analysis. When developing the aggregate timber supply schedule, we found that poorer quality acres were later entrants to the timber base. This conforms with the real world where we find that not only does biological productivity often decrease as access costs increase, but environmental hazards of timber management and benefits to recreational uses of forestland also increase as access costs increase. Therefore, whatever the efficient allocation of acres to timber production, the assignment of the residual acres to other uses may be similar to assigning both classes of acres to their best uses while at the same time observing the most important environmental constraints.

Nevertheless, we must recognize two cautions in developing the narrower land base to a profitable intensity of timber management: (1) potential monocultures and (2) recreational values on good timber sites. Silvicultural intensification on the good sites may conjure visions of forest monocultures. Monocultures mean single species, hybrid seeds, row crops, and heavy doses of pesticides and fertilizers, with associated environmental hazards. The topic needs careful research, but this picture is probably unreasonable in forestry because trees do not grow like corn: Genetic improvement means progeny selection but not hybridization; the uneven forest terrain prevents row crops; pesticide and fertilizer applications, where justified, occur infrequently and at low dose levels. Moreover, experience with intensive fertilization of agricultural lands, in Europe for example, shows no environmental degradation, and while nonpersistent pesticides are more toxic, their period of residence in the ambient environment is limited. Most important, monocultures are unlikely in forestry because it is nearly impossible to exclude floral diversity from the forest understory.

We cannot deny that timber management under efficiency criteria would result in substantial changes in the managed timberland portion of the forest. Notably, harvests would occur every thirty to fifty years, whereas rotations may currently exceed 120 years. The obvious result would be smaller trees on the average. Clearcutting would be the predominant harvest method because it is usually cheaper than alternative, selective, methods. Of course there would be no harvests whatsoever on the expanded recreational forestland base and trees on this land would be both taller and older. Both features of the productive timberland, shorter trees and clearcutting, may be objectional to some. Public policy makers must consider the tradeoff between shorter trees and clearcutting, on the one hand, and, on the other, more costly timber production on more environmentally risky land, with less land reserved for recreational uses.

Forest Resource Valuation

Recreational values on good timberland introduce the next policy implication of our analysis. We know, for example, that campers and hikers enjoy the tallest groves of trees, and that the latter grow on the best land. Similarly, big game require low elevation winter range, and fish require shaded streams running through good timber sites. In each case we expect competition for use of the land, competition between timber and what we might generally call recreational values. Efficiency criteria require that forestland allocations go to the higher net value when both timber and competing recreational values are positive.

Timber values are relatively easy to determine. They equal the land rent in timber as determined by the Faustmann equation. Recreational values are much more difficult. Often there is no reliable market by which to assess them. The absence of a reliable market, combined with the requirement to allocate land between timber and recreational uses, creates a large problem for multiple use-oriented public agencies. This problem has always been apparent to agency land managers, but has recently become more obvious with formalized agency planning and increased public scrutiny.

The problem is not so difficult as it appears. If we know one value, then to learn if there is a higher value we often only need to know the magnitude of the second value. It is sufficient to assess the second imprecisely so long as we can confidently show that one value exceeds the other. That is, once we know the value of the timber opportunity, it is sufficient to learn whether the recreational value is larger or smaller. Recreation information needs are small. Often the approximate number of visitor-days is sufficient. Dividing the annual timber opportunity value by visitor-days per year tells us the minimum value per visit for efficient allocation to recreation. We demonstrated this calculation in our French Pete case study. This approach can be applied with incomplete and imperfect information to all but the marginal cases where timber and competing recreational values per acre are similar. It eliminates the need for additional time-consuming and expensive analysis.

Looking ahead to further research, we might flag an important problem in these marginal cases. The required comparison is for *net* values, therefore recreational values should be *net* of their costs of production. A large body of research focuses on recreation benefits. Very little, most of it obscure, focuses on recreation costs,[2] yet every public forest manager can tell stories about his campground clean-up crews and mountain rescue teams, as well as his wildlife habitat improvement program, and budgeting for each of these. These costs are real and have potentially significant impacts on efficient land allocation.

Looking Ahead

If gains for all interests are to be obtained from economic efficiency and if adjustments for competing positively valued uses of land are not always so difficult, then why have public agencies refrained from applying efficiency criteria? There are probably two answers, one having to do with traditional timber management criteria and public agency incentives, the other having to do with perceived agency responsibilities to communities dependent on a timber economy.

We have alluded to the first. Traditional timber management criteria perhaps once led to results similar to those of economic efficiency criteria. Over the past 50–100 years, much about the timber market has changed and any similarity no longer exists. Meanwhile general agency programs have solidified and expanded.

[2] The exception is William van Hees, "U.S. Forest Service Campground Management: A Cost Analysis" (Ph.D. dissertation, Oregon State University, 1976).

Vested interests, both within and outside the agencies, resist significant changes in them. Moreover, while market incentives reward industrial timber managers, public agency managers obtain their rewards elsewhere. Economic efficiency provides no payoff to agency managers regardless of its societal payoff.

There are some grounds to look for a change on Forest Service lands, however. The agency does have the incentive of satisfying Congress and the courts and two recent federal laws appear to encourage efficiency. The long-term requirements of the Resources Planning Act seem to necessitate some understanding of demand and supply. The first RPA program, the plan as submitted to Congress, uses words such as demand and supply, benefit and cost, although alternative project benefits and costs are derived using traditional timber management criteria. These criteria overlook many costs of production and overemphasize secondary benefits. Therefore, alternative land allocations and levels of production bear little resemblance to efficient levels and estimates of benefits and costs, and demand and supply bear little resemblance to the standard economic estimates.

When the cost accounting and marginal lands clauses of the National Forest Management Act are combined with the planning requirements of RPA, they may help to overcome these inadequacies. (To the Forest Service's credit, it actively supported the drafting and passage of NFMA in spite of the obvious management changes the law now thrusts upon it.) Until 1977 there had been no benefit–expenditure comparisons for the various functions of the national forests. The comparison for the timber function is a step in the direction required by the NFMA. If it is based upon economic rules, then it will also be a step toward estimating production response and supply functions for timber from the national forests. The marginal lands provision requires assessment of land that is marginal for timber production for various reasons, including economic ones. The functional benefit–expenditure account should identify those lands that are marginal for economic reasons.

Sustained yield and reforestation remain legal constraints on efficient harvests of valuable mature standing timber. We demonstrated the large costs to the public treasury of these requirements in the French Pete case study. There are many similar cases on public land, notably on the good quality lands in the Douglas-fir region. The Forest Service cannot change the law, but RPA and NFMA provide vehicles for reporting the costs of these legal requirements to Congress and the public where initiative for change can originate.

The second reason efficiency criteria have not been applied in Forest Service land management decisions is that Forest Service managers recognize there may be distributive costs attached to their implementation. While efficiency may lead to general increases in harvest levels from a smaller land base, the impact will not be uniformly shared by all communities. Instead, harvest increases will fuel economic growth in many areas while harvest decreases will precipitate economic decline in certain other areas where there is a predominance of economically submarginal land. The Forest Service shows legitimate concern for the latter.

Forest Service action to prevent community decline as well as the impact of traditional timber management criteria on community stability must be judged in terms of their beneficial impacts and their costs. Since our concern is for human communities, we might expect focus on the human productive resource, *labor*, and flows of its direct use. Instead, the Forest Service acts to prevent community decline by ensuring periodic *harvest* flows. For communities maintained by a timber resource from an inefficient land base, this is the same as an extended subsidy for which there is no obvious end and for which someone (the public treasury) must pay. Subsidies imply forgoing other nonsubsidized goods or services which the subsidy dollar could have purchased, and they are inflationary. They may be justified, but justification requires a conscious public policy decision. It is incumbent upon Forest Service managers and others concerned with the community impacts of timber harvests to make the case for such decisions, because there is no guarantee that a subsidized timber flow will succeed in preventing community decline. With labor-saving technology over time, for example, a constant timber flow coincides with a declining labor force and a declining community population.

Maintenance of small, geographically isolated communities—and there are many small, isolated, communities dependent on Forest Service timber in the Rocky Mountain and intermountain West—may disregard the public costs of many community services. That is, such communities often cannot themselves support the most rudimentary roads, schools, and health care centers. These services require additional (non-Forest Service) external public financial assistance. Presumably, if these communities did not exist, their citizens would live elsewhere, where social services might be less expensive and of better quality without public assistance.

Thus there are large, and uncertainly effective, public costs for preventing community decline by means of guaranteed flows of timber volume. It must be demonstrated that allowing decline is not the more reasonable option so long as we take precautions to avoid the serious social hardships associated with a *sharp* community decline precipitated by an *immediate* harvest reduction to an efficient level. (We must be prepared to forgo some efficiency rents in order to reduce the potentially high transactions costs of community dislocation.) Accordingly, we might consider a transitional period over which harvests are reduced to the efficient level. Length of the period could be tied to local labor mobility and the remaining life of fixed capital investments. Alternatively, we might consider the costs of retraining or moving the labor force and purchasing the fixed capital.[3]

There is also reason to question the impacts of traditional timber management on *stable* communities. The volume maximization criterion, implying extended rotations, and disregard for annual carrying costs on timber investments, each give preference to capital over labor as a factor of production. Optimally, unemployed or underemployed labor would substitute for some presently employed scarce capital. This might be done by expanding relatively labor-intensive silvicultural practices while decreasing rotation ages. The substitution would continue until the value of the marginal product of capital equals the value of the marginal product of labor. In fact, we observe cases where the discounted value of the marginal product of capital is *negative*. For example, when the quality timberlands of French Pete are managed for 100-year rotations, even the *average* product of capital is so negative as to exceed the combined positive average products of land and labor. Such results are a disservice to local communities with a stock of unemployed labor.

---

[3] A useful guide for several of these issues is Robert H. Haveman and John V. Krutilla, *Unemployment, Idle Capacity, and the Evaluation of Public Expenditures* (Baltimore, Johns Hopkins University Press for Resources for the Future, 1968).

This all suggests a rich potential for research on labor as a basic factor of timber production. Existing research tends to focus on silvicultural inputs such as fertilization, thinning, herbicide treatment, etc. which combine labor and capital.[4] It is not helpful in judging the community impacts of changes in harvest levels.

To present our findings in capsule form: At historically acceptable price trends, a timber shortage is unlikely unless it is a shortage of our own making. The illusion of shortage is the result of misplaced management objectives. Expanded timber production from a contracting land base is the likely result of conversion to efficiently intensive silviculture practices and land allocation. The contracting timberland base suggests decreases in environmental risks due to timber management and expanding forest recreational opportunities. These results would be most noticeable for public lands, which are currently least responsive to economic criteria as well as the center of industry–environmental contention. Applying efficiency criteria to public timber management would also lead to greater returns to the public treasury.

Some community dislocation would occur. This is the policy dual to the efficient forestland management problems. Attention to the transition period and to the relocation of jobs and small communities would be required.

[4] Joe B. Stevens' current research on labor mobility is the exception. "The Oregon Wood Products Labor Force" (Corvallis, Oregon State University, 1978).

A

Appendix: Forest Succession

Hiawatha's "forest primeval" is often thought to be the natural, the Darwinian, if you will, condition of all forests.[1] This forest primeval is not only deep and dark, but for many people the term suggests a wide variety of tree species and age classes. Seedlings begin life under the shelter of their parents and in company with progeny of many other species. The seedlings grow to young trees surrounded by both younger and older siblings. The survivors eventually replace their parents in the forest canopy and produce seed for their own offspring. This implied steady-state concept of forest succession may be romantic, but it does not reflect reality.

Successive Forest Communities

Turning from romance to science, forest succession refers to biota replacement within an ecological community. Fauna as well as flora are involved, but changes in the latter are often a lot easier to observe and they take precedence in the interests of this study.[2]

To better understand forest succession, let us postulate a land area with an unvegetated substrate and then follow the successive

[1] Even the poorest forester does not make this mistake, but many of the rest of us do so regularly.

[2] The material in this appendix is more extensively reviewed in Stephen H. Spurr, *Forest Ecology* (New York, Ronald Press, 1964) pp. 149–224; and David M. Smith, *The Practice of Silviculture* (New York, Wiley, 1962).

plant communities that occupy this area under assumptions that *(1) the microclimate remains unchanged* and *(2) catastrophic environmental disturbances* such as windstorms, fires, avalanches, floods, rock slides, and epidemics *do not interfere.* Primary succession begins after plant substrates are initially exposed and mosses, annuals, forbes, and grasses—depending on site, climate, and species availability—immigrate into the unvegetated area. Succession continues from this pioneer plant stage, through the herbaceous plant and shrub stage, until the first trees arrive.

Trees themselves follow a successional order according to the tolerance of their species, that is, according to their relative capacity to survive and prosper as understory plants and their related ability to respond to openings in the forest and to reach for the canopy. Exposure to light is usually emphasized when tolerance is discussed, although the tolerance of a given species in a particular locale may also be related to moisture, soil, tree age, and associated species. Thus trees are classified as *tolerant* if they can photosynthesize *without* direct sunlight or full crown exposure, yet can respond by growing to the forest canopy when fully exposed to direct sunlight. Trees are classified as *intolerant* if they can photosynthesize only *with* direct sunlight and full crown exposure.

In general, pioneer species are intolerant; midtolerant species characterize the second tree stage, and tolerants characterize late successional stage forest species. Often, but by no means always, groups of species occur together. These groups, called forest types, can also be classified by their tolerance. Intolerant species or types require direct sunlight from their most juvenile growth. This allows them to pioneer open areas, but prevents successful regeneration where there is a forest overstory. Once established, intolerants add height growth quickly and prune themselves naturally as they attempt to reach above their competitors for the available sunlight. Tolerants, on the other hand, can successfully invade an established forest, their seedlings can survive with limited and indirect sunlight, and their juvenile and immature growth can survive many years in the forest understory. Once they reach the overstory, or an opening occurs in the canopy, however, tolerants possess the ability to recover from years of suppression and become dominant in the forest canopy themselves. Tolerants, unlike intolerants, can regenerate under a canopy of their own mature growth.

Due to the natural succession created by tolerants replacing intolerants, pure stands exist only for (1) very intolerant species which have yet to be invaded by those more tolerant and (2) very tolerant species which have out-competed all those less tolerant in the race for canopy closure. In the latter case, midtolerants might invade but never succeed long enough to release their own seeds.

Tolerance is a relative as well as an absolute concept. That is, the most tolerant species or forest type always out-competes those less tolerant, but where there is, for example, no seed source for the most tolerant or where soil or topography vary, a less tolerant species or type may appear at the top of the successional ladder.

So far, the concept of biological succession is straightforward. It was from a basic model as simple as this one that Frederic Clements fabricated his more elaborate structure of plant succession and the concept of climax—the last successional stage.[3] To the biological characteristics of succession discussed above he added, and emphasized, climate. He hypothesized a single final vegetational community, mature, stable, self-maintaining, and self-reproducing.

But the concept of climax is only as good as its assumptions and these are frequently overlooked. In view of the hundreds of years involved in forest successions, the assumption of no interference from natural disturbances is unrealistic. Thus, while it is true that forests may proceed *toward* climax vegetational communities, catastrophic natural disturbances and more gradual, externally originating, climatic changes intercede so frequently that few forests ever attain climax.

Natural disturbances, of course, only cause the forest to revert to some earlier link in the successional chain from which its forward progression begins anew. It is important to recognize, however, that natural disturbances are so natural that some species and types are better selected to cope with disturbance than with their more tolerant competitor species. For example, jack, lodgepole, and Virginia pines are intolerant, early successional species. They are so naturally selected for fire that many of their cones remain closed, failing to discharge seeds until exposed to the heat of fire. There is even a name, "serotinous," for species and cones possessing this characteristic. The seeds of these pines, furthermore, may fail to

---

[3] Frederic E. Clements, *Dynamics of Vegetation: Selections from the Writings of Frederic E. Clements, PhD* (New York, H. W. Wilson, 1949).

germinate unless exposed to the mineral soil, an exposure made possible only by a disturbance such as fire or a landslide which removes the duff on the forest floor.

These three pines are not just unusual exceptions to the rule. All pine species possess a degree of serotiny. The various cotton-woods, another example of intolerant pioneers, are also better selected to cope with natural hazards than with more tolerant competition. They require bare, wet soil for germination—a natural selection for flooding. It is not surprising that pines grow in areas historically threatened by wildfire, and cottonwoods concentrate on river bottoms.

In conclusion, natural succession is not nearly the rigid forward-marching image sometimes held. Natural environmental disturbances cause succession to occur in a more rachetlike sequence, with periods of predictable succession interrupted by natural disturbances before they begin anew from an earlier successional community. On some sites, disturbance is so regular, and the native intolerant species are so naturally selected for it, that succession marches in place, never really progressing toward a climax. Thus we may have mature, stable, self-maintaining forest communities without having climax.

Changes Within Forest Communities

In addition to successional changes *among* vegetational communities, there also occur changes *within* vegetational communities. Like the former, the latter are often misunderstood. It is often assumed that in late successional natural communities a balanced uneven-aged stand structure exists. That is, there is a stable equilibrium among growth, mortality, and reproduction. New trees flow with random periodicity into the structure of truly uneven-aged stands which are continually growing but never really changing.

"Uneven-aged" refers to the fact that trees in such stands are of several ages according to their apparently random periodicity of flow into the stand; it compares with the one "even-aged" characteristic of pioneer stands of intolerants. All-aged stands are an extreme case in which the periodicity is uniformly one year. "Balance" refers to the regularity of flow and uniformity of volume.

Thus, in balanced all-aged stands, there is literally an equal volume of biomass in each age class of trees from age one to the age of mortality. Or, to put it a different way, in a balanced all-aged stand an equal volume can be harvested—by man or mortality— each and every year, perpetually.

Balanced *uneven*-aged stand structure, however, is rarely observed even in mature, late successional stands of naturally growing timber. Most natural stands, regardless of successional status, have an irregular distribution of age and diameter classes in which certain young and middle-aged cohorts may be lacking. In fact, many stands of mixed species that appear to be uneven-aged are actually even-aged. The size variance that gives an uneven-aged appearance is explained by the fact that some trees are suppressed by their sibling competitors. Balanced uneven-aged stands come into existence naturally only as an even-aged stand is gradually replaced as the fortuitous result of a long series of irregular but minor disturbances. But, severity as well as periodicity of disturbances is ordinarily irregular in time and in space. Therefore balance is rare and a balanced all-aged stand would surely be unique.

Conclusion

Most of the current misconceptions about forest succession can be traced to the *dauerwald* or continuous forest concept inherited from German forestry and accepted as dogma in the United States as late as the 1930s and 1940s. The continuous forest concept involves selective harvest of uneven-aged stands without silvicultural programs for reestablishment or arrangement of age classes within the structure of the timberstand. The continuous forest seemed natural because it did not require any attention to regeneration. But, as matter of fact, regeneration is the weak link in the system—even for very tolerant species. The explanation for the neglect of regeneration is that the continuous forest concept was first introduced in localities where natural regeneration is nearly automatic. Of course, regeneration problems which arose when the concept was applied elsewhere explain the eventual rejection of *dauerwald* as a universal truth.

The two points to be learned from this appendix on forest succession are that (1) succession and climax are not nearly as rigid as sometimes thought. Disturbances may even be the rule, preventing succession and climax on some forest sites. And, as a corollary, (2) the natural forest is unlikely to include trees of all age classes or even of some regular periodicity of age classes. With these two points in mind it is easy to comprehend why, even where stands are mixed with respect to age classes and species, forest managers seldom recommend selective cutting of a portion of the timberstand *every* year. Furthermore, totally aside from aesthetic values, the best of foresters and the best of ecologists agree that clearcutting, the harvesting of the entire stand in a single year, is an ecologically sound management regimen for *some* species and on *some* sites.

Silvicultural systems are designed for harvest *and* regeneration under the assumption that the land will continue to be used for forestry. Given the local characteristics of site, topography, climate, competing species, and animal and insect populations, the best way to harvest and regenerate varies from selectively harvesting a few trees each year through a variety of intermediate harvest practices to clearcutting the entire stand at once. Selective harvests, where and when properly applied, encourage continued production in a forest naturally varied in species and age classes. Where improperly applied, they result in the poorest trees being left as seed sources, a change in the species mix, and stagnant stands. Clearcutting, where and when properly applied, encourages continued production in a forest which is (usually, not always) naturally less varied in species and age classes. It can be thought of as the forest managers' way *not* of altering the natural environment, but rather of simulating natural disturbances[4] and, therefore, replacing stagnating stands and encouraging regeneration. Where clearcutting is improperly applied, the forest manager probably failed to ask himself how big and how frequent were the natural disturbances he intended to simulate. "Darwinian" environments are not interrupted by normal forest practices properly applied.

[4] It might be argued that such simulations help *restore* the natural frequency and severity of disturbances because, after all, forest managers also try to minimize the impacts of fire and epidemics. Thus, natural balances upset by minimizing the impacts of natural disasters *may* be compensated by the man-made "disaster" of a clearcut harvest.

B

Appendix: Special Cases of the Production Model

In this appendix we examine the trend in timber production models from the earliest preference for volume maximization through modern economic value maximization models, and conclude with a glimpse at the trends in technology and their implications for future production modeling. Our contribution lies in the suggestion that each model may have been rational in its own historical economic and biological context. The optimal production period (rotation length) has been the focus of debate between biological and economic managers.[1] Volume maximization may call for rotations twice as long as prevail under value maximization. The difference is not trivial; for the commercially important coastal Douglas-fir species, for example, it may be thirty-five years. We examine the production period, and the debate, and predict the latter will vanish as new timber production technologies become widespread.

We first examine the simple (or traditional) volume and value maximization models and explain the local technical rationality of each. Each is a special case of the more general model, which we introduce here. It is an important characteristic of the general model that the *optimal rotation is constant neither in time nor in space.*

---

[1] The standard forest management text teaches both objectives. Kenneth P. Davis, *Forest Management* (New York, McGraw-Hill, 1974). The National Forest Management Act of 1976, for example, refers to characteristics of each objective. P.L. 94-588 §6(m)9LO, 90 Stat. 2956, amending 16 USC §1604 (Supp. IV 1974).

Finally, we discuss the technical production trend and its implication for rotation length and the volume versus value maximization debate. We can demonstrate that the difference in optimal rotation lengths may be temporary, restricted to currently observed economic and biological conditions. As timber production changes from harvesting naturally grown timber to a more crop-oriented technology, we can show that harvest volume becomes a more constant function of time. As a result, (1) rotation length becomes less important to volume maximization and (2) the value-maximizing rotation is extended. We see evidence of both in industrially managed stands of Douglas-fir today. It is in anticipation of this result that we predict the old debate over volume or value maximization will lose meaning.

Traditional Models

The first model is the simple biological model, also known as the maximum sustainable yield (MSY) model. Its origin—and the origin of modern forestry—can be traced to middle-eighteenth-century Germany. The prevailing German economy was stable, featuring closure from external influences and a stable technology that rewarded craftsmanship more than innovation. Undeveloped transportation and communications networks, reinforced by high customs barriers, minimized market exchange. Small, self-sufficient, political and economic units were the rule.[2]

The relative value of wood as a fuel was higher than it is today. Accordingly, productive timberland had a higher relative value and was located closer to the center of the economic unit.[3] An additional inventory was not readily available on adjacent land —as it often is today—and collective action was necessary to prevent exhaustion of the common timber resource. The result was a commons-type commitment to maximum even flows of timber

[2] Richard W. Behan, "Forestry and the End of Innocence," *American Forests* vol. 81, no. 5 (May 1975) pp. 16ff; Ernest M. Gould Jr., "Forestry and Recreation" (Petersham, Mass., Harvard Forest Papers no. 6, 1962); Hugh M. Raup, "Some Problems in Ecological Theory and Their Relation to Conservation," *Journal of Ecology* vol. 52 (Supplement) (March 1964).

[3] John H. von Thunen, *Der Isolierte Staat in Beziehung auf Landwirtschaft und Nationalökonomie* (The Isolated State in Relation to Land Use and National Economy), (Berlin, Schmaucher Zarchlin, 1875).

volume. Moreover, sound ecological justification apparently accompanied this economic justification of the simple biological model. The continuous forest, or *dauerwald*, concept was accepted in those areas of northern Germany where the biological model was applied.[4] That is, regeneration was expected to be natural and immediate (costly silvicultural management was thought to be unnecessary) because vigorous understory trees were always ready to replace mature trees after the latter were harvested.

The objective of the biological model is to maximize *continuous* annual harvest volume V from a fixed area of land. The model can be expressed mathematically in terms of its cumulative biological production function Q, which is variant only with time T in the usual logistic pattern of density-determined biological populations.[5]

$$V^8 = \max_{T} Q(T)/T \qquad \text{(B-1)}$$

If (1) price and technology are constant, as in the stable German economy, and (2) the cost of silvicultural effort is zero, as in *dauerwald,* then Eq. (B-1) identifies the year of maximum annual returns to perpetual timber management on the land.

Logistic functions are smooth and possess exactly one inflection point. It is a property of them that necessary and sufficient conditions for a maximum are

$$Q_T T = Q \qquad \text{(B-2)}$$

$$Q_{TT} < 0 \qquad \text{(B-3)}$$

where the subscripts indicate derivatives of the function with respect to the subscript. The natural growth rate Q_T/Q at the optimal harvest time is $1/T$. The rotation age is chosen such that, in foresters' terminology, when average annual harvest or mean annual productive increment (MAI) Q/T is at its maximum, current annual increment (CAI) Q_T is positive but decreasing.[6]

[4] Steven H. Spurr, *Forest Ecology* (New York, Ronald Press, 1964) pp. 149–224.

[5] A. J. Lotka, *Elements of Physical Biology* (Baltimore, Williams and Wilkins, 1925).

[6] It is important to distinguish this continuous production solution from the *single period* volume maximization. The latter problem is to maximize $Q(T)$. Its solution occurs where the marginal product of time Q_T is zero, or at the absolute peak of the production function.

The Simple Economic Model

Germany remained the center of learning in forestry, but the characteristic features of a closed economy and stable technology faded into its past. With them, any normative justification of volume maximization also faded. A stronger central government with developing external interests replaced the closed and locally oriented economy. Ideas from the outside world, together with local industrialization, assured technical change. Subsequently, alternative investment opportunities developed and relative values adjusted: in particular, coal replaced timber as a fuel, causing relative timber values to decrease and productive timberland to shift away from the center of the isolated economic unit toward the marginal productive lands adjacent to unmanaged, natural timberland. Rationing timber consumption through collective community action was no longer necessary.

In 1849, Faustmann[7] introduced the correct simple and deterministic competitive economic model, the objective of which is to maximize value V or specifically, to maximize the present value of perpetual returns to the fixed factor of production, an acre of timberland. Value is the sum of revenues minus costs. Revenue is the expected price p times the volume harvested $Q(T_1)$ discounted from the time of harvest T_1 to the initial moment of land availability, by the opportunity cost of capital r. Since trees grow naturally—that is, without silvicultural inputs—harvest volume continues to be only a function of time, and there are no costs other than the opportunity costs of capital and land. The cost of land is the economic rent R for the duration of the timber production period ("soil expectation" in the forestry literature).[8]

$$V^9 = \max_{T_1} pQ(T_1)e^{-rT_1} - R \int_0^{T_1} e^{-rt}\, dt \qquad \text{(B-4)}$$

where T_1 is the length of the production period, a single rotation.

---

[7] Martin Faustmann, "On the Determination of the Value which Forest Land and Immature Stands Possess for Forestry" (1849) in M. Gane, ed., *Institute Paper 42* (Commonwealth Forestry Institute, Oxford University, 1968).

[8] William R. Bentley and Dennis Teeguarden, "Financial Maturity: A Theoretical Review," *Forest Science* vol. 11, no. 1, pp. 76–87 (March 1965); Mason M. Gaffney, "Concepts of Financial Maturity of Timber and Other Assets" (Raleigh, North Carolina State College Agricultural Economics Information Series, no. 62, 1962).

If timber production is the best use of the land, then we can—as did Faustmann—substitute for the rent term a term explaining perpetual use of the land for timber production.

$$V^9 = \max_{T_n} p \left\{ Q(T_1) \exp(-rT_1) + Q(T_2) \exp[-r(T_1 + T_2)] \right.$$
$$\left. + \ldots + Q(T_n) \exp\left(-r \sum_{i=1}^{n} T_i\right) + \ldots \right\}$$
$$= \max_{T_n} p \sum_{n=1}^{\infty} Q(T_n) \exp\left(-r \sum_{i=1}^{n} T_i\right) \qquad \text{(B-4a)}$$

Since all parameters continue unchanged from one production period to the next, the identical problem confronts the forest manager following each harvest. Therefore, each succeeding production period is of the same length ($T_i = T_j$ for all i, j), and Eq. (B-4a) is usually stated as

$$V^9 = \max_T pQ(T)e^{-rT}(1 - e^{-rT})^{-1} \qquad \text{(B-4b)}$$

The necessary and sufficient conditions for a maximum are

$$Q_T = rQ(1 - e^{-rT})^{-1} \qquad \text{(B-5)}$$

$$Q_{TT} < rQ_T \qquad \text{(B-6)}$$

Timber is said to be "financially mature" when its natural growth rate is $r(1 - e^{-rT})^{-1}$, which is equal to the opportunity cost of capital adjusted upward to compensate for the implicit land rent. The greater the cost of capital, the shorter the production period. *Price is not a factor in the production period decision.*

We can demonstrate the relationship between the simple economic and simple biological models by examining the natural growth rate as the cost of capital approaches zero. By l'Hopital's rule,

$$\lim_{r \to 0} r(1 - e^{-rT})^{-1} = 1/T \qquad \text{(B-7)}$$

which is characteristic of a biological maximum [Eqs. (B-2) and (B-3)]. As expected, the optimal economic production period is shorter than the optimal biological production period when the cost of capital is positive. For smaller costs of capital, the value-maximizing harvest age increases until it converges with the volume-maximizing age. If capital costs were low for eighteenth century Germany, then the volume-maximizing harvest age approximated the value-maximizing age.

A More General Economic Model

As the North American market developed, German-trained American foresters initially applied the old models. But new economic factors increased in importance and doubts developed over the reliability of the *dauerwald* concept. The simple economic model remains a useful, if incomplete, tool. Contemporary applications of it require modifications to reflect a multitude of different timber and land conditions. We introduced some of the more generally important modifications in chapters 3 and 4 and we summarize them here.

Some of the original natural bounty of mature timber ("old growth") exists in North America to this day. As this stock has been drawn down over time, relative timber prices (stumpage) have risen, much as prices rise with the slow depletion of a mine that provides a large market share of some given mineral. Eventually this stock will be exhausted, all timber harvested will be the result of a renewable production process, and the rate of price increase will drop to zero. Until then, we expect relative stumpage prices to continue rising. Let ρ be an exogenous function of the declining stock of mature timber explaining the rate of price increase. (Expectations about both technical change and future demand may also affect this rate.)

Related to the stock of old growth and the westward development pattern of North America is the fact that transportation costs have become important. The relative value of timberland is now such that it is physically located beyond agricultural land and on the fringe of productive land. A natural stock of old growth is often just beyond the fringe of *managed* timberland. Therefore, as prices rise, making timber a more attractive investment, some timber managers are presented with a very real tradeoff between intensifying silvicultural effort on currently managed land or expanding harvests to less accessible, currently unmanaged, land.

Since prices are quoted on the stump (stumpage), they must be adjusted for extraction costs x from the particular timberstand in question in order to reduce locational bias in their estimation.

Meanwhile, we have come to learn that *dauerwald* is unrepresentative of the way most forests grow. It is unrepresentative of the softwood forests that provide the bulk of our commercial timber harvests, and it becomes even less representative as we develop a more crop-oriented timber production technology.

North American softwood forests are not continuous in age distribution. Natural regeneration following harvests is often not immediate: in the highly productive coastal Pacific Northwest it may take up to twenty-five years and in the drier Rocky Mountains it may take centuries. The production period must be adjusted for this regeneration lag. Where time T previously referred to timber-stand age, when adjusted for the regeneration lag it more accurately reflects land use.

Eventually stumpage prices have risen to a level where they can justify more than natural management of the land, implicitly the only management in the traditional economic model. Introduction of silvicultural effort can shift the regeneration lag, and even make it negative if the effort includes planting advanced-age seedlings immediately following harvest of the old timberstand. Silvicultural management may also include changing to a faster-growing or more valuable species, or planting select progeny from within a species. Thus, both the level and the rate of cumulative biological production are now functions of time and silvicultural effort E. Effort is measured in terms of some standardized unit (such as one man and one machine for one hour). Its factor cost is w.

The full objective function of the generalized economic model is

$$
\begin{aligned}
V^{10} = \max_{T_n, E} \Bigg\{ & p \sum_{n=1}^{\infty} Q(T_n, E) \exp\left[(\rho - r) \sum_{i=1}^{n} T_i \right] \\
& - x \sum_{n=1}^{\infty} Q(T_n, E) \exp\left(-r \sum_{i=1}^{n} T_i \right) \\
& - wE \sum_{n=1}^{\infty} \exp\left(-r \sum_{i=0}^{n-1} T_i \right) \Bigg\}
\end{aligned}
\tag{B-8}
$$

Relative stumpage prices continue changing until, say, the *N*th period when the remaining stock of old growth is fully harvested.

(Expectations about both technical change and future demand may also cause continuing price changes.) Therefore,

$T_i \neq T_j$ for $i,j < N$

$T_i = T_j = T_n$ for $i,j \geq N$

Changing production periods make this a more difficult problem than that expressed by Eq. (B-4a). It is possible, however, to simplify the problem somewhat, and still develop a degree of understanding about it. Consider that subsequent to each harvest the forest manager confronts the same problem *except* for the permanently higher price. One approach, therefore, is to determine the optimality conditions given one price and, implicitly, one production period, then reexamine them for a higher price—much as the manager reexamines subsequent to each harvest.

Following this approach, the problem can initially be stated as

$$V^6 = \max\left[(p - x)\, Q(T,E)e^{-rT} - wE\right](1 - e^{-rT})^{-1} \quad (3\text{-}8)$$

Equation (3-8) has the additional merit of being identical with Eq. (B-8) after the Nth rotation, when the last stand of old growth is gone.

The necessary and sufficient conditions for a maximum are

$$(p - x)\, Q_{EE}e^{-rT^*} = w \qquad\qquad\qquad (\text{B-9})$$

$$Q_{EE} \leq 0 \qquad\qquad\qquad (\text{B-10})$$

$$(p - x)Q_T = r[(p - x)Q^* - wE^*](1 - e^{-r_2 T^*})^{-1} \quad (\text{B-11})$$

$$(p - x)Q_{TT} \leq 2r^2\, (p - x)\, Q_T\, (1 - e^{-rT^*})^{-1}$$
$$- r^2\left[(p - x)Q^* - wE^*\right](1 - e^{-rT^*})^{-2} \qquad (\text{B-12})$$

and $V^6{}_{EE}\, V^6{}_{TT} > (V^6{}_{TE})^2$. These conditions possess the standard intuitive logic, that is, declining marginal revenues equal nondeclining marginal costs. Specifically, when rotation length is held constant at T^*, the constant factor cost equals the declining marginal value product of effort. And, when effort is held constant at E^*, the declining value of marginal physical product equals the increasing opportunity cost of delaying subsequent crops $(p - x)\, Q_T(1 - e^{-rT^*}) = r[(p - x)\, Q^* - wE^*]$.

Price can no longer be ignored in the general economic model. Dividing all terms in Eq. (B-11) by $(p - x)$, it is clear that the optimal rotation age is dependent on the factor cost–stumpage price ratio.

$$Q_T/[Q^* - w(p - x)^{-1} E^*] = r(1 - e^{-rT^*})^{-1} \qquad \text{(B-13)}$$

Permanent increases in stumpage prices or permanent decreases in the factor cost–stumpage price ratio cause shorter rotations. Thus, we expect successive crops to be harvested at earlier ages until the secular price rise levels off for the Nth crop. (On the other hand, in chapter 4 we found that the *rate* of price change has a negative impact on the rotation age.) The net impact or the optimal rotation of both the rate of price change and the change in the price level is indeterminate. We also note, from Eq. (B-9) that increasing prices justify expanding levels of silvicultural inputs.

There are several additional interesting characteristics of this model. We discussed them, and their responsiveness to price changes, in chapters 3 and 4. For purposes of this appendix, the most interesting of these is that the optimal rotation age increases for less accessible land. Thus, we conclude from the general economic model that there is not just one *optimal rotation age; rather, the optimal rotation varies over time (or with secular price increases) and space.*

The relationships between the general economic model and the other two models should be clear. For constant access conditions within the perimeter of efficient extraction and when relative stumpage prices are unchanging, there is no regeneration lag, the factor costs are zero, the general and simple economic models are identical. When the cost of capital is also zero, the optimality conditions for the general economic model are identical with those of the simple biological model.

Summary

Table B-1 compares the assumptions of the general economic model with those of the traditional or simple biological and economic models—also known as volume and value maximizing models, respectively. The objective of each is to maximize perpetual returns to the single-acre landowner, but the two traditional models

Table B-1. Comparison of Revised and Traditional Models: Assumptions

	General model	Traditional models	
		Biological	Economic
1. Production function	$Q = Q(T,E)$	$Q = Q(T)$	$Q = Q(T)$
2. Land costs	Perpetual timber management	Perpetual timber management	Perpetual timber management
3. Regeneration lag, t_r	$t_r \gtreqless 0$	$t_r = 0$	$t_r = 0$
4. Regeneration costs	$wE \geq 0$	$wE = 0$	$wE = 0$
5. Cost of capital	$r \geq 0$	$r = 0$	$r \geq 0$
6. Rate of relative stumpage price change	$\rho \geq 0$	$\rho = 0$	Independent determination[a]
7. Extraction costs	$x \geq 0$	Independent determination[a]	$x \geq 0$[b] Independent determination[a]

[a] That is, when extraction costs or the changes in relative prices of timber are calculated, they are external to these traditional models. See the discussion of extraction in chapter 4.

[b] In the traditional economic model, if extraction is argued to be considered in stumpage price determination, then this adds a characteristic to p (r ?) which is not in the traditional model.

do this while assuming that some generally important parameters are zero valued. In this sense they are only special forms of the general case. These special forms may have been appropriate in their own historical economic and biological contexts, but they are inconsistent with contemporary timber production technology.

The optimality conditions for the three models are compared in table B-2. The generalized conditions for an optimum (a value maximum) are that marginal revenues equal marginal costs. In the general economic model, these conditions apply for inputs of productive time, silvicultural effort, and land of varying accessibility, as well as for known price expectations. In the traditional models, they apply only to the first of these under constant prices. The optimal rotation is the frequent focus of comparison—and contention. It is longest with the biological model. In the general economic model it varies with other input levels and with price expectations.

Table B-2. Comparison of Revised and Traditional Models: Conditions

	General model		Traditional models	
	Constant prices	Changing prices $(p < p')$	Biological	Economic
1. Optimal level of silvicultural effort, E^*	$w = (p - x)Q_E e^{-rT}$ (Factor cost = marginal value product of silvicultural effort)	$E^*(p) < E^*(p')$	—	—
2. Optimal rotation age, T^*	$Q_T/[Q^* - wE^*(p - x)^{-1}] = r/(1 - e^{-rT^*})$ (Value of marginal economic growth rate = cost of capital adjusted for implicit land rent)	$T^*(p) > T^*(p')$	$Q_T/Q^* = 1/T^*$ (Zero interest rate solution, harvest at culmination MAI)	$Q_T/Q^* = r/(1 - e^{-rT^*})$ (Natural growth rate = cost of capital adjusted for implicit land rent)
3. Optimal production level, Q^*	$Q^* = wE^*(p - x) + Q_T(1 - e^{-rT^*})/r$	$Q^*(p) > Q^*(p')$[a]	$Q^* = Q_T T^*$	$Q^* = Q_T(1 - e^{-rT})/r$
4. Location, land rent relationship (x = extraction cost, R = rent)	$dR/dx < 0$; rental value of acre on extramarginal boundary $= 0$	$\max x(p) < \max x(p')$	—	—
5. x, E relationship	$dE^*/dx \leq 0$	—	—	—
6. x, T relationship	$dT^*/dx \geq 0$	—	—	—

[a] See chapter 4 for this important result.

Looking Ahead

Even the generalized economic model is rapidly becoming outdated. An examination of the technological trends in timber production may allow us to anticipate the eventual form of the economic model. As the stock of old growth disappears, timber production is changing from a harvest to a crop orientation. Gradually, the various segments of the industry, public and private, are introducing technologies which ultimately lead to perennial management of the land, that is, to continual and perpetual treatment of the land and trees so that silvicultural activities such as weeding, thinning, and fertilizing and their associated costs, occur throughout the life of the timber crop instead of just during stand establishment. As a result, the biological production function stretches vertically and changes form, and expected revenues increase throughout the growing period.

The new technologies have not been introduced everywhere because (1) some producers are uncertain about their impacts and (2) some technologies require a new seed crop. (The latter will be introduced gradually, of course, as current timberstands are harvested and replaced.) Furthermore, our theory tells us that the crop orientation will *never* be introduced everywhere. At the perimeter of productive timberland (least accessible sites), we expect only the minimal level of silvicultural effort, and beyond this perimeter we expect only natural growth. Nevertheless, on inframarginal land, where new technologies are introduced, we expect the production gains to be great. Timber production is probably at the foot of a leaning curve. Initial gains alone may be substantial, particularly because many of them can be directly transferred from agriculture. There is already some affirmative empirical evidence of this from industrial timberlands.[9]

Seed Improvement

There are two classes of technologies important to the new, crop-oriented, timber production: (1) seed improvement and (2) truly perennial activities. Seed improvement is a particularly active field of investigation today. The initial planting introduces new, improved seed while each successive crop, at the time of its estab-

---

[9] George Weyerhaeuser and others, "What Is High Yield Forestry?" *American Forests* vol. 70, no. 11 (November 1974) pp. 17–32.

lishment, incorporates subsequent improvements. Therefore, each production function effectively stretches along its vertical axis, and production at the nth planting is represented by

$$Q^n(T,E) = e^{n\tau T} Q(T,E) \tag{B-14}$$

where τ is a function of expanding knowledge in forest genetics. Following Eq. (B-7), we now have,

$$
V^{11} = \max_{T_n, E} \left\{ p \sum_{n=1}^{\infty} Q(T_n, E) \exp\left[(\rho + \tau - r) \sum_{i=1}^{n} T_1 \right] \right.
$$

$$
- x \sum_{n=1}^{\infty} Q(T_n, E) \exp\left[(\tau - r) \sum_{i=1}^{n} T_i \right]
$$

$$
\left. - wE \sum_{n=1}^{\infty} \exp\left(-r \sum_{i=0}^{n-1} T_i \right) \right\} \tag{B-15}
$$

Recall our discussion of expected price increases—described by ρ in Eqs. (B-8) and (B-15). Clearly, expected seed improvements have a similar impact on optimal management practice. Specifically, they lead to shorter optimal rotations as there is a payoff for replacing current timberstands with better quality second growth. Restated another way, there is an opportunity cost to ignoring expected technological advancement.

Perennial Technologies

Most technologies are not restricted to seed stock of a specific vintage. Rather, they can be applied to the standing timber (e.g., thinning or pruning) or the site itself (e.g., weeding or fertilizing) as they are perfected. Perennial timberstand management is an attempt to apply these technologies so as to take full advantage of the site's *annual* productive capacity. Once seedlings are established on a site, they grow until they fully occupy the site, that is, until tree spacing is such that (1) there are no openings in the forest canopy through which sunlight can penetrate and (2) the standing timber fully exploits the nutritional value of the soil. Before the stand achieves this fully stocked condition, some soil nutrients and some sunlight are unused; therefore, the full potential of the land is unrealized. Beyond full stocking, the site's full-growth potential is exploited, but it either (1) concentrates in those few stems which compete best or (2) divides among too many stems, and the stand stagnates; that is, each stem grows, but at a suppressed rate. In the former case, those stems which cannot compete thin themselves naturally and the site potential accrues to the remaining stems until the timberstand is once again too dense and another natural thinning occurs. Natural thinning means that those trees which cannot compete die and deteriorate. The commercial volume of their accumulated growth is lost. In the case of stagnating stands, we do not lose the volume of naturally thinned timber; instead, we lose the higher values per unit volume associated with larger trees.

The single year of most rapid growth identifies the biological productive capacity for a given site and seed quality. A new fertilizing process, new seed, or some other process, is associated with a new production function, therefore, a new productive capacity. For a given production function, Q in figure B-1(a), the productive capacity is the slope of Q at its steepest for any moment (year) in time, at t_c—known as culmination of current annual increment (CAI).

Thinning maintains the stand growth rate in the neighborhood of culmination CAI. Thinning removes dead or stagnant stems, allowing the site potential to concentrate on more competitive, better spaced stems.[10] Subsequent production from the residual growing stand is diagrammed as Q^{-g} in figure B-1(a) with thinning occurring at approximately culmination CAI. Growth continues at approximately the rate of culmination CAI until t_c' when the thinned stand is once more fully stocked and begins to stagnate. Accumulating the thinned volume and the residual growing volume gives us *gross* yield Q^g. Figure B-1(b) demonstrates the case of repeated thinnings. The high growth rate is maintained for a longer period but eventually tapers off as all remaining trees become biologically mature. After maturity they stagnate, not from competition, but from old age.

In addition to the explicit advantage of maintaining high production rates per unit of time, there are three less obvious advan-

10 Pruning, like thinning, concentrates growth. Thinning concentrates growth in select trees within the stand. Pruning concentrates growth within select parts (the bole) of individual trees. Pruning, however, is generally uneconomic in North America at current relative prices.

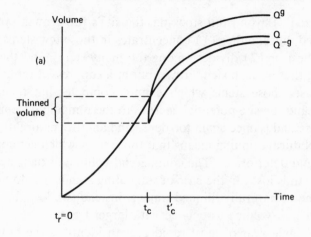

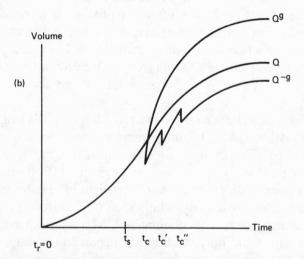

Figure B-1. Biological productive potential: Cases of (a) single and (b) repeated thinnings. (Culmination CAI occurs at t_c for production described by Q and again at t'_c for thinned stand production describd by Q-g.)

tages to thinning: (1) Planned thinnings are just intermediate and partial harvests—the accumulated growth on thinned trees is not lost to mortality as it is in naturally grown stands, but can be sold commercially. (2) After repeated thinnings, the postponed final harvest is composed of older, larger trees. Larger trees have a larger portion of recoverable fiber in their clear straight stems. This implies higher quality, therefore higher price per unit of final harvest volume. And (3), also as a result of postponing final harvest, site preparation and planting costs are delayed—or, what is the same, occur less often—therefore, thinning costs are somewhat offset by a reduction in stand establishment costs.

A reexamination of figure B-1 reveals that even thinning fails to increase the growth rate in the earliest years of production when spacing is not a constraint on growth. To take better advantage of the site's potential during the early years, we could plant more densely, but then earliest thinnings would be of unmerchantable size. Such thinnings are called precommercial. There is a limit to their application because they are expensive and either encourage high-grading or provide no immediate return. (High-grading, in this case, means thinning the few merchantable trees regardless of spacing in order to obtain immediate financial returns. Slower growing, poorly spaced trees remain, guaranteeing a poorer long-run return for the precommercial thinning effort.) The tradeoff is between assured regeneration, dense early growth, but precommercial thinning, on one hand; and a willingness to accept less regeneration, more undesirable biological competition, and eventually less growth, but no precommercial thinning costs, on the other hand. A partial solution is to plant older seedlings, seedlings of, say, age t_s where t_s is the age at which the slope of the production function first approaches some tolerable range of culmination CAI.

In conclusion, initial dense planting and regular thinnings thereafter *maintain* the natural productive maximum of the site. Additionally, site improvements *increase* the natural productive maximum by altering the nutrient flow or the level of undesirable biological competition on the site. In the ultimate case, where one or another timberstand or site improvement occurs virtually perennially, the rate of annual growth is both increased and maintained at a high level for a longer period of time. Figure B-2 demonstrated this. Cumulative biological production is a function of time T and silvicultural effort E, which varies such that $E^3 > E^2 > E^1$. Natural production Q^1 is the usual logistic growth function. In this example, advanced age seedlings were planted (the regeneration lag is minus t_r). Site improvements imply an additional input of silvicultural effort and have the effect of increasing production throughout its range. The result is a production function like Q^2 with a slope which is greater than the slope of Q^1. Stand improvements (thin-

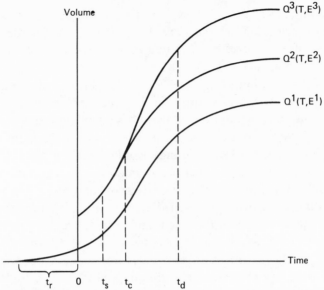

Figure B-2. Biological productive potential: The case of perennial management.

ning) imply additional effort, yet (when added to site improvements such as fertilization) extend the period of maximum annual growth from t_c (the year of culmination of natural stand CAI) to t_d. The result is cumulative production described by Q^3.

Anticipated Solution

The full mathematical description of this anticipated model requires a complicated variational calculus model. However, such a full description is not necessary—reference to figure B-2 is sufficient—for a discussion of the general implications for volume and value maximization and the rotation age.

For more accessible land, where the level of silvicultural inputs is significant, the anticipated production function is steeper due to both seed improvement and perennial technologies. The total revenue function is even steeper yet due to the price–quality–stand age relationship. More to our point, however, the production and revenue functions bear a more linear relation to productive time. Recall that the combination of advanced age seedlings and precommercial thinning causes a reduction in the period of slow juvenile growth. Later commercial thinnings and fertilization extend the period of peak growth.[11]

It should be clear from this summary that the *volume* maximizing rotation age is no longer single-valued. Rather, annual harvest volume is at its maximum for a number of years; for example, all years in the interval (t_c, t_d) for function Q^3 in figure B-2. It is intuitive that there is only one *value* maximizing rotation, however. For value maximization, final harvest must occur after the timberstand attains merchantable size (t_c) but before growth rates begin to decline (t_d). That is, the *optimal economic rotation occurs in the interval of indifference to biological managers.*

Thus, we expect the old issue of contention between biological and economic managers to diminish with the development of a crop-oriented timber production technology. On more accessible land, with a substantial level of silvicultural inputs, the optimal economic rotation falls in the range of the biological optimum. This is the important land where the economic rent returned to timber management is greatest and where the bulk of North America's commercial timber originates.

Summary

The first part of this appendix compared the basic biological and economic models for timber management. It found that each was justified in its specific historical context. These findings are summarized in tables B-1 and B-2 and will not be repeated here.

The current trend in timber management is away from harvesting old growth and toward a more crop-oriented technology. This trend includes new technologies for seed, site, and stand improvement. Some of these technologies may be applied almost continuously over the lifetime of a single timber crop. They are all expected to yield considerable increases in annual harvest volume per acre.

[11] On less accessible land, with little or no silvicultural inputs (where the general economic model of the previous section is more representative), our chapter 3 analysis tells us that optimal economic and biological production periods diverge. At the margin of economically productive timberland, where regeneration lags are substantial and mining of volunteer stands is justified (if the biological model adjusts for regeneration lags), both optima may be large and annual production per acre small. Therefore, this divergence of optimal economic and biological production periods may be of little consequence.

The model that incorporates these technologies must allow for perennial input costs, increased timberstand growth rates—which continue at a high level throughout much of the rotation—and stumpage prices that are closely related to log size and stand age. It yields a result previously overlooked in timber production models: Expectations of future technical change affect current management practice. They imply shorter rotations in order to replace the slow-growing current crop with a preferred second crop.

The rotation age itself has been, and continues to be, a focal point in the debate over preference for biological or economic harvest models. Optimal economic rotations have normally been shorter than optimal biological rotations by a considerable number of years. We find that, as perennial timberland management develops, the period over which *volume* is maximized expands until it takes in the optimal economic rotation. This suggests that the debate over volume or value maximization will lose importance as perennial management becomes widespread.

Index

Access to timber: alternatives for, 150; costs of, 114–116; in French Pete, 149–150; for public lands, 144–145; stumpage price and, 118–199

ACE. *See* Allowable cut effect

Alder, regeneration lag in, 93

Allowable cut: economic efficiency replacement of, 35–41; explanation of, 13; for periodic Forest Service harvests, 29

Allowable cut effect (ACE), 20

Allowable cut model: with efficiency constraints, 35–40; explanation of, 13; Forest Service version, 26–29; objections to 20–21, 34; objective of, 14; variations of, 21

Amenity valuation, 112–113, 160, 175

Area control, 16–17

Ayres, Robert U., 136n

Baden, John, 3n, 33n, 167n

Balance structure for timberstands, 193–194

Balmer, William E., 98n

Barlow, Thomas J., 33

Barnett, Harold J., 68n, 117n

Beaverhead National Forest, 41

Behan, Richard, 164n, 197n

Behavioral production model. *See* Profit maximization model

Behrens, William W., III, 135n

Bell, Enoch F., 19n, 22n, 27n

Bentley, William R., 34n, 44n, 73n, 199n

Berman, Mathew D., 72n

Beuter, John H., 2n, 135n

Biological model, 14, 45, 197–198

Biota replacement, 190

Bolsinger, Charles L., 90n, 93n

Bowes, Michael D., 151n, 164n

Bradley, Paul G., 117n

Briegleb, Philip A., 46n

British Columbia, 70, 92

Brown, George, 33n

Bruce, David, 89, 101, 102n

Bruce, Donald, 88n, 155n

Bureau of Indian Affairs, 21

Bureau of Land Management, 21, 86

Burns, Robert, 147n, 151n

CAI. *See* Current annual increment

California, 86, 87n

Callahan, James C., 68n, 117n

215

About the author

Before obtaining his M.S. in forestry and his Ph.D. in economics from the University of Michigan, the author was a smoke-jumper with the U.S. Forest Service, a ranch field hand, butcher's assistant, and Russian linguist. In addition, courtesy of the U.S. Army, he ran the only telephone exchange in Korea during the U.S.S. *Pueblo* crisis.

While at the University of Michigan, he was a Rockefeller Environmental Quality Fellow and acted as a consultant for the Havasupi Indians in the Grand Canyon. This book was written while he was a member of the RFF research staff. He now teaches at Duke University's Center for Resource and Environmental Policy Research.